ANTHOLOGY
OF JESUS

To the only wise God Our Saviour be Glory and Majesty, Dominion and Power, both now and ever.

ANTHOLOGY
OF JESUS

Arranged and Selected by
Sir James Marchant

Edited by
Warren W. Wiersbe

KREGEL PUBLICATIONS
Grand Rapids, MI 49501

Library of Congress Cataloging in Publication Data

Marchant, James, Sir, 1867-1956, Compiler.
    Anthology of Jesus.
    Reprint of the 1926 ed. published by Cassell, London; some of the original selections have been eliminated and a new foreword has been added.
    Bibliography: p.
    Includes index.
    1. Jesus Christ — Literary collections.
I. Wiersbe, Warren W. II. Title.
PN6071.J4A57   1981   808.8'0382   80-25038
ISBN 0-8254-4015-7

Printed in the United States of America

CONTENTS

Contents

FOREWORD

This book has been a treasured volume in my library, standing on the shelf in company with Fenelon's *Spiritual Letters* and *Christian Perfection,* Oxenham's *Bees In Amber, The Oxford Book of Christian Verse,* and *The Imitation of Christ.* I have often turned to it in the quiet hours of the evening, and it has never failed to point my heart to Jesus Christ.

Anthology of Jesus was compiled by James Marchant and was first published in England by Cassell and Company in 1926. That same year, a slightly revised edition was published in the United States by Harpers. Marchant described the book as "a basket of flowers, gathered from many lands, from many ages, from saints and martyrs, from apostles and prophets, poets, priests and kings." You will find a variety of worshippers and witnesses in these pages, and it is this variety that gives richness to the book.

At the request of the publisher of this edition, I have edited the original Cassell's edition and eliminated some selections. The original volume had as its purpose the exalting of Jesus Christ, and that is the aim of this present edition. But allow the original editor to say it for himself: "This anthology has been designed to quicken faith and love, and to turn the hearts of this

vii

Foreword

generation... to Him Who alone can bring them salvation and peace without money and without price.''

Some of the contributors to this work held some doctrinal views that perhaps some of us might not agree with; but this disagreement must not rob us of the blessings of these selected writings.

My own heart and mind have been greatly enriched as I have read these selections and meditated on the Biblical truths that they present. I trust that this will be your experience as well.

WARREN W. WIERSBE

PREFACE

Here is a basket of flowers, gathered from many lands, from many ages, from saints and martyrs, from apostles and prophets, poets, priests and kings.

To these Jesus was, and still is to a host in Heaven and on earth which no man can number, Lord and Savior, the Prince of Peace, the Rose of Sharon, and the Bright Morning Star, the Fairest among ten thousand, and the Altogether Lovely One.

These flowers are the flowers of the soul of a great company of His disciples, many of whom now behold Him face to face. Amongst them are blossoms reverently placed on His shrine by some who could not follow Him, but who were constrained by truth to declare that He is the greatest amongst the sons of men.

In these pages, the disciples of Jesus may follow the story of His earthly life in the Holy Land, from the morning when shepherds heard the Heavenly choir singing above the green pastures of Bethlehem, to the evening when a cloud on Olivet received Him out of their sight. They may here obtain a glimpse of His Resurrection Life in His Church throughout the centuries, of His influence upon the social and moral life of peoples, upon art and literature, music and song, upon the lives alike of the most despised and rejected, and of those clad in purple and fine linen.

Preface

In the twentieth century as in the first, Jesus is the center and circumference of His Church and of the life of His disciples. In their highest moments one and all exclaim with the apostle Paul, "I live, yet not I, but Christ liveth in me: and the life which I now live in the flesh, I live by the faith of the Son of God, who loved me, and gave Himself for me."

This anthology has been designed to quicken faith and love, and to turn the hearts of this generation, worn with sorrow and suffering, heavy-laden, and sorely disappointed with seemingly ineffectual sacrifices, to Him Who alone can bring them salvation and peace without money and without price.

JAMES MARCHANT

ANTHOLOGY OF JESUS

PROLOGUE

1

On the Threshold

I stand at the door. . . . I am the door.
Revelation 3:20, John 10:9

1. MATHESON

"BEHOLD, I stand at the door and knock."
Why does He not come in ? Is not this Divine
Spirit omnipotent ? Has He not power to enter
where He will, to breathe where He chooses, to blow
where He listeth ? Why, then, does He stand
without, knocking at the door of a frail human heart ?
Could He not break down that door in a moment,
in the twinkling of an eye, and annihilate that opposing
barrier which disputes His claim to universal empire ?
Yes, but in so doing He would annihilate also the
man. What makes me a man is just my power to
open the door. If I had no power to open or to
forbear opening I would not be responsible. The
Divine Spirit might then, indeed, do with me what
He will, but I would not be worth His possession.
I would be simply as the unconscious stars which He
fills with light, as the blind winds which He directs
on their way. But if the stars and the winds had been

enough He would never have said, " Let us make man." He made me because He meant me to be more than a star, more than a breath of heaven. He meant me to respond to Himself, to open on His knocking at the door. He could have no joy in breaking down the door, in taking the kingdom of my heart by violence ; there would be no response in that, no answer of a heart to His heart, no acceptance of a will by His Will. Therefore, He prefers to stand without till I open, to knock till I hear, to speak till I respond. He would not have my being to be lost in His, for His being is love, and love demands love.

Whether Thou comest to me in sunshine or in rain, I would take Thee into my heart joyfully. Thou art Thyself more than the sunshine, Thou art Thyself compensation for the rain ; it is Thee and not Thy gifts I crave ; knock and I shall open unto Thee.

2. À KEMPIS

CHRIST will come to thee, holding out to thee His consolation, if thou prepare Him a fit dwelling within thee.

Many a visit does He make to the interior man ; sweet is His communication with him, delightful His consolation, great His peace, and His familiarity exceedingly amazing. Give place, then, for Christ, and deny entrance to all others.

" He that followeth Me, walketh not in darkness," saith the Lord. These are the words of Christ, by which we are taught to imitate His life and manners,

2

if we would be truly enlightened, and be delivered from all blindness of heart. Let, therefore, our chief endeavour be to meditate upon the life of Jesus Christ.

When thou hast Christ thou art rich, and He is sufficient for thee. He will provide for thee and faithfully supply thy wants in all things, so that thou needest not trust to men.

" Son," says Christ to us, " leave thyself, and thou shalt find Me."

3. CHRISTINA ROSSETTI

BUT Christ can give thee heart Who loveth thee:
Can set thee in the eternal ecstasy
Of His great jubilee :
Can give thee dancing heart and shining face,
And lips filled full of grace,
And pleasures as the rivers and the sea
Who knocketh at His door.
He welcomes evermore :
Kneel down before
That ever-open door.
The time is short, and smite
Thy breast, and pray with all thy might.

4. FAIRBAIRN

THE greatest problems in the field of history centre in the Person and Life of Christ. Who He was, what He was, how and why He came to be it, are questions that have not lost and will not lose

3

their interest for us and for mankind. For the problems that centre in Jesus have this peculiarity : they are not individual, but general—concern not a person, but the world. How we are to judge Him is not simply a curious point for historical criticism, but a vital matter for religion. Jesus Christ is the most powerful spiritual force that ever operated for good on and in humanity. He is to-day what He has been for centuries—an object of reverence and love to the good, the cause of remorse and change, penitence and hope to the bad ; of moral strength to the morally weak, of inspiration to the despondent, consolation to the desolate, and cheer to the dying. He has created the typical virtues and moral ambitions of civilized man ; has been to the benevolent a motive to beneficence, to the selfish a persuasion to self-forgetful obedience ; and has become the living ideal that has steadied and raised, awed and guided youth, braced and ennobled manhood, mellowed and beautified age. In Him the Christian ages have seen the manifested Good, the Eternal living in time, the Infinite within the limits of humanity ; and their faith has glorified His sufferings into a sacrifice by the Creator for the creature, His death into an atonement for human sin. No other life has done such work, no other person been made to bear such transcendent and mysterious meanings. It is impossible to touch Jesus without touching millions of hearts now living and yet to live. He is, whatever else He may be, as a world's imperishable wonder, a world's everlasting problem, as a pre-eminent object of human faith, a pre-eminent subject of human thought.

4

On the Threshold

5. DIDON

JESUS CHRIST is the great name in history. There are others for whom men have died ; He alone is adored by all people, in all nations, and in all times.

He who bears this name is known throughout the world. Even among the savage and degenerate tribes of the human race, His apostles preach without ceasing that He died upon the cross ; and the off-scourings of mankind may be saved by loving Him. Those who are neutral, in the modern world, recognize that none is better for the weak and miserable.

The greatest intellects of the past would be forgotten if memorials, as palaces, obelisks or tombs ; if written testimonies, as papyrus or parchments, bricks, columns or medals, had not preserved their memory. Jesus survives in the conscience of the faithful : there is His witness and indestructible monument. The Church founded by Him fills time and space with His name. She knows Him, she loves Him, she adores Him.

6. ST. MATTHEW

COME unto me, all ye that labour and are heavy laden, and I will give you rest.

Take my yoke upon you, and learn of me ; for I am meek and lowly in heart ; and ye shall find rest unto your souls,

For my yoke is easy and my burden is light.

7. THE ALEXANDRIAN APOSTLE

GOD, who at sundry times and in divers manners spake in time past unto the fathers by the prophets,

Hath in these last days spoken unto us by his Son, whom he hath appointed heir of all things, by whom also he made the worlds;

Who being the brightness of his glory, and the express image of his person, and upholding all things by the word of his power, when he had by himself purged our sins, sat down on the right hand of the Majesty on high;

Being made so much better than the angels, as he hath by inheritance obtained a more excellent name than they.

For unto which of the angels said he at any time, Thou art my Son, this day have I begotten thee? And again, I will be to him a Father, and he shall be to me a son?

And again, when he bringeth in the firstbegotten into the world, he saith: And let all the angels of God worship him.

And of the angels he saith: Who maketh his angels spirits, and his ministers a flame of fire.

But unto the Son he saith: Thy throne, O God, is for ever and ever: a sceptre of righteousness is the sceptre of thy kingdom.

———————

Behold, I stand at the door and knock.

He that Should Come

Before Abraham was, I am.—John 8:58

8. LACORDAIRE

THE proportions of the work of Christ in the times which preceded Him are more striking than all the divine proportions of His life and His after-life. For when a man lives, He is a power; He has an action; it is possible to conceive that certain circumstances may have favoured a man of rare genius, and have given him great ascendancy over his contemporaries. But what are we able to do upon that which precedes us, upon the past? Who among us, however eminent he may be, is able to make an ancestor for himself? Who among us, desiring to found a doctrine, is able to create for himself an *avant-garde* of generations already faithful to a teaching which had not been heard? Who among us will present his doctrinal ancestry to the world, if he be not truly the son of a doctrine anterior to himself? Ah! the past is a land closed against us; the past is not even a place wherein God can act, unless He act there beforehand, and by way of preparation. Had Jesus Christ been like one of us, fallen without a providential pre-existence between the past and the future, He would in vain have demanded from history accomplished and closed a pedestal which would bear Him back twenty centuries beyond His cradle. Instead of this, Abraham, Isaac, Jacob, David, Isaiah, Jeremiah, Ezekiel, Daniel, a whole people, the human race itself, came to meet and salute Him in the arms of the aged Simeon, exclaiming in the name of all the past, of which he is the last representative : "Lord, now lettest Thou Thy servant depart in peace, according to Thy word : For mine eyes have seen Thy salvation, which Thou hast prepared before the face of all people ; A light to lighten the Gentiles, and the glory of Thy people Israel."

9. PASCAL

SUPPOSING one single man to have left a book of predictions concerning Jesus Christ as to the time and manner of His coming, and supposing Him to have come agreeably to these predictions, the argument would be of almost infinite force ; yet here the evidence is stronger beyond all comparison ; a succession of men for the space of four thousand years follow one another, without interruption or variation, in foretelling the same great event. A whole people are the harbingers of the Messias, and such a people as subsisted four thousand years to testify in a general body their assured hope and expectation, from which no severity of threats or persecutions could oblige them to depart. This is a case which challengeth in a far more transcendent degree our assent and wonder.

He that Should Come

10. DEAN STANLEY

IT is acknowledged by all students of the subject that the Hebrew prophets made predictions concerning the fortunes of their own and other countries which were unquestionably fulfilled. It is a simple and universally recognized fact that, filled with these Prophetic images, the whole Jewish nation—nay, at last the whole Eastern world—did look forward with longing expectation to the coming of this future Conqueror. Was this unparalleled expectation realized ? And here again I speak of facts which are acknowledged by Germans and Frenchmen, no less than by Englishmen, by critics and by sceptics, even more fully than by theologians and ecclesiastics. There did arise out of this nation a Character by universal consent as unparalleled as the expectation which had preceded Him. Jesus of Nazareth was, on the most superficial no less than on the deepest view we take of His coming, the greatest name, the most extraordinary power, that has ever crossed the stage of history. And this greatness consisted not in outward power, but precisely in those qualities on which from first to last the Prophetic order had laid the utmost stress—justice and love, goodness and truth.

11. GARVIE

THE utterances about pre-existence we can deal with apart from the metaphysical explanations and the doctrine of the Logos. What remains is the response to the challenge of His enemies. " Before

Abraham was, I am." The contrast here between
γενέσθαι and εἰμί indicates a timeless existence.
The term pre-existence is contradictory, as expressing
such timeless existence, since it suggests priority in
time, and to speak of a continuity of consciousness
between that timeless existence and the whole of the
life in time is to make a development under human
conditions and limitations altogether inconceivable.
The only intelligible explanation of such a saying,
accepting its authenticity, is this, that the more Jesus'
claim was challenged the more certain He became
of His relation to God as Son to Father, and that this
certainty included a distinct intuition that this relation
had not and could not have begun in time, but was
eternal as God Himself.

12. LAURENCE HOUSMAN

COMEST Thou peaceably, O Lord ?
    " Yea, I am Peace !
Be not so fearful to afford
Thy Maker room ! for I am the Reward
    To which all generations of increase
    Looking did never cease.

" Down from amid dark wings of storm
    I set My Feet
To earth. Will not My earth grow warm
To feel her Maker take the form
    He made, when now, Creation's purpose
      meet,
    Man's body is to be God's Mercy-seat ? "

He that Should Come

Lord, I am foul : there is no whole
    Fair part in me
    Where Thou canst deign to be !
This form is not Thy making, since it stole
    Fruit from the bitter Tree.
" Yet still thou hast the griefs to give in toll
That I may test the sickness of man's soul."

O Lord, my work is without worth !
    I am afraid,
Lest I should mar the blissful Birth
Quoth Christ, " 'Ere seas had shores, or earth
    Foundations laid,
    My Cross was made ! "

" Naught canst thou do that was not willed
    By Love to be,
    To bring the Work to pass through Me.
No knee
    Stiffens, or bends before My Sov'reignty,
But from the world's beginning hath fulfilled
Its choice betwixt the valleyed and the hilled.
    For both, at one decree,
My Blood was spilled."

Yet canst Thou use these sin-stained hands ?
    " These hands," quoth Christ,
    " Of them I make My need :
Since they sufficed to forge the bands
    Wherein I hunger, they shall sow the seed !
    And with bread daily they shall feed
My Flesh till, brought and bound, It stands
    A Sacrifice to bleed."

13. DIDON

SUCH were the elements fused in mankind. towards the eighth century of Rome, in the 192nd Olympiad, and according to Jewish chronology, at the end of four thousand years from the creation. It was, according to the first word which fell from the lips of Jesus, " the fulness of time." The empire, paganism, philosophy, official Judaism, all human forces had accomplished their evolution ; the world was dying, enslaved by Roman policy, degraded and brought to despair by false religions, asking philosophers in vain for the secrets of life and virtue. Judaism itself was in the death-throe, faithless to its destiny. There was never a more critical moment ; but God was over all, and among his elect people humble souls prayed and hoped. Beyond Judaism, a vague expectation, to which poets, historians and the Sibylline books bear witness, was astir, and kept the world in suspense : such a presentiment as goes before all the great events of history.

The birth of Jesus was at hand.

3

His Advent

Good tidings of great joy.—Luke 2:10

14. ST. LUKE

THE angel said to her : Hail, full of grace.
The Lord is with thee ! Blessèd art thou among
women.

And when she saw him, she was troubled at his
saying, and cast in her mind what manner of salutation
this should be. And the angel said unto her, Fear
not, Mary : for thou hast found favour with God.
And, behold, thou shalt conceive in thy womb, and
bring forth a son, and shalt call his name Jesus. He
shall be great, and shall be called the Son of the
Highest : and the Lord God shall give unto him the
throne of his father David : and he shall reign over
the house of Jacob for ever ; and of his kingdom
there shall be no end.

And so it was that . . . the days were accom-
plished that she should be delivered. And she brought
forth her first-born son, and wrapped him in swaddling
clothes, and laid him in a manger because there was
no room for them in the inn.

15. MILTON

I

IT was the winter wild,
While the heaven-born child
All meanly wrapt in the rude manger lies;
Nature in awe to Him
Had doffed her gaudy.trim,
With her great Master so to sympathize.
It was no season then for her
To wanton with the Sun her lusty paramour.

IV

No war or battle's sound
Was heard the world around;
The idle spear and shield were high up hung;
The hookèd chariot stood,
Unstained with hostile blood;
The trumpet spake not to the armèd throng;
And kings sat still with awful eye,
As if they surely knew their sovran Lord was by.

VIII

The shepherds on the lawn,
Or ere the point of dawn,
Sat simply chatting in a rustic row;
Full little thought they than
That the mighty Pan
Was kindly come to live with them below.
Perhaps their loves, or else their sheep,
Was all that did their silly thoughts so busy keep.

His Advent

At last surrounds their sight
A globe of circular light,
That with long beams the shame-faced Night arrayed.
The helmed Cherubim,
And sworded Seraphim,
Are seen, in glittering ranks with wings displayed,
Harping, in loud and solemn quire,
With unexpressive notes to Heaven's new-born
Heir.

Such music—as 'tis said—
Before was never made,
But when of old the Sons of Morning sung;
While the Creator great
His constellations set,
And the well-balanced World on hinges hung,
And cast the dark foundations deep,
And bid the weltering waves their oozy channel
keep.

16. CHRISTINA ROSSETTI

IN the bleak mid-winter
Frosty wind made moan,
Earth stood hard as iron,
Water like a stone;
Snow had fallen, snow on snow,
Snow on snow,
In the bleak mid-winter
Long ago.

Our God, heaven cannot hold Him,
   Nor earth sustain :
Heaven and earth shall flee away
   When He comes to reign :
In the bleak mid-winter
   A stable-place sufficed
The Lord God Almighty
   Jesus Christ.

Enough for Him Whom cherubim
   Worship night and day,
A breastful of milk
   And a manger full of hay ;
Enough for Him Whom angels
   Fall down before,
The ox and ass and camel
   Which adore.

Angels and archangels
   May have gathered there,
Cherubim and seraphim
   Thronged the air,
But only his mother
   In her maiden bliss
Worshipped the Belovèd
   With a kiss.

17. ELIZABETH BROWNING

WE sate among the stalls at Bethlehem.
   The dumb kine from their fodder turning them,
Softened their hornèd faces
To almost human gazes
Towards the newly Born.

His Advent

The simple shepherds from the star-lit brooks
    Brought visionary looks,
As yet in their astonied hearing rung
    The strange, sweet angel-tongue.
The Magi of the East, in sandals worn,
    Knelt reverent, sweeping round,
With long pale beards, their gifts upon the
      ground—
    The incense, myrrh, and gold,
These baby hands were impotent to hold.
So, let all earthlies and celestials wait
    Upon Thy royal state !
    Sleep, sleep, my Kingly One !

18. DANTE GABRIEL ROSSETTI

THIS is that blessed Mary, pre-elect
   God's Virgin. Gone is a great while, and
     she
Dwelt young in Nazareth of Galilee.
Unto God's will she brought devout respect,
Profound simplicity of intellect,
And supreme patience. From her mother's
     knee
Faithful and hopeful ; wise in charity ;
Strong in grave peace ; in pity circumspect.
So held she through her girlhood ; as it were
An angel-watered lily, that near God
Grows and is quiet. Till, one dawn at home
She woke in her white bed and had no fear
At all, yet wept till sunshine, and felt awed
Because the fullness of the time was come.

17

19. G. K. CHESTERTON

THE Christ-Child lay on Mary's lap,
His hair was like a light.
(O weary, weary were the world,
But here is all aright.)
The Christ-Child lay on Mary's breast,
His hair was like a star.
(O stern and cunning are the Kings,
But here the true hearts are.)
The Christ-Child lay on Mary's heart,
His hair was like a fire.
(O weary, weary is the world,
But here the world's desire.)
The Christ-Child stood on Mary's knee,
His hair was like a crown,
And all the flowers looked up at Him,
And all the stars looked down.

20. ALICE MEYNELL

NO sudden thing of glory and fear
Was the Lord's coming; but the dear
Slow Nature's days followed each other
To form the Saviour from His Mother
—One of the Children of the year.
The earth, the rain, received the trust
—The sun and dews, to frame the Just.
He drew His daily life from these,
According to His own decrees
Who makes man from the fertile dust.
Sweet summer and the winter wild,
These brought Him forth, the Undefiled.
The happy Springs renewed again
His daily bread, the growing grain,
The food and raiment of the Child.

His Advent

21. MARTIN

MANY a Hebrew in those days was looking
for *the Consolation of Israel.* Many were
searching the Scriptures of the prophets to see *what
time or what manner of time the Spirit of Christ which
was in them did point unto.* And the Temple shep-
herds, as they lay around their fire, talked of the
one theme which was then talked of wherever the
poor in spirit met together. One, it may be, had a
scroll from the Book of Isaiah, and, turning its charac-
ters towards the firelight, read to his fellows,

The government shall be upon his shoulder ; and
his name shall be called Wonderful, Counsellor,
Mighty God, Everlasting Father, Prince of Peace.

And presently another played on his lute marriage
music of the Messianic psalm men called *Shoshannim,*
that is *Lilies,* for was it not a music liquid, and as
gold set in white, like the canopied flowers of the
field ? As he played his fellows sang,

Thy throne, O God, is for ever and ever :

A sceptre of equity is the sceptre of Thy kingdom.

Thou hast loved righteousness, and hated wicked-
ness :

Therefore God, Thy God, hath anointed Thee

With the oil of Gladness above Thy fellows.

All Thy garments smell of myrrh, and aloes, and
cassia ;

Out of ivory palaces stringed instruments have made
Thee glad.

One after another the Shepherds became aware of a
being from another sphere standing just outside their
circle, listening. Their drawing together in medita-
tion and song brought them all into the same conviction
about him.

Suddenly there was with the angel, who, it is said, *stood by them, a multitude of the heavenly host.* As at twilight in an unlighted room a flame will, in a moment, break out from a black coal-fire and illumine ceiling and walls and every furnishing, so the earth seemed suddenly inundated with light. There were heavenly beings all about the Shepherds. Up past the sheepfold, covering the fields and the hillsides, far away towards the desert and the Jordan valley, they crowded the landscape with their splendour. And they were praising God.

Just what they sang we can hardly tell.

For the angels were singing not to man but to God. And what may be the language of worlds higher than ours, who shall say? It must transcend all earthly dialects, as truly as our English speech transcends the chatter of monkeys in a forest. But the central fact is that the Elect Shepherds did overhear for a moment the worship of sinless hosts, and that that worship interpreted itself in their minds as a garment of praise woven of two strands—the Glory of God and the Peace of Man.

So the angels sang, and then ceased, and the Shepherds heard no more. The glory contracted, narrowed into a stream of silver that passed along those hills, and faded into the light of splendid stars, and all the earth was dark and still, except for the leaping fire of the bivouac and the tinkle of a sheep-bell.

22. LACORDAIRE

THE field of the shepherds is still there; flocks feed in winter under the olives, as in the days of

Jesus, in the fields where the grass still grows green, and the anemones flower. Worship has never left the place where shone the brightness of the birthday dawn of Christ. On Christmas evening the people of Bethlehem flock to the church of St. Helena, of which only the ruins remain, and in its desolate crypt they pray to the shepherds of Beir-Saour, their ancestors, who were the first apostles. Clad in their long white veils, seated in groups on the broken walls, beneath the shade of the circling olives, the women, seen from afar, recall the mysterious beings who heralded the advent of Jesus. The crowd has an air of cheerfulness and calm, which harmonizes well with the memories of which the plain is full; and with that Eastern light which colours the whole and gives to the sterile rock itself an appearance of richness and of life.

23. GEORGE HERBERT

THE shepherds sing; and shall I silent be?
   My God, no hymne for Thee?
My soul's a shepherd too; a flock it feeds
   Of thoughts and words and deeds:
The pasture is Thy word; the streams Thy grace,
   Enriching all the place.
Shepherd and flock shall sing, and all my powers
   Out-sing the daylight houres.

24. ST. LUKE

AND Mary said, My soul doth magnify the Lord,
   And my spirit hath rejoiced in God my Saviour.
For he hath regarded the low estate of his hand-

maiden : for, behold, from henceforth all generations shall call me blessed.

For he that is mighty hath done to me great things ; and holy is his name.

And his mercy is on them that fear him from generation to generation.

He hath showed strength with his arm ; he hath scattered the proud in the imagination of their hearts.

He hath put down the mighty from their seats' and exalted them of low degree,

He hath filled the hungry with good things ; and the rich he hath sent empty away.

He hath holpen his servant Israel, in remembrance of his mercy ;

As he spake to our fathers, to Abraham, and to his seed for ever.

4

His Name

Thou shalt call His name Jesus.—Matthew 1:21

25. SPURGEON

WHEN a person is dear, everything connected with him becomes dear for his sake. Thus so precious is the person of the Lord Jesus in the estimation of all true believers, that everything about Him they consider to be inestimable beyond all price. "All Thy garments smell of myrrh, and aloes, and cassia," said David, as if the very vestments of the Saviour were so sweetened by His person that he could not but love them. Certain it is, that there is not a spot where that hallowed foot hath trodden—there is not a word which those blessed lips have uttered—nor a thought which His loving Word has revealed—which is not to us precious beyond all price. And this is true of the *names* of Christ—they are all sweet in the believer's ear. Whether He be called the Husband of the Church, her Bridegroom, her Friend; whether He be styled the Lamb slain from the foundation of the world—the King, the Prophet, or the Priest—every title of our Master—Shiloh, Emmanuel, Wonderful, the Mighty Counsellor—every name is like the honeycomb dropping with honey, and luscious are the drops that distil from it. But if there be one name sweeter than another in the believer's ear, it is the name of *Jesus*. Jesus! it is the name which moves the harps of heaven to melody. Jesus! the life of all our joys. If there be one name more charming, more precious than another, it is this name. It is woven into the very warp and woof of our psalmody. Many of our hymns begin with it, and scarcely any, that are good for anything, end without it. It is the sum total of all delights. It is the music with which the bells of heaven ring; a song in a word; an ocean for comprehension, although a drop for brevity; a matchless oratorio in two syllables; a gathering up of the hallelujahs of eternity in five letters.

> "Jesus, I love Thy charming name.
> 'Tis music to mine ear."

("I remember with strange vividness," writes the Rev. W. J. FULLERTON, "the Sunday evening when Charles Spurgeon preached the sermon from which the above is taken. It was a subject in which he revelled, it was his chief delight to exalt his glorious Saviour, and he seemed in that discourse to be pouring out his very soul and life in homage and adoration before his Gracious King. But I really thought he would have died there, in face of all those people. At the end he made a mighty effort to recover his voice; but utterance well-nigh failed, and only in broken accents could the pathetic peroration be heard— 'Let my name perish, but let Christ's name last for ever! Jesus! *Jesus!* Jesus! Crown Him Lord of all! You will not hear me say anything else. These are my last words in Exeter Hall for this time. Jesus! Jesus! Jesus! Crown *Him* Lord of all!' and then he fell back almost fainting in the chair behind him.")

His Name

26. AN EARLY ENGLISH WRITER

AH! ah! that wonderful name! Ah! that delightable name! This is the name that is above all names, the highest name of all, withou which no man hopes for health. This name is in mine ear heavenly sound, in my mouth honeyful sweetness.

Soothly, Jesu, desirable is Thy name, lovable and comfortable. None so sweet joy may be conceived, none so sweet song may be heard, none so sweet and delightable solace may be had in mind

Soothly, nothing so slackens fell flames; destroys ill thoughts; puts out venomous affections; does away curious and vain occupations from us.

This name *Jesu*, leally holden in mind, draws out vices by the root; plants virtues; sows charity; pours in savour of heavenly things; wastes discord; forms again peace; gives lasting rest; does away grievousness of fleshly desires; turns all earthly things to nought; fills the loving with ghostly joy. . . .

Also know all that the name of *Jesus* is healthful, fruitful, and glorious. Therefore who shall have health that loves it not? Or who shall bear the fruit before Christ, that has not the flower? And joy shall he not see that in his joying loved not the name of *Jesu*.

27. RICHARD CRASHAW.

I SING the Name which None can say
But touch't with An interiour Ray:
The Name of our New Peace; our Good
Our Blisse: and Supernaturall Blood:
The Name of All our Lives and Loves.
Hearken, and Help, ye holy Doves!

The high-born Brood of Day; you bright
Candidates of blissefull light,
The Heirs Elect of Love; whose Names belong
Unto the Everlasting life of Song;
All ye wise Soules, who in the wealthy Brest
Of This unbounded Name build your warm Nest.

28. WESLEY

THOU hidden Source of calm repose,
    Thou all-sufficient Love Divine;
My help and refuge from my foes,
    Secure I am if Thou art mine;
And lo! from sin, and grief, and shame,
I hide me, Jesus, in Thy name.

Thy mighty name salvation is,
    And keeps my happy soul above;
Comfort it brings, and power, and peace,
    And joy, and everlasting love;
To me, with Thy dear name, are given
Pardon, and holiness, and heaven.

Jesus, my all-in-all Thou art—
    My rest in toil, my ease in pain,
The medicine of my broken heart,
    In war my peace, in loss my gain;
My smile beneath the tyrant's frown;
In shame, my glory and my crown.

In want, my plentiful supply;
    In weakness, my almighty power;
In bonds, my perfect liberty;
    My light in Satan's darkest hour
My help and stay whene'er I call;
My life in death, my heaven, my all.

5

The Temple and the Home

Now his parents went to Jerusalem every year at the feast of the passover. . . . And he went down with them, and came to Nazareth, and was subject unto them. . . . And Jesus increased in wisdom and stature, and in favour with God and man.
—Luke 2:41, 51, 52

29. DIDON

HIS parents, like all pious Jews, made each year, at the feast of the Passover, their journey to Jerusalem. He went with them; as His first step in life after His years of childhood, and His first public act of submission to the Law.

After a two-hours' march they came at last to Mount Scopus, to a place now called Naschevat, whence the Holy City suddenly appeared like a radiant vision; the Temple with its golden roof covered Mount Moriah; on Zion rose the palace of Herod and those of the high priests; all the domes shone white in the rising sun : sixty towers rose upon the walls, like giant sentinels round the city of the great King Scopus, with one summit crowned by Nabi Samuel, forming a semicircle of rocks and stones, grey and desolate, severely framing the Holy City to the north; the Mount of Olives rises to the east, covered with cypresses, cedars, and other sombre trees; on the horizon to the south, quite close, is the undulating chain of the mountains of Bethlehem, and in the far distance the hills of Moab faded into the sky. The sight of Jerusalem filled the pilgrims with unspeakable emotion, and they chanted, to express it, the Psalm of Degrees, " How goodly are Thy tabernacles, O Lord of Hosts ! " . . .

Those who know the manners of the East, and have seen the Jewish synagogues or the Moslem mosques, at the hour of teaching, will not wonder at this scene. A circle is made round the doctors, all sit on mats, listening, asking, answering by turns ; young and old are seated side by side, the teachers and the disciples with their legs crossed, on the same carpet, and all may speak. History does not tell us, but we may easily guess the questions of Jesus and His answers. He Who was to proclaim Himself as the Son of God and the expected Messiah, to preach the Sermon on the Mount, to show the emptiness of Jewish observances, to bring to all the Spirit of Salvation, must have showed some ray of the infinite wisdom with which He was filled. If human genius always reveals itself the divine wisdom of Christ must have done the same. What is really surprising is the shade in which Jesus remained so long voluntarily hidden. And when they saw Him thus admired by the most celebrated teachers and by the crowd, His parents " were amazed : and His mother said unto Him, Son, why hast Thou thus dealt with us ? Behold, Thy Father and I have sought Thee sorrowing. And He said unto them, How is it that ye sought Me ? Wist ye not that I must be about My Father's business?" The mind of Jesus is revealed for the first time in this mysterious speech : His whole Self was there in its fulness, with His title of Divine Sonship, His Sovereign initiative, His heavenly vocation ; His life, in its smallest detail, would be only the accomplishment of this that was spoken in His twelfth year. Neither Mary nor Joseph understood all its depth. Jesus went down with them to Nazareth, where He resumed His humble and laborious existence, waiting for His manifestation, the call of God.

30. MILTON

" ERE yet my age
Had measured twice six years, at our great feast
I went into the temple, there to hear
The teachers of our law, and to propose
What might improve my knowledge or their own ;
And was admired by all : yet this not all
To which my spirit aspired : victorious deeds
Flamed in my heart, heroic acts, one while
To rescue Israel from the Roman yoke ;
Then to subdue and quell, o'er all the earth
Brute violence and proud tyrannic power,
Till truth were freed, and equity restored."

31. LUTHER

CHRIST, our blessèd Saviour, forebore to preach and teach until the thirtieth year of His age, neither would He openly be heard ; no, though He beheld and heard so many impieties, abominable idolatries, heresies, blasphemings of God, etc. It was a wonderful thing He could abstain, and with patience endure them, until the time came that He was to appear in His office of preaching.

32. MARTIN

IN His youth He must have been laying the foundations of future health, because afterwards when the full pressure of the toils of manhood was upon Him, He bore His terrific burdens without breaking down. His powers of endurance are often evident to the reader of the Gospels. In His public work He could be intensely busy, often forfeiting His meals, and spending His nights in prayer. The people flagged at His preaching, and once, at least, He had to find a meal for them in the wilderness, but there is no record that He partook of it Himself. Physically He must have arrested the eyes of men everywhere. The ring of health and strength was in His voice, so that the evangelists sometimes write, *Jesus cried and said.* The evil-minded shrank before Him when His anger showed. And all these things, I say, were founded in a youth that was without weakness, slackness, vice, and that was strenuous and pure in body as in mind.

6

His Baptism

Suffer it to be so now.— Matthew 3:15

33. LACORDAIRE

ABOUT the end of the year 27, perhaps in the first days of the year 28, Galilee, like all the other provinces, was filled with the name of John the Baptist; the people of Galilee, under the impulse which carried all the Jews with it, came in their turn to ask for baptism. This was for Jesus the hour of God. The Carpenter of Nazareth was thirty years old; he joined the caravans of his country and descended into the valley of Jordan to the very place that John had chosen for His baptism.

Thither came Jesus, lost in the crowd. John knew Him not, but as Jesus approached a sudden vision revealed Him. Above the head of Jesus, John saw the heavens open; and the Spirit of God, under the bodily form of a dove, descending and lighting upon Him.

This was the expected sign. John then understood that which no human knowledge, no genius could teach him; he must needs experience one of those unspeakable emotions which show that God is there. He saluted Jesus of Nazareth, and refused to baptize Him, saying, " I have need to be baptized of Thee, and comest Thou to me ? And Jesus answering said unto him, Suffer it to be so now : for thus it becometh us to fulfil all righteousness. Then He suffered him."

The depth of these words is the guarantee of their authenticity ; they throw an unexpected light on the soul of Jesus, they show that He had a perfect knowledge of His Messianic vocation, and that in submitting to the rite instituted by John, He already began to realize it.

The greatest men have only their genius, their will, and their passions ; amongst the most holy, the inspiration of God is added to all these springs of personal energy, an inspiration often ephemeral, always limited, which allows the weakness of man still to manifest itself ; but this public consecration revealed in Jesus the fullness of the Spirit, and this Spirit was the sovereign principle of all His thoughts and will, of His discourses, actions, and plans. Jesus was to communicate the Spirit to us. The scene of His baptism, which contains the secret of regeneration, was to reproduce itself even to the end of the world ; water was to be one day, by special institution, consecrated to be the sacrament of man's regeneration, and the baptism of water was to become the baptism of the Spirit. Whoever, at the call of Christ, will quit his vices, his ignorance, and his selfishness, through repentance, sacrifice, and faith, whoever will enter into the words of Jesus, will see, like Him, the gates of heaven open, the sons of earth and of corrupt mankind will become the sons of God, they will hear in the depths of their conscience the Spirit murmur this ineffable name, and they will learn of Him to call God their Heavenly Father.

His Baptism

34. MILTON

NOW had the great Proclaimer, with a voice
More awful than the sound of trumpet, cried
Repentance, and heaven's kingdom nigh at hand
To all baptized : to His great baptism flocked
With awe the regions round, and with them came
From Nazareth the son of Joseph deemed
To the flood Jordan, came, as then obscure,
Unmarked, unknown ; but Him the Baptist soon
Descried, divinely warned, and witness bore
As to His worthier, and would have resigned
To Him his heavenly office, nor was long
His witness unconfirmed : on Him baptized
Heaven opened, and in likeness of a dove
The Spirit descended, while the Father's voice
From Heaven pronounced Him His belovèd Son.

7

The Temptation

Tempted like as we are.— Hebrews 4:15

35. MILTON

The Son of God,
Musing, and much revolving in His breast
How best the mighty work He might begin
Of Saviour to mankind, and which way first
Publish His God-like office, now mature,
One day walked forth alone, the Spirit leading,
And His deep thoughts, the better to converse
With solitude ; till far from track of men,
Thought following thought, and step by step led on
He entered now the bordering desert wild,
And, with dark shades and rocks environ'd round,
His holy meditations thus pursued. . . .
Sole, but with holiest meditations fed,
Into Himself descended, and at once
All His great work to come before Him set ;
How to begin, how to accomplish best
His end of being on Earth, and mission high.

36. FAIRBAIRN

THE place where it happened is not without
significance. Into what wilderness Jesus was
led to be tempted we do not know—whether the
wild and lonely solitudes watched by the mountains
where Moses and Elijah struggled in prayer and

The Temptation

conquered in faith, or the steep rock by the side of the Jordan overlooking the Dead Sea, which later tradition has made the arena of this fell conflict. Enough, the place was a desert, waste, barren, shelterless, overhead the hot sun, underfoot the burning sand or blistering rock. No out-branching trees made a cool restful shade ; no spring upbursting with a song of gladness came to relieve the thirst ; no flowers bloomed, pleasing the eye with colour and the nostrils with fragrance : all was drear desert. Now, two things may be here noted—the desolation, and the solitude. The heart that loves Nature is strangely open to her influences. The poet sees a glory in the light of setting suns, and the round ocean and the living air, which exalts and soothes him ; but a land of waste and cheerless gloom casts over his spirit a shadow as of the blackest darkness. And Jesus had the finest, most sensitive soul that ever looked through human eyes. He loved this beautiful world, loved the stars that globed themselves in the heaven above, the flowers that bloomed in beauty on the earth beneath, the light and shade that played upon the face of Nature, now brightening it as with the smile of God, now saddening it as with the pity that gleams through a cloud of tears. Think, then, how the desolation must have deepened the shadows on His spirit, increased the burden that made Him almost faint at the opening of His way. And He was in solitude—alone there, without the comfort of a human presence, the fellowship of a kindred soul. Yet the loneliness was a sublime necessity. In His supreme moments society was impossible to Him. The atmosphere that surrounded the Temptation, the Transfiguration, the Agony, and the Cross, He

35

alone could breathe; in it human sympathy slept or died, and human speech could make no sound. Out of loneliness He issued to begin His work; into loneliness He passed to end it. The moments that made His work divinest were His own and His Father's.

37. H. C. G. MOULE

THERE is no more mysterious scene in the whole story of the Gospels than the temptation in the wilderness. That dark enigma, the existence and the awful power of a personal Lord of Evil, recognized everywhere as a fact in the New Testament, appears here in all its darkness. And, darkness is indeed a living midnight, when we see it face to face with the sinless Son of God and Man. Who shall fathom the depth of the secret reasons which constrained the Lord, under the immediate power and guidance of the Holy Spirit poured on Him without measure, to submit Himself to the personal, positive, and profoundly subtle assaults of the Evil Spirit, alone and in the waste ?

All that we can know is that the dreadful encounter was a vital factor in His incarnate experience, and that the endurance of it, and then the victorious sequel, like all that He did and suffered, were of infinite import for our blessing.

This at least we know, that the Lord Jesus Christ is now, in the power of that strife and of that victory, able to enter into the very depth of every moral struggle of His disciples, and "able to succour also them that are tempted," with the sympathetic power of an almighty but all-sensitive Fellow-Sufferer.

The Temptation

38. LACORDAIRE

THE destiny of Jesus did not call Him to delay long in the desert; He only halted there.

The greatest among religious men go into the desert to seek energy, Jesus retired there to show it; they seek solitude and peace, Jesus sought strife; they ask in it a refuge against evil, Jesus came there to pray, to endure the assaults of Satan and to overcome him. He Who had been proclaimed by God Himself to be the Son of God, could not free Himself from the sad conditions of humanity; He had already made, in His baptism, a public profession of expiation and sacrifice, He was to submit himself to the law of trial, under a mysterious and difficult form which defies human reason and of which the historian must seek to penetrate the enigma.

Jesus was fasting in the desert. For forty days and forty nights, like Moses and Elias, he neither ate nor drank, nor felt the pangs of hunger. All the needs of life were at rest. In a momentary freedom from this slavery, earth had no hold on him. None can tell to how great a degree of liberty, independence, and spiritual freedom, a soul absorbed by God may bring its own body. Time exists no longer for the spirit which God withdraws from all terrestrial things, from all which can change and perish, and steeps in his eternal light.

39. MATHESON

AND the devil, taking him up into an high mountain, showed unto him all the kingdoms of the world in a moment of time.

The tempter had tried the Son of Man through the

power of depression ; he now tries Him by the power of exaltation. He had sought to vanquish Him by the scourge of poverty ; he now seeks to overcome Him by the vision of plenty. He had brought Him down into the valley and had tempted Him by the dangers of humiliation ; he now carries Him up to the mountain and tempts Him by the dangers of elevation.

O Thou Divine Spirit, that hast proved Thy strength alike over the valley and over the mountain, let me find my strength in Thee. I need Thee, that I may be strong everywhere. I long to be independent of all circumstances alike of the cloud and of the sunshine. I want a power to keep me from being depressed in the vale and to prevent me from being giddy on the height ; to save me from sinking in despondency and to rescue me from soaring in pride. I want both a pillar of fire and a pillar of cloud ; a refuge from the night of adversity and a shield from the day of prosperity. I can find them in Thee. Thou hast proved Thy power both over the night and over the day ; Thou hast vanquished the tempter in the valley and Thou hast conquered the tempter on the hill. Come into my heart, and Thy power shall be my power. The earth shall be mine and the fullness thereof. I shall be victorious over all circumstances, at home in all scenes, restful in all fortunes. I shall have power to tread upon scorpions, and they shall do me no hurt ; the world shall be mine when Thy Spirit is in me.

40. À KEMPIS

I PRAISE and highly exalt Thee for ever, for Thy mighty conflict with the devil ; for the many vexations of the wicked tempter ; for the scorn of all his evil suggestions; for meeting his proposals by fitting answers taken from the Word of God; and for the glorious victory over the three great vices, achieved by Thee; to the perpetual confusion of Satan, and the strengthening of our infirmity.

41. FARRAR

THE Temptation was real, not a mere semblance. Our Lord, under stress of genuine temptation, had to win the victory, in man and for man, by evincing self-denial, self-control, disregard for selfish advantage; absolute renunciation of power, honour, and self-gratification; and complete self-surrender to His Heavenly Father's will. If the struggle had not been an actual struggle, there would have been no significance in the victory. The Gospels represent Jesus as subject to temptations from without, not only at this crisis, but during all His life. He said to Peter, " Get thee behind Me, Satan : thou art a *stumbling-block* unto Me "; and He said to His Apostles, " Ye are they which have continued with Me in My temptations." The only difference between the temptations of Christ and our own is that His came from without, but ours come also from within. In Him " the tempting opportunity " could not appeal to " the susceptible disposition." With us sin acquires its deadliest force, because we have yielded to it. We can only conquer it when, by the triumph of God's grace within us, we are able to say with the dying hero of Azincour, " Get thee hence, Satan; thou hast no part in me; my part is in the Lord Jesus Christ."

8

His Miracles

The whole multitude sought to touch him : for there went virtue out of him, and healed them all.
—Luke 6:19

42. SEELEY

BETWEEN the astonishing design and its astonishing success there intervenes an astonishing instrumentality—that of miracles. It will be thought by some that in asserting miracles to have been actually wrought by Christ we go beyond what the evidence, perhaps beyond what any possible evidence, is able to sustain. Waiving then for the present the question whether miracles were actually wrought, we may state a fact which is fully capable of being established by ordinary evidence, and which is actually established by evidence as ample as any historical fact whatever—the fact, namely, that Christ *professed* to work miracles. We may go farther, and assert with confidence that Christ was believed by His followers really to work miracles, and that it was mainly on this account that they conceded to Him the pre-eminent dignity and authority which He claimed. The accounts we have of these miracles may be exaggerated ; it is possible that in some special cases stories have been related which have no foundation whatever ; but, on the whole, miracles play so important a part in Christ's scheme that any theory which would represent them as due entirely to the imagination of His followers or of a later age destroys the credibility of the documents not partially but wholly, and leaves Christ a personage as mythical as Hercules.

43. STORRS

THE impressive moral lessons always implied in the miracles of the Lord constitute a just and forcible argument for them. The spiritual meanings so illustriously set before men surpass any limits of time, and are equally vital for each generation. Goethe missed the true lesson of one of the miracles referred to by him : but even then he saw in it a secondary significance, of secular value :—

" I have been reading in the New Testament, and thinking of a picture Goethe showed me," wrote Eckermann, " of Christ walking on the water, and Peter coming towards Him, at the moment when the apostle begins to sink in consequence of losing faith for a moment. ' This,' said Goethe, ' is a most beautiful history, and one which I love better than any. It expresses the noble doctrine, that man, through faith and animated courage, may come off victor in the most dangerous enterprises, while he may be ruined by a momentary paroxysm of doubt.' "

44. CHANNING

CHRIST'S miracles are in unison with His whole character, and bear a proportion to it, like that which we observe in the most harmonious productions of nature : and in this way they receive from it great confirmation. And the same presumption in their favour arises from His religion. That a religion carrying in itself such marks of divinity and so inexplicable on human principles, should receive outward confirmations from Omnipotence, is not surprising. The extraordinary character of the religion accords with and seems to demand extraordinary interpositions in its behalf. Its miracles are not solitary, naked, unexplained, disconnected events, but are bound up with a system, which is worthy of God, and impressed with God; which occupies a large space, and is operating with great and increasing energy, in human affairs.

45. DALE

ACCORDING to the Christian case, the miracles of Christ belong to the life and work of One who has changed, and changed immeasurably for the better, the moral and religious condition of great nations, and whose power after the lapse of eighteen centuries is still unspent. In the narratives which record the miracles of Christ the miracles are not the most wonderful elements: His teaching, His unique Personality, the Divine perfection revealed under human conditions in His character and history, are more wonderful still. Finally, His appearance has proved to be the transcendent fulfilment of a great hope which, for many centuries, had been the stay, the strength, and the consolation of the race from which He sprang, a race to which had come an exceptional knowledge of God. That Christ should have worked miracles does not surprise me. It would have surprised me if He had not.

His Miracles

46. CRASHAW

CRASHAW once wrote on the Miracle of Cana
of Galilee :
" The Conscious Water knew its Lord, and blushed."

47. MATHESON

" AND their eyes were opened ; and Jesus straitly
charged them, saying, ' See that no man know
it.' " Why conceal the miraculous cure ? Because
He wanted to be loved, not for His wealth, but for
His soul. . . . The Son of Man fears to be first
known as the Son of God. He is afraid you judge
the work by its title-page—accept the rhythm for the
sake of the ring. Therefore, He veils Himself :
He enters into a cloud ; He puts on the disguise
of a servant ; He works wonders by stealth ; He flies
from fame ; He buries underground the trophies
of His glory. He wants me to love Him for Himself
—through the mean apparel, through the human
weakness, through the common pain. He wants me
to find His pearl in the dust, His beauty in the manger,
His crown in the cross. He wants me to see Him
by His own light—spirit light, soul light. He meets
with me on the road to Emmaus, and talks with me,
and makes my heart burn ; but He tells me not at
first that His name is Jesus. Perhaps I call Him
by other names—nature, art, science, culture,
humanity. Be it so ; mine eyes are holden by *His*
hand. He covers my face, that I may not see His
glory. He makes me love Him in disguise. He
veils His coronet, that I may come to His inner
beauty. Oh, blest disguise ! Oh, glorious veil !

Oh, revealing silence !   My heart finds itself in thee.
It has loved a captive, and He is found to be a king :
it has adored a manger, and it proves to be a palace.
I bless His mighty name that He won my love
unknown.

48. HEBER

THE winds were howling o'er the deep,
    Each wave a watery hill ;
The Saviour waken'd from His sleep ;
    He spake, and all was still.

The madman in a tomb had made
    His mansion of despair :
Woe to the traveller who stray'd
    With heedless footsteps there !

He met that glance, so thrilling sweet ;
    He heard those accents mild ;
And, melting at Messiah's feet,
    Wept like a weaned child.

49. ORIGEN

THAT He also raised the dead, and that this
is no fiction of those who composed the Gospels,
is shown by this : that if it had been a fiction, many
individuals would have been represented as having
risen from the dead.   But, as it is no fiction, they
are very easily counted of whom this is related to have
happened. . . .   I would say, moreover, that, agree-
ably to the promise of Jesus, His disciples performed
even greater works than these miracles of Jesus which

were perceptible only to the senses. For the eyes of those who are blind in soul are ever opened : and the ears of those who are deaf to virtuous words listen readily to the doctrine of God, and of the blessed life with Him : and many who were lame in the feet of the ' inner man,' as Scripture calls it, having now been healed by the word, do not simply leap, but leap as the hart, which is an animal hostile to serpents, and stronger than all the poison of vipers.

50. TENNYSON

WHEN Lazarus left his charnel-cave,
And home to Mary's house returned,
Was this demanded—if he yearn'd
To hear her weeping by his grave ?

" Where wert thou, brother, those four days ? "
There lives no record of reply,
Which telling what it is to die
Had surely added praise to praise.

From every house the neighbours met,
The streets were fill'd with joyful sound,
A solemn gladness even crown'd
The purple brows of Olivet.

Behold a man raised up by Christ !
The rest remaineth unreveal'd ;
He told it not ; or something seal'd
The lips of that Evangelist.

51. A. H. CLOUGH

I SAW again the spirits on a day,
  Where on the earth in mournful case they lay;
Five porches were there, and a pool and round,
Huddling in blankets, strewn upon the ground,
Tied-up and bandaged, weary, sore, and spent,
The maimed and halt, diseased and impotent.
For a great angel came, 'twas said, and stirred
The pool at certain seasons, and the word
Was, with this people of the sick, that they
Who in the waters here their limbs should lay
Before the motion of the surface ceased
Should of their torment straightway be released.
So with shrunk bodies and with heads down-dropt,
Stretched on the steps, and at the pillars propt,
Watching by day and listening through the night,
They filled the place, a miserable sight.

But what the waters of that pool might be,
Of Lethe were they, or Philosophy;
And whether he, long waiting, did attain
Deliverance from the burden of his pain
There with the rest; or whether, yet before
Some more diviner stranger passed the door
With his small company into that sad place,
And breathing hope into the sick man's face,
Bade him take up his bed, and rise and go.

52. STALKER

JESUS never, indeed, had a house of His own
  to which He could invite people. But on the two
occasions when He fed the five thousand and the four
thousand He acted as entertainer on a colossal scale.

His Miracles

It was a character in which He was thoroughly Himself; for it displayed His consideration for the common wants of man. Spiritual as He was and intent on the salvation of the soul, He never under-valued or overlooked the body. On the contrary He recognized on it the stamp and honour of its Maker, and He knew quite well that it is often only through the body that the soul can be reached. The great majority of His guests were doubtless poor, and it gratified His generous heart to confer a benefit on them. It was, indeed, but common fare He gave them; the table was the ground, the tablecloth was the green grass, and the banqueting hall was the open air; but never did His guests enjoy a better meal, for love presided at the table and it is love that makes an entertainment fine.

As we see Him there, beaming with genial delight over the vast company, it is impossible not to think of such words of His as these: " I am the bread of life "; " The bread which I shall give is My flesh, which I will give for the life of the world." In His teaching He delighted to represent the gospel as a feast, to which He invited all the sons of men in the beautiful spirit of a royal host.

53. LONGFELLOW

BLIND Bartimeus at the gates
Of Jericho in darkness waits;
He hears the crowd—he hears a breath
Say, " It is Christ of Nazareth!"
And calls in tones of agony,
" Jesus, have mercy now on me!"

The thronging multitudes increase ;
Blind Bartimeus, hold thy peace !
But still, above the noisy crowd,
The beggar's cry is shrill and loud ;
Until they say, " He calleth thee ! "
" Fear not, arise, He calleth thee ! "

Then saith the Christ, as silent stands
The crowd, " What wilt thou at My hands ? "
And he replies, " O give me light !
Rabbi, restore the blind man's sight."
And Jesus answers,
                " Go in peace
Thy faith from blindness gives release ! "

Ye that have eyes yet cannot see,
In darkness and in misery,
Recall those mighty Voices Three,
" Jesus, have mercy now on me !
Fear not, arise, and go in peace !
Thy faith from blindness gives release ! "

54. GARVIE

IT is in connexion both with the teaching and the
example of Jesus that the miracles may be with
most advantage considered. They must not be
regarded as external credentials of supernatural power
to enforce the authority of Jesus as teacher. That
teaching appeals to reason, conscience, affection, and
aspiration, and needs no such enforcement. The
miracles are necessary constituents of His message
and mission of grace, in which He revealed the love

of the Father to men, and showed the characteristics
of His own religious experience, moral character,
and mediatorial function. We shall not accordingly
give the miracles their due place if we lay stress on
the supernatural power which may have been dis-
played and not on their witness to His confidence
in God and compassion for man.

55. JOHN CHARLES EARLE

WIDE fields of corn along the valleys spread;
 The rain and dews mature the swelling vine;
I see the Lord is multiplying bread;
 I see Him turning water into wine;
 I see Him working all the works divine
He wrought when Salemward His steps were led;
 The selfsame miracles around Him shrine;
He feeds the famished; He revives the dead;
 He pours the flood of light on darkened eyes;
He chases tears, diseases, fiends away;
 His throne is raised upon these orient skies;
His footstool is the pave whereon we pray.
 Ah, tell me not of Christ in Paradise,
For He is all around us here to-day.

9

With His Disciples

*And he ordained twelve, that they should be with him,
and that he might send them forth to preach.*
　　　　　　　　　　　　　—Mark 3:14

56. ALEXANDER WHYTE

WHAT a never-to-be-forgotten time the twelve
disciples must have had when at leisure and
alone with their Master up among the hillsides and
watersheds of Galilee ! To have had His generous
discharge for a short season from their far too hard
work, and then to have been continually and un-
interruptedly with Him when He was in His holiday
mind—what a memorable experience that must have
been ! "Come away," He said to the overworked
twelve, "and I will take you to a place apart that no
man knows. For if this goes on, we shall all sink
under it before we have half-finished the work that
has been given us to do. There are so many coming
and going that we have no leisure so much as to eat."
And having so said, He arose and led His disciples
into a hill country that no man knew but He Himself.
And all their after days His disciples remembered
their first holiday with their Divine Master : the place
of it, and the occupations of it, and the recreations
and amusements of it, so high up among the delectable
mountains of Israel. Jesus of Nazareth had known
the whole of that hill country, every foot of it, from the

days of His youth. He knew all the places where
the water-springs rose and ran among the hills. He
knew where the fowls of heaven had their habitation
which sing among the branches. He took and con-
ducted His disciples to where the hills were watered
from the chambers of God, where the grass grew
for the cattle and herbs for the service of man.
The trees of the Lord were full of sap in the place
He chose for them to make their tabernacles, the
cedars of Lebanon which God had planted with His
own hands ; where the birds build their nests, and
where, as for the stork, the fir-trees are her house. The
high hills all around their retreat were a refuge for the
wild goats, and the rocks for the conies. And away up
there, for days and for weeks, they held their Summer
School of natural and revealed theology. No ; the
Stoics were not the founders of natural theology.
The prophets and the psalmists of Israel first founded
that heavenly science, and Jesus of Nazareth and
His twelve disciples were the devoted scholars and
the direct successors of those ancient prophets and
psalmists. The Eighth Psalm and the Nineteenth
Psalm and the Hundred-and-fourth Psalm are all full
of natural theology ; and those twelve theologians,
with their Master at their head, had a memorable
holiday-time singing those psalms and offering those
prayers up among the highlands of northern Israel.

57. STALKER

IT would be a very inadequate account of His
relation to the Twelve merely to point out the
insight with which He discerned in them the germs
of fitness for their grand future. They became

very great men, and in the founding of the Christian
Church achieved a work of immeasurable importance.
They may be said, in a sense they little dreamed of,
to sit on thrones ruling the modern world. They
stand like a row of noble pillars towering afar across
the flats of time. But the sunlight that shines on
them, and makes them visible, comes entirely from
Him. He gave them all their greatness; and theirs
is one of the most striking evidences of His. What
must He have been Whose influence imparted to
them such magnitude of character and made them
fit for so gigantic a task! At first they were rude
and carnal in the extreme. What hope was there
that they would ever be able to appreciate the designs
of a mind like His, to inherit His work, to possess
in any degree a spirit so exquisite, and transmit to
future generations a faithful image of His character?
But He educated them with the most affectionate
patience, bearing with their vulgar hopes and their
clumsy misunderstandings of His meaning. Never for-
getting for a moment the part they were to play in the
future, He made their training His most constant
work. They were much more constantly in His
company than even the general body of His disciples,
seeing all He did in public and hearing all He said.
They were often His only audience, and then He
unveiled to them the glories and mysteries of His
doctrine, sowing in their minds the seeds of truth,
which time and experience were by and by to fructify.
But the most important part of their training was one
which was perhaps at the time little noticed, though
it was producing splendid results,—the silent and
constant influence of His character on theirs. He
drew them to Himself and stamped His own image

on them. It was this which made them the men they became. For this, more than all else, the generations of those who love Him look back to them with envy. We admire and adore at a distance the qualities of His character; but what must it have been to see them in the unity of life, and for years to feel their moulding pressure! Can we recall with any fullness the features of this character whose glory they beheld and under whose power they lived?

10

His Teaching

Never man spake like this man.— John 7:46

58. A. H. CLOUGH

ACROSS the sea, along the shore,
In numbers more and ever more,
From lonely hut and busy town,
The valley through, the mountain down,
What was it ye went out to see,
Ye silly folk. of Galilee ?
The reeds that in the wind doth shake ?
The weed that washes in the lake ?
The reeds that waver, the weeds that float ?
A young man preaching in a boat. . . .

A prophet ?   Boys and women weak !
    Declare, or cease to rave ;
Whence is it He hath learned to speak ?
    Say, who His doctrine gave ?
A prophet ?   Prophet wherefore he
    Of all in Israel tribes ?—
He teacheth with authority,
    And not as do the scribes.

59. ROUSSEAU

WHAT a touching grace in His instructions !
What sweetness, yet what purity, in His
manners !   What loftiness in His maxims !   What
profound wisdom in His discourses !   What presence

of mind, what delicacy of art, yet what justice, in His replies! What an empire over His passions! Where is the man, where the sage, who knows thus to act, to suffer, and to die, without weakness, and without ostentation? What prejudice, what blindness, must be in him who dares to compare the son of Sophroniscus with the Son of Mary? What a distance lies between them! . . . Greece abounded in virtuous men before he (Socrates) had defined virtue. But whence had Jesus drawn for His disciples that exalted and pure morality of which He alone has presented at once the lessons and the example? Out of the midst of the fiercest fanaticism the highest wisdom made itself heard, and the artlessness of the most heroical virtues glorified the vilest of all the nations. The death of Socrates, philosophizing quietly with his friends, is the pleasantest that one could desire: that of Jesus, expiring amid torments, insulted, railed at, cursed by a whole nation, is the most horrible that anyone could fear. Socrates, taking the poisoned cup, blesses him who presents it, and who weeps beside him. Jesus, in the midst of a frightful anguish, prays for his maddened executioners. Yes! if the life and the death of Socrates are those of a philosopher, the life and the death of Jesus are those of a God.

60. BAUR

THE word with which the Founder of Christianity began His preaching of the Gospel—that the followers of His doctrine are not only the poor in spirit, to whom belongs the Kingdom of Heaven, but also the meek, who shall inherit the Earth— was brought to fulfilment in the external history of

Christianity, in that course of its first three centuries which concerns the world's history. . . . Only to its own principle, as the interior effectual power, can Christianity be indebted for all which it has outwardly become in the progress of time ; and the greater the effects which have proceeded from this principle, the more certain becomes the attestation thus given of the divinity of its origin. . . . Christianity itself describes that which it purposes to accomplish in man, the substance of the change which shall be fully effected through it, as a regeneration and renewal of the whole man : so as such a power transforming man it has to attest itself historically through the moral regeneration brought about by it in the public life of mankind. But this is certainly that which gives its weightiest significance to the period of the first three centuries of Christianity, when we regard it from the most universal point of view, that of moral and religious consideration. Let us fix our thought, as here must be done, not on that which Christianity wrought in separate individuals in the hidden deeps of their inner life, but on its effects in the larger contemplation ; on what came from it in the common public life of Nations, as the noblest fruit of its efficacious activity. So with all justice may it be said that the world, through Christianity, if only in the bounded circles over which its influence could directly extend, actually became a morally purer and better world. This shows itself, as in the nature of the case could not be otherwise, as an undeniable historical fact, at all the points at which Christianity came into closest and most immediate contact with the dominant moral corruption of the heathen world.

His Teaching

61. BUNSEN

I BELIEVE that the true Christian philosopher cannot but discern, through all the deviations and all the aberrations in that history of the religious mind which He has to observe and to record during fifteen centuries, and through all the bitter contention and conflicting anathemas of priests and theologians, . . . one sublime and original thought, which, even in dark misunderstanding and in deep corruption, constitutes the redeeming feature and the Divine power in the minds of believers. This thought is nothing less than that great fundamental Christian idea of the reunion of the mind of mortal man with God, by thankful sacrifice of self, in life, and therefore also in worship.

62. MONTAIGNE

THE Christian religion has all the marks of the utmost justice and utility, but none more apparent than the severe injunction it lays upon all to yield obedience to the magistrate, and to maintain and defend the laws. What a wonderful example of this has the Divine wisdom left us, which, to establish the salvation of mankind, and to conduct His glorious victory over death and sin, would do it after no other way but at the mercy of our ordinary political organization; subjecting the progress and issue of so high and so salutary an effect, to the blindness and injustice of our customs and observances; sacrificing the innocent blood of so many of His own elect, and so long a loss of many years, to the maturing of this inestimable fruit !

63. STORRS

THE love of noble or gentle landscape, which has come to be a source of such keen and wide pleasure among western peoples in more recent times, is in harmony with, as it seems plainly to have sprung from, the picturesque and exalting instructions of the Gospel; and nothing else so links the earth, in lily and mountain, and winding waters, with blooms above and rivers of life, as does the astonishing record of the Christ.

64. SHELLEY

. . . MY neighbour, or my servant, or my child, has done me an injury, and it is just that he should suffer an injury in return. Such is the doctrine which Jesus Christ summoned his whole resources of persuasion to oppose. " Love your enemy; bless those that curse you " : such, He says, is the practice of God, and such must ye imitate if ye would be the children of God.

65. TOLSTOI

I NOW understood the words of Jesus : " *Ye have heard that it hath been said, ' An eye for an eye, and a tooth for a tooth ' : but I say unto you, That ye resist not evil.*" Jesus' meaning is : You have thought that you were acting in a reasonable manner in defending yourself by violence against evil, in tearing out an eye for an eye, by fighting against evil with criminal tribunals, guardians of the peace, armies ; but I say unto you, " Renounce violence ; have nothing to do with violence ; do harm to no one, not even to your enemy."

His Teaching

I understand now that in saying " Resist not evil," Jesus not only told us what would result from the observance of this rule, but established a new basis for society conformable to His doctrine and opposed to the social basis established by the law of Moses, by Roman law, and by the different codes in force to-day. He formulated a new law whose effect would be to deliver humanity from its self-inflicted woes. His declaration was : " You believe that your laws reform criminals ; as a matter of fact, they only make more criminals. There is only one way to suppress evil, and that is to return good for evil, without respect of persons. For thousands of years you have tried the other method, now try mine,— try the reverse."

66. DALE

THE impression of "authority," and of an authority of an altogether unique kind, produced by His earlier ministry is deepened as His teaching becomes fuller and more explicit. There is a new accent in all His words, even in the simplest of them ; and there are passages in His discourses in which He assumes prerogatives and powers such as no prophet had ever claimed before. He forgives the sins of men. He calls to Himself all that labour and are heavy-laden, and promises that He will give them rest. He declares that where two or three are gathered together in His name, He is in the midst of them ; reminding us of the great Jewish saying, which was perhaps already current in our Lord's time, that where two of the devout sons of Abraham are studying the Divine law together, *there* is the Shechinah, the glory which is an assurance of the presence of the

God of Israel. He is the Shepherd of the flock of God, whether they are in the Jewish fold, or scattered over the great waste and wilderness of heathenism ; He has come to lay down His life for the sheep, and they are to become one flock under one Shepherd. To all that listen to His voice and follow Him He gives eternal life ; and He says that they shall " never perish, and no one shall snatch them out of My hand." The life which He gives is not given once for all ; those who receive it are continuously dependent upon Him ; " apart " from Him they wither and die, like the branches apart from the vine. He Himself is " the Way, the Truth, and the Life " ; " no one cometh to the Father " but by Him. He is in the Father, and the Father is in Him. To have seen Him is to have seen the Father. He will pray the Father, and the Father will send His disciples another Comforter—a Divine Person— to teach, strengthen, and defend them. He Himself will send the Comforter, and the Comforter will glorify Him. He associates Himself with the Eternal : " He that loveth Me shall be loved of My Father ; and I will love him, and will manifest Myself unto him. . . . My Father will love him, and We will come to him, and make Our abode with him." He is to die, but His Blood is to be " shed for many unto remission of sins." . As for Himself, He has no sins that need remission

67. WATSON

HIS service was to lay down the infallible principles on which we could think rightly on religion. They can be all found in the Gospels ; they lie to any man's hand. Jesus gave the few axioms of the spiritual science on which its whole reasoning can be surely built. He placed us in possession of the mine, leaving the ages to mint its contents and make the gold current coin.

What has to be laid down in the strongest terms and held in perpetual remembrance is that Jesus gave in substance final truth, and that no one, apostle or saint, could or did add anything to the original deposit, however much he might expound or enforce it.

Like a father He placed in the hands of His children the sum of all His wisdom, not expecting them at once to understand it, but charging them to study it, in the good hope that one day they would enter into its fullness. The Church has been the child, and the long history of doctrine and morals has been the attempt to possess Jesus' words, while all the time He Himself was the Saviour of every one that trusted in Him. Her history as the disciple of Jesus has been a progress from the second century unto this present. After the Apostolic days, still bright with the after-glow of Jesus, there was her childhood, simple, poetical, audacious—a time of allegories; her manhood, strenuous, reasonable, comprehensive—a time of doctrines; then will come her maturity, calm, charitable, certain—a time of fellowship. We have not seen this last period, and must remind ourselves at every turn that the Church has not yet compassed the mind of the Master.

68. THEODORE PARKER

THAT mightiest heart that ever beat, stirred by the Spirit of God, how it wrought in his bosom! What words of rebuke, of comfort, counsel, ad-

monition, promise, hope, did He pour out! words
that stir the soul as summer dews call up the faint
and sickly grass. What profound instruction in His
proverbs and discourses! what wisdom in His homely
sayings, so rich with Jewish life! what deep divinity
of soul in His prayers, His action, sympathy, resig-
nation!

Try Him as we try other teachers. They deliver
their word; find a few waiting for the consolation,
who accept the new tidings, follow the new method,
and soon go beyond their teacher, though less mighty
minds than He. Such is the case with each founder
of a school of philosophy, each sect in religion.
Though humble men, we see what Socrates and Luther
never saw. But eighteen centuries have passed
since the tide of humanity rose so high in Jesus:
what man, what sect, what church, has mastered
His thought, comprehended His method, and so
fully applied it to life? Let the world answer in
its cry of anguish. Men have parted His raiment
among them, cast lots for His seamless coat; but
that spirit which toiled so manfully in a world of sin
and death, which died and suffered and overcame
the world,—is that found, possessed, understood!
Nay, is it sought for and recommended by any of
our churches?

69. FRANCES POWER COBBE

ONE thing we may hold with approximate
certainty, and that is, that all the *highest* doctrines,
the purest moral precepts, the most profound spiritual
revelations, recorded in the Gospels, were actually
those of Christ Himself. The originator of the

His Teaching

Christian movement must have been the greatest
soul of His time, as of all time. If He did not speak
those words of wisdom, who could have recorded
them for Him? It would have taken a Jesus to
forge a Jesus.

70. W. R. CASSELS

IT must be admitted that Christian ethics were not
in their details either new or original. The
precepts which distinguish the system may be found
separately in early religions, in ancient philosophies,
and in the utterances of the great poets and seers of
Israel. The teaching of Jesus, however, carried
morality to the sublimest point attained, or even
attainable, by humanity. The influence of His
spiritual religion has been rendered doubly great by
the unparalleled purity and elevation of His own
character. Surpassing in His sublime simplicity
and earnestness the moral grandeur of Sakya Muni,
and putting to the blush the sometimes sullied, though
generally admirable, teaching of Socrates and Plato,
and the whole round of Greek philosophers, He
presented the rare spectacle of a life, so far as we can
estimate it uniformly noble and consistent with His
own lofty principles, so that the "imitation of
Christ" has become almost the final word in the
preaching of His religion, and must continue to be
one of the most powerful elements of its permanence.
His system might not be new, but it was in a high
sense the perfect development of natural morality,
and it was final in this respect among others, that,
superseding codes of law and elaborate rules of life,

63

it confined itself to two fundamental principles:
Love to God and love to man. While all previous
systems had merely sought to purify the stream, it
demanded the purification of the fountain. It placed
the evil thought on a par with the evil action. Such
morality, based upon the intelligent and earnest accep-
tance of Divine Law, and perfect recognition of the
brotherhood of man, is the highest conceivable by
humanity, and although its power and influence must
augment with the increase of enlightenment, it is
itself beyond development, consisting as it does of
principles unlimited in their range and inexhaustible
in their application. Its perfect realization is that
true spiritual Nirvana which Sakya Muni less clearly
conceived, and obscured with Oriental mysticism:
extinction of rebellious personal opposition to Divine
order, and the attainment of perfect harmony with
the Will of God.

71. GARVIE

EFFORTS have been made to discredit the
originality of Jesus by showing that many of
His characteristic sayings can be paralleled elsewhere.
For instance, it is said that the Golden Rule is found
in a negative form in Confucius, but in a positive in
Lao-tsze. There is a likeness between the kind of
life enjoined by Gautama the Buddha and that
presented in the moral teaching of Jesus. In the
Jewish fathers there are sayings about forgiveness
which very closely resemble what He taught. It is
assumed that in His teaching about the last things
He reproduced the apocalyptic ideas of His own
age. Regarding this argument it may be said

that it would be very strange if Jesus had never
said what had been said before Him. God had not
been without witness in other lands and former
times, speaking not through the succession of Hebrew
prophets alone " by divers portions and in divers
manners." To be saying what nobody else has
ever thought of saying is proof of folly and vanity
rather than of wisdom and virtue. Jesus came, not
to startle the world with unheard-of novelties, but
to carry the moral and religious development of
mankind to a new stage, transcending and yet ful-
filling the previous stages, continuous with them
as well as contrasted to them.

72. SABATIER

THE Christian principle appears in its simple
and naked form, in the form of feeling and of
inspiration, in the soul of Jesus. It is described,
explained, expanded, in His Gospel. The Gospel,
in fact, is merely the popular translation and the
immediate application of the principle of the piety
of Jesus in the social *milieu* in which He lived.
Everything springs from His filial consciousness as a
natural and wonderful efflorescence : His messianic
vocation, His twofold ministry of preaching and
healing, His deeds and His discourses, His ethics
and His doctrine, the absolute gift of Himself in life
and death. We must place ourselves at this luminous
centre if we would see the rest dart forth like rays.
In it is found the inner, living unity of His teaching
and His destination. He promulgates no law or
dogma ; He founds no official institution. His
intention is quite different : He wishes, before every-

thing else, to awaken the moral life, to rouse the soul from its inertia, to break its chains, to lighten its burden, to make it active, free and fruitful   He regards His work as finished when He has communicated His life, His piety, to a few poor consciousnesses that He found asleep and dead.   Never man spake like this man, because never had man less concern about what we call " orthodoxy "—that is, about abstract and accurate formulas.   He prefers the language of the people to the language of the schools ; He makes use of images, parables, paradoxes, of current and traditional ideas, of every form of expression which, taken literally, is the most inadequate in the world, but which, on the other hand, is the most living and stimulating.   Each of His sentences or parables is enclosed in a hard shell that has to be broken before you can get at the kernel.   Jesus wished to force His hearers to interpret His words, because He called them to an inward, personal, autonomous activity, because He wished to put an end to the religion of the letter and of rites, and to found the religion of the spirit.   Even now, he that does not give himself to this labour of interpretation and assimilation in reading the Gospel,—he who does not penetrate through the letter and the form to the inspiration and the inmost consciousness of the Master —cannot understand or profit by His teaching. He who does not collaborate with Him while listening to Him, who does not pierce through His words to His soul, will come away empty.   He only gives to those who have, or at least desire to have.   He only leads the seeker to the truth.   He only pardons those who repent, or comforts those who mourn, or fills the hungerer and the thirster after righteousness.

His Teaching

THE Master stood upon the mount, and taught,
    He saw a fire in His disciples' eyes :
" The old law," they said, " is wholly come to naught !
    Behold the new world rise ! "

" Was it," the Lord then said, " with scorn ye saw
The old law observed by Scribes and Pharisees ?
I say unto you, see *ye* keep that law
    More faithfully than these !

" Too hasty heads for ordering worlds, alas !
Think not that I to annul the law have will'd ;
No jot, no tittle from the law shall pass,
    Till all hath been fulfill'd."

So Christ said eighteen hundred years ago.
And what then shall be said to those to-day,
Who cry aloud to lay the old world low
    To clear the new world's way ?

" Religious fervours ! ardour misapplied !
Hence, hence," they cry, " ye do but keep man blind !
But keep him self-immersed, preoccupied,
    And lame the active mind ! "

Ah ! from the old world let some one answer give :
" Scorn ye this world, their tears, their inward cares ?
I say unto you, see that *your* souls live
    A deeper life than theirs !

" Say ye : The spirit of man has found new roads,
And we must leave the old faiths, and walk therein ?—
Leave them the Cross as ye have left carved gods,
    But guard the fire within !

" Bright, else, and fast the stream of life may roll,
And no man may the other's hurt behold :
Yet each will have one anguish—his own soul
    Which perishes of cold."

Here let that voice make end ; then let a strain.
From a far lonelier distance, like the wind
Be heard, floating through heaven, and fill again
    These men's profoundest mind :

" Children of men ! the unseen Power, whose eye
For ever doth accompany mankind,
Hath looked on no religion scornfully
    That men did ever find.

" Which has not taught weak wills how much they can?
Which has not fall'n on the dry heart like rain ?
Which has not cried to sunk, self-weary man :
    Thou must be born again !

" Children of men ! not that your age excel
In pride of life the ages of your sires,
But that *you* think clear, feel deep, bear fruit well,
    The Friend of man desires."

74. FINDLAY

AS for the Master Himself, so for His followers,
there can be no rest till the work is done, if they
are still to follow Him. They must not stand still,
must not even look back, till the furrow is ploughed ;
they must not stop to bring away the things or say
good-bye to the people at home ; they must not

cling to parents or wife, but must say farewell to all
that has made life worth living up till then.   If they
would " go and preach the kingdom of God " they
must " launch out into the deep," and make the joint
adventure fearlessly, for no one who is not prepared
to do violence to his own tastes and inclinations can
force his way into the Kingdom in strenuous days
such as those are when Jesus sets the pace.   Hard
thinking, deep and instant repentance, drastic dealing
with themselves, is what He demands of them ; and
the speed grows greater till He outstrips His most
willing followers, for His work cannot wait their
leisure.   Thus, as we draw up to the Cross, He is
left more and more alone, for He is pressing on to
regions never visited before by the foot of living man ;
for a moment He Himself hesitates, and there is an
hour of agony ; but He goes on past all our power to
follow Him even in thought, and by-and-by comes
back with blessing upon His lips and unshadowed
peace upon His face.   When He left His friends
behind, He told them at least to be ready, with " loins
girt up and lamps burning," for His return.   That He
did come back, that there was something in His
demeanour when He came which quieted all their
fears, and made them strong enough to be left, is
proved not only by the change in the tone of His
words, by the new serenity which breathes upon
us still as we read them, but still more by the change
which came to them.   Up till now they had cowered
in a room with doors shut for fear of the Jews ; after
Pentecost, the consummation of Easter, even prison
walls cannot hold them in, and they, like Him, are
borne out and out and out, till they cover the wide
world with the message He had brought them.

11

The Words of Jesus

Thou hast the words of eternal life.
—John 6:68

75. D'ARCY

THE Words of Jesus.—First, by whatever process
the Gospels reached their present form, whether,
that is, the evangelists made use of materials already
existing, or depended upon a body of oral tradition,
or were supernaturally guided in the writing of every
word, the fact remains that the words of our Lord
shine by their own light, they carry with them their
own credentials. There are no other words like
them anywhere. Like the Person who uttered
them, they are unique. They are simple yet pro-
found, calm yet intense, " mild yet terrible." They
have a peculiar force which expresses authority.
They do not persuade or entreat or reason with the
hearer: they penetrate, they convict, they reveal.
The charm and the wonder of them are as fresh to-day,
for the unlearned as well as for the learned, as when
the people were astonished at His doctrine.

76. PASCAL

OUR Lord discourseth of the sublimest subjects
in a phrase so plain and natural as if it had not
been deeply considered, but withal so pure and exact

as to show that it proceeded from the greatest depth of thought. The joining of this accuracy with this simplicity is admirable.

77. STEVENSON

NOW, every now and then, and indeed surprisingly often, Christ finds a word that transcends all commonplace morality; every now and then He quits the beaten track to pioneer the unexpressed, and throws out a pregnant and magnanimous hyperbole; for it is only by some bold poetry of thought that men can be strung up above a level of everyday conceptions to take a broader look upon experience or accept some higher principle of conduct. To a man who is of the same mind that was in Christ, who stands at some centre not too far from His, and looks at the world and conduct from some not dissimilar or, at least, not opposing attitude—or, shortly, to a man who is of Christ's philosophy—every such saying should come home with a thrill of joy and corroboration; he should feel each one below his feet as another sure foundation in the flux of time and chance; each should be another proof that in the torrent of the years and generations, where doctrines and great armaments and empires are swept away and swallowed, he stands immovable, holding by the eternal stars.

78. BERGUER

JESUS in this sense was a poet; a truer and a better one than the greatest among men. He possessed as no other did the insight into those underlying harmonies which attune all things to the majestic

unity of God. He felt as no one else has done the
inexpressible joy of those harmonies and that rhythm,
and, too, the poignant tragedy which sometimes comes
from it. It is something of that radiant, sublime
poetry which is expressed in the name of Father which
He taught us to spell and attribute to God. As we
follow Him along the lightened paths where He walked
we learn to forsake the artificial, laboured poetry of
words and recognize true poetry, that which quickens
life with a breath of sincerity and which infuses
into it divine and consoling energies.

79. STALKER

THOUGH the encouragement of hospitality, and
through it of love, was one reason for which
Jesus went to the tables of those who invited Him,
He carried there a still higher purpose. When He
went to dine at the house of Zacchæus, He said,
" To-day is salvation come to this house "; and
salvation came to many a house when He entered it.
Hospitality affords unrivalled opportunities of con-
versation, and Jesus made use of these to speak words
of eternal life. If you carefully examine His words,
you will be surprised to find how many of them are
literally table-talk—words spoken to His fellow-
guests at meals. Some of His most priceless sayings,
which are now the watchwords of His religion, were
uttered in these commonplace circumstances, such as
" They that are whole have no need of a physician,
but they that are sick "; " The Son of man is come
to seek and to save that which was lost "; and many
more.

The Words of Jesus

80. FENELON

" MY yoke is easy, and my burden is light." Let
not the word *yoke* terrify us ; we feel the
weight of it, but we do not bear it alone. Jesus
Christ will enable us to bear it, He will teach us the
charm of justice and truth, the chaste delights of
virtue ; His religion supports man against himself,
against his corrupt desires, and makes him strong in
spite of his weakness. O ye of little faith, what do
ye fear ? You suffer, but you may suffer with peace,
with Love for God. You must fight, but you shall
gain the victory ; God is on your side, and He will
crown you with His own hands. You weep, but
He Himself shall wipe away your tears.

Is it to be lamented that we are delivered from the
heavy yoke of the world, and have only to bear the
light burden that Jesus Christ imposes ? Do we
fear being too free from self, from the caprices of
our pride, the violence of our passions, and the
tyranny of the world ?

81. RUSKIN

OBEY the word (of Christ) in its simplicity, in
wholeness of purpose, and serenity of sacrifice
. . . and truly you shall receive sevenfold into your
bosom in this present life and in the world to come
life everlasting. All your knowledge will become to
you clear and sure, all your footsteps safe, in the
present brightness of domestic life you will foretaste
the joy of Paradise, and to your children's children
bequeath not only noble fame but endless virtue.

82. ROBERTSON

HERE we end our study of the words of Jesus, which, the more they are pondered, used, and compared with all other wisdom, approve themselves the more as supreme in value and authority. Whichever way we turn we feel that from Him comes the one great and sure light of life. Nearly two thousand years have passed, bringing many conflicts and many discoveries; our own age is passing with its new problems and great widening of men's thoughts; yet still the words rise to our lips as they rose to the lips of Peter, conscious of mysteries he could not penetrate—" Lord, to whom shall we go ? Thou hast the words of eternal life." But precious as are the words of Jesus, the faith of the Church recognizes that He is Himself greater than all His utterances; and His own teaching, which we have here reviewed, has shown us that a greater blessing comes to us by Him than even that teaching itself. Greater than the gift of His words is the gift of the divine life which we have through communion with Him; and the assurance descends to us from the throne to which He has been exalted, " Because I live, ye shall live also."

83. ST. MATTHEW

HEAVEN and Earth shall pass away, but my words shall not pass away.

12

His Kingdom

My kingdom is not of this world.—John 18:36

84. SEELEY

THE achievement of Christ, in founding by His
single will and power a structure so durable and
so universal, is like no other achievement which
history records. The masterpieces of the men of
action are coarse and common in comparison with it,
and the masterpieces of speculation flimsy and in-
substantial. When we speak of it the common-
places of admiration fail us altogether. Shall we
speak of the originality of the design, of the skill dis-
played in the execution ? All such terms are
inadequate. Originality and contriving skill operated
indeed, but, as it were, implicitly. The creative
effort which produced that against which, it is said,
the gates of hell shall not prevail, cannot be analysed.
No architects' designs were furnished for the New
Jerusalem, no committee drew up rules for the
Universal Commonwealth. If in the works of
Nature we can trace the indications of calculation,
of a struggle with difficulties, of precaution, of in-
genuity, then in Christ's work it may be that the same
indications occur. But these inferior and secondary
powers were not consciously exercised ; they were
implicitly present in the manifold yet single creative
art. The inconceivable work was done in calmness ;

before the eyes of men it was noiselessly accomplished, attracting little attention. Who can describe that which unites men? Who has entered into the formation of speech which is the symbol of their union? Who can describe exhaustively the origin of civil society? He who can do these things can explain the origin of the Christian Church. For others it must be enough to say, " the Holy Ghost fell on those that believed." No man saw the building of the New Jerusalem, the workmen crowded together, the unfinished walls and unpaved streets; no man heard the clink of trowel and pickaxe; it descended *out of heaven from God.*

85. WATSON

EVERY prophet of the first order has his own message and it crystallizes into a favourite idea. With Moses the ruling idea was law; with Confucius, it was morality; with Buddha, it was Renunciation; with Mohammed, it was God; with Socrates, it was the Soul. With the Master, it was the Kingdom of God. The idea owed its origin to the Theocracy, its inspiration to Isaiah, its form to Daniel, its popularity to John Baptist. When the forerunner's voice was stifled in the dungeon of Herod, Jesus caught up his word and preached the Utopia of John with a wider vision and sweeter note. The hereditary dream of the Jew passed through the soul of Jesus and was transformed. The local widened into the universal; the material was raised to the spiritual. A Jewish state with Jerusalem for its capital, and a greater David for its king, changed at the touch of Jesus into a moral kingdom whose throne should be in the heart and its borders conterminous with the race.

86. D'ARCY

DOMINATING the whole realm of His moral ideas is the great conception of the Kingdom. It is essentially a *Social Ideal*, a glorious vision of a universe of souls bound together by love. In it, the supreme blessing is a common blessing, a blessing for all and a blessing for each. This Kingdom exists already on earth wherever the principle of love prevails. But its realization here and now is imperfect. In its perfect form it is the absolute Ideal, the *Summum Bonum*, the great end which all human conduct should strive to realize, for which all should work and pray, and in the realization of which all its members shall find their eternal realization.

The Kingdom grows, not only in the heart and life of the individual, but also in the life of the human race. To this latter side of moral progress, our Lord devotes a number of striking parables. These teach us that the Kingdom is to be in the world as a great reorganizing principle. Like the leaven, it is to spread through the whole till all is leavened. Here our Lord's teaching touches on the political and ecclesiastical organizations of the world, and implies that all will ultimately be made to subserve the coming of the Kingdom. The profound and prophetic character of this part of the teaching, taken together with the history of Christianity, especially in the earlier centuries, shows that our Lord did not omit from the range of His ethical vision all consideration of duty to the State, as superficial critics have frequently asserted.

Lastly, Christ kept steadily before Him the great final realization of the Ideal. He constantly looked at the present in the light of the future, and He impressed most forcibly on the minds of His hearers the necessity of ever living and working with the great end in view. Thus, He knew, the worker would be lifted above the mere worldly standpoint and would be kept true to the master-rule of all high and holy living. He made His people pray, " Thy Kingdom come."

87. THOMPSON

O WORLD invisible, we view thee,
  O world intangible, we touch thee,
O world unknowable, we know thee,
Inapprehensible, we clutch thee !

*   *   *

Not where the wheeling systems darken,
  And our benumbed conceiving soars !
The draft of pinions, would we hearken,
  Beats at our clay-shuttered doors.

The angels keep their ancient places,
  Turn but a stone and start a wing !
'Tis ye, 'tis your estrangèd faces
  That miss the many-splendoured thing.

But when so sad, thou canst not sadder
  Cry ; and on thy so sore loss
Shall shine the traffic of Jacob's ladder
  Pitched between heaven and Charing Cross.

Yea, in the night, my Soul, my daughter
  Cry—clinging Heaven by the hems
And lo, Christ walking on the water
  Not of Genesareth but Thames !

13

The Way, the Truth, the Life

I am the way, the truth, and the life.
—John 14:6

88. À. KEMPIS

MY son, the more thou canst go out of thyself, so much the more wilt thou be able to enter into Me.

As to desire no outward thing produceth inward peace, so the forsaking of ourselves inwardly, joining us unto God.

I will have thee learn perfect resignation of thyself to My will, without contradiction or complaint.

Follow thou Me : " I am the way, the truth, and the life." (John xiv, 6.) Without the way, there is no going ; without the truth, there is no knowing ; without the life, there is no living. I AM the way, which thou oughtest to follow ; the truth, which thou oughtest to trust ; the life, which thou oughtest to hope for.

I AM the way inviolable, the truth infallible, the life that cannot end.

I AM the straitest way, the highest truth, the true life, the blessed life, the life uncreated.

If thou remain in My way, thou shalt know the truth, and the truth shall make thee free, and thou shalt lay hold on eternal life.

If thou wilt enter into life, keep the commandments. (Matt. xix, 17.)

If thou wilt know the truth, believe Me.

If thou wilt be perfect, sell all. (Matt. xix, 21.

If thou wilt be My disciple, deny thyself utterly. (Luke ix, 23.)

If thou wilt possess a blessed life, despise this life present.

If thou wilt be exalted in heaven, humble thyself in this world. (John xii, 25.)

If thou wilt reign with Me, bear the cross with Me. (Luke xiv, 27.)

For only the servants of the cross can find the way of blessedness and of true light.

89. LACORDAIRE

LET us first see how Jesus Christ declared Himself. Did He declare Himself as a creator ? Did He say : I am the inventor of truth ? No, gentlemen ; He said : " I am the truth." (St. John xiv, 6.) He said : " I am not come to destroy the law, but to fulfil it " ; (St. Matt. v. 17) which means : I am the truth of all times and places ; I am that truth which was in the bosom of the Father ; which appeared to the first man in the innocence of the terrestrial paradise ; which the patriarchs, his successors, knew ; which Noah, on quitting the ark, received and promulgated afresh ; which Abraham, in the fields of Chaldæa and Syria, saw and heard ; which Moses, at the foot of Sinai, received, graven by the hand of God. I am that truth which is the first and the last, and which no man has ever been able totally to set aside.

The Way, the Truth, the Life

Behold, gentlemen, what Jesus Christ said of Himself,
and what the Church still says of Him daily. He did
not seek, nor do we seek for Him, a success of creation ;
we have never pretended that Christianity commenced
with the appearance of Christ under Augustus.   To
have given it a character of novelty would have been
to ruin Christianity.   From the first day of the world,
from the first word of God, from the first divine ray
which shone in our soul, it was Christ who acted, who
spake, and who revealed Himself; and that revelation
spread over the whole earth with the dispersion of
the primordial branches of the human race.

90. DANTE

CHRIST said not to his first conventicle,
  ' *Go forth and preach impostures to the world,*'
But gave them truth to build on, and the sound
Was mighty on their lips ; nor needed they
Beside the Gospel other spear or shield
To aid them in their warfare for the faith.

91. TENNYSON

THOUGH truths in manhood darkly join
  Deep-seated in our mystic frame,
  We yield all blessing to the name
Of Him that made them current coin ;

For Wisdom dealt with mortal powers
  Where truth in closest words shall fail,
  When truth embodied in a tale
Shall enter in at lowly doors.

And so the Word had breath and wrought
  With human hands the creed of creeds
  In loveliness of perfect deeds,
More strong than all poetic thought;

Which he may read that binds the sheaf
  Or builds the house, or digs the grave,
  And those wild eyes that watch the wave
In roarings round the coral reef.

92. DOSTOEVSKY

I BELIEVE there is nothing lovelier, deeper, more sympathetic and more perfect than the Saviour; I say to myself with jealous love that not only is there no one else like Him, but that there could be no one. I would say even more. If any one could prove to me that Christ is outside the truth, and if the truth really did exclude Christ, I should prefer to stay with Christ and not with truth. There is in the world only one figure of absolute beauty : Christ. That infinitely lovely figure is as a matter of course an infinite marvel.

93. MOULE

HAD the earliest Christian martyrdoms been theatrical displays of unnatural courage they would have borne feeble witness to the solidity of the facts which the martyrs confessed, and for confessing which they died. The body might in that case have been given to the stoning, or the steel, by a motive no better than a diseased spiritual ambition, a personal and emulous desire for a high place in the coming glory as the reward of special pain. But

Stephen, James, Peter, and Paul died not so. They did not choose or court death. They chose Christ and His truth, and died rather than deny it. And here, in their calmness and spiritual sanity, in their willingness not to die if it could be avoided rightly, lies the weight and power of their *witness*. It appears as a witness indeed ; not a display of their courage so much as an indication of the strong solidity of the basis of truth beneath their feet.

94. JOHN OXENHAM

LORD, I would follow, but—
First, I would see what means that wondrous call
That peals so sweetly through Life's rainbow hall,
That thrills my heart with quivering golden chords,
And fills my soul with joys seraphical.

Lord, I would follow, but—
First, I would leave things straight before I go,—
Collect my dues, and pay the debts I owe ;
Lest when I'm gone, and none is here to tend,
Time's ruthless hand my garnering o'erthrow.

Lord, I would follow, but—
First, I would see the end of this high road
That stretches straight before me, fair and broad ;
So clear the way I cannot go astray,
It surely leads me equally to God.

Lord, I would follow,—yea,
Follow I *will*,—but first so much there is
That claims me in life's vast emergencies,—
Wrongs to be righted, great things to be done ;
Shall I neglect these vital urgencies ?

Who answers Christ's insistent call
Must give himself, his life, his all,
Without one backward look.
Who sets his hand unto the plow,
And glances back with anxious brow,
His calling hath mistook.
Christ claims him wholly for His own ;
He must be Christ's and Christ's alone.

95. ABBOT MARMION

CHRISTIANITY is a mystery of death and life, but it is especially a mystery of life. As you know, death was not included in the Divine Plan ; it was the sin of man that brought it upon the earth ; sin, which is the negation of God, has produced the negation of life, namely, death. If, therefore, Christianity required renunciation, it is in order to immolate that in us which is contrary to life ; we must remove the obstacles that are opposed to the free development within us of the Divine life which Christ brings us : He is the great Author of our holiness, without Him we can do nothing. . . .

Let us contemplate what took place in Jesus Christ, for we must always regard Him in all things. Is He not the model of holiness? He is God and man. His state of Son of God is the source whence flows the Divine value of all His acts ; but He is also man, *Perfectus homo*. Although united in an ineffable manner to the Divine Person of the Word, His human nature in no way lost its own activity, its special manner of acting ; this nature was the source of perfectly authentic human actions. Jesus Christ prayed, worked, ate, suffered, slept : those were human actions, which showed that Our Lord was truly man ; I dare even say that none has ever been so much man as He, for His human nature was incomparably perfect. Only, in Him, the human nature subsisted in the Divinity.

96. CHRISTINA ROSSETTI

HE died for me : what can I offer Him ?
    Towards Him swells incense of perpetual prayer
His court wear crowns and aureoles round their hair :
His ministers are subtle Cherubim ;
Ring within ring, white intense Seraphim
Leap like immortal lightnings through the air,
What shall I offer Him ? Defiled and bare
My spirit broken and my brightness dim ?
" Give Me thy youth." " I yield it to Thy rod,
As Thou didst yield Thy prime of youth for
    me."
" Give Me thy life." " I give it breath by breath ;
As Thou didst give Thy life so give I Thee."
" Give Me thy love." " So be it, my God, my
    God
As Thou hast loved me, even to bitter death."

97. DINAH M. CRAIK

JESUS, Redeemer ;—Thou sole Redeemer !
    I, a poor dreamer, lay hold upon Thee :
Thy will pursuing, though no end viewing,
    But simply doing as Thou biddest me.

Though Thee I see not, either light be not,
    Or Thou wilt free not the scales from mine eyes,
I ne'er gainsay Thee, but only obey Thee :
    Obedience is better than sacrifice.

Though on my prison gleams no open vision,
    Walking Elysian by Galilee's tide,
Unseen I feel Thee, and death will reveal Thee :
    I shall wake in Thy likeness, satisfied.

14

His Portrait

Yea, he is altogether lovely.—Song of Solomon 10:16
Thou art fairer than the children of men.

Psalm 45:2

98. CAMPBELL

IT is remarkable that in the gospels we have so little reference to a subject on which modern readers would greatly desire information. What was Jesus like in appearance ? Was He tall or short, robust or frail, handsome or the reverse ? Did He resemble in any degree the conventional portrait of Him which has now become all but universal in Christendom ? How did He dress ; and what characteristic features, if any, did He possess ? What sort of voice, look, gesture, such as we are wont to associate with those dear to us, would those who knew Him always remember as specially His ?

On all these points the evangelists are strangely silent. All we can gather from them is—and they are impressively at one in regard thereto—that He carried with Him a suggestion of great personal force and at the same time of wonderful winsomeness.

There is one incident which illustrates this even more than the saying " Suffer little children to come unto Me," which finds a place in all the synoptics, and that is the placing of a little child in the midst of the wondering circle of quarrelling men and bidding them imitate him if they would attain to membership in the Kingdom of God. This child must have been content to stand between Jesus' knees with Jesus' arms around him ; no hint is offered to the contrary. And where did He find the child ? The suggestion is that he was there already, standing looking up into the Master's face, and that Jesus had simply drawn him to His side to point His discourse. Children could have felt no fear of Jesus. Evidently, therefore, there must have been something attractive and kind in His very look when it rested on a little one, something tender and winning.

The erring and the downtrodden discerned this also. The woman taken in adultery remained near' Him when her accusers fled discomfited, the woman that was a sinner washes His feet with her tears, regardless of the opinion of those about her ; little Zacchæus blurts out his promise of amendment in the presence of a company that scorned him, sure of the Master's sympathy and understanding—all that was good in him rose up and found expression under the serene gaze of those kind eyes.

And what eyes Jesus must have had. All of the evangelists repeatedly draw attention to the way in which He looked at people. Evidently they were struck by this. Those who listened to Jesus habitually must often have spoken about it—that look at Peter in the judgment hall, for instance, the look that He gave to the churlish Pharisees before the act of healing in the synagogue; most of all, perhaps, the smiling sympathy with which He regarded the rich young ruler. As to His voice, we are told that " the common people heard Him gladly," which they would

not have done if there had not been a certain charm
in the cadences of the voice that uttered the words
of eternal life. " Never man spake like this man,"
was the testimony of the officers of the Sanhedrin
sent to arrest Him. In their absorption in what He
was saying and in His way of saying it they forgot
their commission, and later felt they could not carry
it out.

His dress, His walk, His demeanour would all be in
keeping. There would be a dignity and simplicity
about these which accord with the rest of what we
are told about Jesus. He was not rich, so His gar-
ments must have been those of the ordinary person of
His class in that day. Perhaps it is not very different
now. He may have worn the praying shawl of white
with coloured edges which was common in that day,
as at present, principally in the synagogue, but also
outside. The long straight undergarment worn by
natives of Palestine by night and day, and extending
from the neck to the ankles, no doubt formed part
of Jesus' costume. This too may have been white,
and was probably fastened with a girdle. On His
head would be a large white or coloured napkin,
folded diagonally. A sleeveless cloak or coat of
goat's or camel's hair or wool, for outdoor use, and
sandals for the feet would complete the wearing
apparel, as in Tissot's realistic pictures.

99. MATHESON

SPIRIT of Christ, Spirit of the "altogether
lovely," in Thee alone is realized my ideal of
the beautiful. There are patterns hung up in my

heart to which I can find nothing outside that answers. The light within my soul is a light that never shone on sea or land. All attempts to copy it are vain. There are spots in every sunbeam, there are thorns in every rose, there are crosses in every life. I have never seen the perfect landscape, I have never beheld the cloudless day. I have never looked upon the faultless human soul. Never till I found *Thee*. But Thou hast answered to the pattern in my heart, Thou hast realized the ideal in my spirit. Thou art the spotless sunbeam, Thou art the thornless rose, Thou art the cloudless day, Thou art the faultless life. My imagination cannot transcend Thee; though I shut my eyes a hundred times, I can fancy nothing more beautiful. In the vision of Thee I have received the fulfilment of my dream; Thou hast realized my pattern for the courts of the house or the Lord.

100. SPURGEON

THE entire person of Jesus is but as one gem, and His life is all along but one impression of the seal. He is altogether complete; but not only in His several parts, but as a gracious all-glorious whole. His character is not a mass of fair colours mixed confusedly, not a heap of precious stones laid carelessly one upon another; He is a picture of beauty and a breastplate of glory. In Him, all the "things of good repute" are in their proper places, and assist in adorning each other. Not one feature in His glorious person attracts attention at the expense of others; but He is perfectly and altogether lovely.

Oh, Jesus! Thy power, Thy grace, Thy justice, Thy tenderness, Thy truth, Thy majesty, and Thine immutability make up such a man, or rather such a God-man, as neither heaven nor earth hath seen elsewhere. Thy infancy, Thy eternity, Thy sufferings, Thy triumphs, Thy death, and Thine immortality are all woven in one gorgeous tapestry, without seam or rent. Thou art music without discord; Thou art many, and yet not divided; Thou art all things, and yet not diverse. As all the colours blend in one resplendent rainbow, so all the glories of heaven and earth meet in Thee, and unite so wondrously, that there is none like Thee in all things; nay, if all the virtues of the most excellent were bound in one bundle, they could not rival Thee, Thou mirror of all perfection. Thou hast been anointed with the holy oil of myrrh and cassia, which Thy God hath reserved for Thee alone; and as for Thy fragrance, it is as the holy perfume, the like of which none other can ever mingle, even with the art of the apothecary; each spice is fragrant, but the compound is divine.

101. SAMUEL RUTHERFORD

O THE fair face of the man Jesus Christ! O time, time, why dost thou move so slowly! Come hither, O love of Christ! What astonishment will be mine when I first see that fairest and most lovely face! It would be heaven to me just to look through a hole of heaven's door to see Christ's countenance!

102 . CHRISTINA ROSSETTI

IS this the face that thrills with awe
Seraphs who veil their face above ?
Is this the face without a flaw
    The face that is the face of love ?
Yea, this defaced, a lifeless clod,
    Hath all creation's love sufficed,
Hath satisfied the love of God,
    This face the face of Jesus Christ.

15

His Love and Tenderness

Greater love hath no man than this, that a man lay down his life for his friends.—John 15:13

103. ST. PAUL

WHO shall separate us from the love of Christ ? shall tribulation, or distress, or persecution, or famine, or nakedness, or peril, or sword ?

As it is written, For thy sake we are killed all the day long ; we are accounted as sheep for the slaughter.

Nay, in all these things we are more than conquerors, through Him that loved us.

For I am persuaded that neither death, nor life, nor angels, nor principalities, nor powers, nor things present, nor things to come,

Nor height, nor depth, nor any other creature, shall be able to separate us from the love of God, which is in Christ Jesus our Lord.

104. MOMERIE

IF you do not love Him, it must be because you do not know Him. Either He is seldom in your thoughts, or you think of Him as a dogma rather than a person. Try and picture Him to yourself as of old He lived, and talked, and worked in Palestine. Remember how wonderfully, like no one before or since, He combined all conceivable excellences. He had the tenderness of the most womanly woman, and at the same time the strength of the manliest man. Though invincible by the temptations which assailed Himself, He was always ready to make the most generous allowance for those who failed and fell. He lived much with God, but this seemed to bring Him only nearer to man. He delighted in solitary communion with the Father, but He was fond also of mingling with His neighbours at their social meetings and festivities. He was keenly alive to the paramount importance of the Spirit and eternity; and yet no one was ever so thoughtfully considerate for men's temporal and bodily welfare,—He ministered to them in their bereavements and in their diseases, He was not unmindful even of their hunger and thirst. He had the most sensitive nature, which yearned inexpressibly for sympathy, and yet He never, for the sake of sympathy, swerved from the path of duty. Though all His followers deserted Him, under the conviction that their confidence had been misplaced, He persevered unto the end. He avoided no effort, He shirked no sacrifice, He shrank from no anguish, by which He might serve the race in revealing God and reconciling man. Think of this and much more in that sad, beautiful, sublime career. Think of Him till you love Him and your love has made you like Him. Nothing short of this will make you what Christ would call a Christian. " Except ye eat the flesh and drink the blood of the Son of man, ye have no life in you."

His Love and Tenderness

105. À KEMPIS

O HOW powerful is the pure love of JESUS, which is mixed with no self-interest, nor self-love! Are not all those to be called mercenary, who are ever seeking consolations?

Do they not show themselves to be rather lovers of themselves than of Christ, who are always thinking of their own profit and advantage?

Where shall one be found who is willing to serve God for nought?

106. YOUNG

WE are entitled to assert that compassion for humanity held the place of a master-force in the soul of Jesus Christ. The man is worse than blind, who does not perceive the charm of a subduing tenderness streaming fresh from His heart, and shed over His whole public life. It is related that once as He looked upon the multitudes who had assembled to listen to His teaching, " He had compassion on them, because they were as sheep that had no shepherd." This short sentence descends to the deepest depth of His being, and lays open the spring of all His movements; He had compassion on the multitudes. Spiritual truth was precious to Him; He felt also the burden of a great mission, and He was tenderly alive to all the rights and claims of God. But He pitied and loved the multitude : their spiritual condition, their destinies, their necessities, and their sorrows oppressed His heart. In addition to all the force of fidelity to God, to Himself, and to truth, of which He was conscious, there were impulses of love and pity that gushed up ever warm and fresh in His bosom, and imparted a subduing tone to all His ministrations. Jesus saw an inexpressible worth in human nature. It is fallen and ruined, but it is a precious ruin. The wonderful powers yet left to the soul and the amazing destiny before it, ineffably bright or unutterably dark, were present to His mind, and were the source of that yearning affection which ruled His life. He loved man as man.

107. ANTHONY HORNECK

O MY Jesus! I am not worthy to love Thee! Yet because Thou biddest me love Thee and hast told me that my Soul was created on purpose to love Thee, I cheerfully resign my Love and Affection to Thee! I desire to love Thee! I wish for nothing more than that I may passionately love Thee. Whom have I in Heaven to love but Thee? And there is none on Earth that I desire to love more than Thyself. For Thou art altogether lovely, and Thy Love surpasses all the Love of Friends, and the dearest Relations I have.

O my blessed Redeemer! I desire to love Thee with all my Heart, and with all my Strength: Thou gavest me this Heart and this Strength: And on whom can I bestow it better, than on Thee, the Author of it? Oh, that all that is within me might be turned into Desires, and Inclinations, and Sighs, and Languishings, and Breathings after Thee!

108. SPURGEON

T HE love of Christ in its sweetness, its fulness, its greatness, its faithfulness, passeth all human comprehension. Where shall language be found

His Love and Tenderness

which shall describe His matchless, His unparalleled
love towards the children of men ?   It is so vast and
boundless that, as the swallow but skimmeth the
water, and diveth not into its depths, so all descrip-
tive words but touch the surface, while depths im-
measurable lie beneath.   Well might the poet say,

"O love, thou fathomless abyss !"

for this love of Christ is indeed measureless and
fathomless ; none can attain unto it.   Before we can
have any right idea of the love of Jesus, we must
understand His previous glory in its height of majesty,
and His incarnation upon the earth in all its depths
of shame.   But who can tell us the majesty of Christ ?
When He was enthroned in the highest heavens He
was very God of very God ; by Him were the heavens
made, and all the hosts thereof.   His own almighty
arm upheld the spheres ; the praises of cherubim and
seraphim perpetually surrounded Him ;   the full
chorus of the hallelujahs of the universe unceasingly
flowed to the foot of His throne : He reigned supreme
above all His creatures, God over all, blessed for
ever.   Who can tell His height of glory then ?
And who, on the other hand, can tell how low He
descended ?   To be a man was something, to be a
man of sorrows was far more ; to bleed, and die, and
suffer, these were much for Him who was the Son
of God ; but to suffer such unparalleled agony—to
endure a death of shame and desertion by His Father,
this is a depth of condescending love which the most
inspired mind must utterly fail to fathom.   Herein
is love ! and truly it is love that " passeth knowledge."
O let this love fill our hearts with adoring gratitude,
and lead us to practical manifestations of its power.

109. HERBERT

LOVE bade me welcome ; yet my soul-drew back,
  Guilty of dust and sin.
But quick-eyed Love, observing me grow slack
  From my first entrance in,
Drew nearer to me, sweetly questioning
  If I lack'd anything.

"A guest," I answered, "worthy to be here."
  Love said, "You shall be he."
"I, the unkind, ungrateful ? Ah, my dear,
  I cannot look on Thee."
Love took my hand and smiling did reply,
  "Who made the eyes but I ?"

"Truth, Lord ; but I have marr'd them : let my shame
  Go where it doth deserve."
"And know you not," says Love, "who bore the
    blame ?"
  "My dear, then I will serve."
"You must sit down," says Love, "and taste my
    meat."
  So I did sit and eat.

110. LACORDAIRE

THERE is a Man whose tomb is guarded by love,
  there is a Man whose sepulchre is not only glorious
as a prophet declared, but whose sepulchre is loved.
There is a Man whose ashes, after eighteen centuries,
have not grown cold ; who daily lives again in the
thoughts of an innumerable multitude of men ;
who is visited in His cradle by shepherds and by

His Love and Tenderness

kings, who vie with each other in bringing to Him
gold and frankincense and myrrh. There is a Man
whose steps are unweariedly retrodden by a large
portion of mankind, and who, although no longer
present, is followed by that throng in all the scenes
of His bygone pilgrimage, upon the knees of His
mother, by the borders of the lakes, to the tops of the
mountains, in the byways of the valleys, under the
shade of the olive trees, in the still solitude of the
deserts. There is a Man, whose every word still
vibrates and produces more than love, produces
virtues fructifying in love. There is a Man, who
eighteen centuries ago was nailed to a gibbet, and
whom millions of adorers daily detach from this
throne of His suffering, and, kneeling before Him,
prostrating themselves as low as they can without
shame, there, upon the earth, they kiss His bleeding
feet with unspeakable ardour. There is a Man, who
was scourged, killed, crucified, whom an ineffable
passion raises from death and infamy, and exalts
to the glory of love unfailing which finds in Him
peace, honour, joy, and even ecstasy. There is a
Man, pursued in His sufferings and in His tomb
by undying hatred, and who, demanding apostles
and martyrs from all posterity, finds apostles and
martyrs in all generations. There is a Man, in fine,
and only one, who has founded His love upon earth,
and that Man is thyself, O Jesus! who hast been
pleased to baptize me, to anoint me, to consecrate
me in Thy love, and whose name alone now opens
my very heart, and draws from it those accents which
overpower me and raise me above myself.

But among great men who are loved? Among
warriors? Is it Alexander? Cæsar? Charlemagne?

Among sages? Aristotle? Plato? Who is loved among great men? Who? Name me even one; name me a single man who has died and left love upon his tomb. Mahomet is venerated by Mussulmans; he is not loved. No feeling of love has ever touched the heart of a Mussulman repeating his maxim: "God is God, and Mahomet is His prophet." One Man alone has gathered from all ages a love which never fails; Jesus Christ is the sovereign Lord of hearts as He is of minds, and by a grace confirmatory of that which belongs only to Him, He has given to His saints also the privilege of producing in men a pious and faithful remembrance.

111. WATSON

THE passion for Jesus has no analogy in comparative religion; it has no parallel in human experience. It is a flame of unique purity and intensity Thomas does not believe that Jesus is the Son of God, or that, more than any other man, He can escape the hatred of fanaticism; but he must share the fate of Jesus. "Let us also go," said this morbid sceptic, "that we may die with Him." At the sight of His face seven devils went out of Mary Magdalene; for the blessing of His visit, a chief publican gave half his goods to the poor. When a man of the highest order met Jesus he was lifted into the heavenly places and became a Christed man, whose eyes saw with the vision of Christ, whose pulse beat with the heart of Christ. Browning has nothing finer than "A Death in the Desert," wherein he imagines the love of St. John to Jesus. No power is able to rouse the apostle from his last sleep, neither words nor

cordials. Then one has a sudden inspiration : he
brings the Gospel and reads into the unconscious ear,
  " I am the resurrection and the life,"
with the effect of an instantaneous charm :
  " Whereat he opened his eyes wide at once
  And sat up of himself and looked at us."

112. MATHESON

O LOVE that wilt not let me go,
    I rest my weary soul in Thee ;
I give Thee back the life I owe,
That in Thine ocean depths its flow
    May richer, fuller be.

O Light that followeth all my way,
    I yield my flickering torch to Thee ;
My heart restores its borrowed ray,
That in Thy sunshine blaze its day
    May richer, fairer be.

O Joy that seekest me through pain,
    I cannot close my heart to Thee ;
I trace the rainbow through the rain,
And feel the promise is not vain
    That morn shall tearless be.

O Cross that liftest up my head,
    I dare not ask to fly from Thee ;
I lay in dust life's glory dead,
And from the ground there blossoms red
    Life that shall endless be.

113. AN EARLY ENGLISH WRITER

SO sweet a love on earth none is
For one who loves Him heartily;
To love Him well were greatest bliss
For called *King of Love is He.*
With this true love I would, I wis,
So firmly to Him bounden be,
That all my heart were wholly His,
And other loving liked not me.

If I by nature love my kin,
(I ever think thus in my thought)
By ties of kin I should begin
At Him that made me first of nought.
My soul He set His likeness in,
And all this world for me He wrought;
As Father true my love to win
My heritage in heaven He bought.

114. MOULE

OH, sweet it is to know, most simply, that the
soul loves Him; not as it should love Him,
truly, and not " more than these," with a glance of
self-consciousness around; but that indeed it does
love Him.

115. AN EARLY ENGLISH WRITER

SWEET Jesú, now will I sing
To Thee a song of love-longing;
Make in mine heart a well to spring
Thee to love above all thing.

Sweet Jesú, mine heart's true light,
Thou art day withouten night;
Give to me both grace and might
That so I may love Thee aright.

    *   *   *   *   *

Jesu, my life, my Lord, my King!
To Thee my soul hath great longing,
Thou hast it wedded with Thy ring;
When Thy will is, to Thee it bring!

Jesu, all fair, my lover bright!
I Thee beseech with all my might,
Bring my soul into Thy light,
Where all is day and never night.

Jesu, help Thou at mine ending;
Take my soul at my dying;
Send it succour and comforting;
That it dread no wicked thing.

Jesu, Thy bliss hath no ending,
There is no sorrow and no weeping,
But peace and joy with great liking:
Sweet Jesú, us thereto bring! Amen.

116. EDMUND SPENSER

O BLESSED Well of loue! O Flowre of Grace!
O Glorious Morning Starre! O Lampe of Light!
Most liuely image of Thy Father's face,
Eternall King of Glorie, Lord of Might,
Meeke Lambe of God, before all worlds behight
How can we Thee requite for all this good?
Or what can prize with Thy most precious blood?

Yet nought Thou ask'st in lieu of all this loue,
But loue of us, for guerdon of Thy paine :
Ay me ! what can us lesse than that behoue ?
Had He required life for us againe,
Had it beene wrong to aske His own with gaine ?
He gaue us life ; He it restorèd lost ;
Then life were least that us so litle cost.

117. JACOB BEHMEN

O THOU deepest and most precious Love of God in Christ Jesus ! Grant to me Thy pearl; press Thou it into my very soul; take Thou my soul in Thine arms. O Thou sweetest Love, I am indeed impure before Thee, destroy Thou only mine impurity by Thy death ! Lead Thou the hunger and thirst of my soul by Thy death and resurrection out into Thy triumph ! . . . O Highest Love, as Thou hast indeed appeared unto me, remain also in me and uphold me in Thyself. Keep me so that I may not be able to depart from Thee ; satisfy my hunger with Thy love ; feed Thou my soul with Thy heavenly essence, and refresh it with Thy blood. . . . O Thou life and strength of the Godhead, Who hast promised to us : " We will come unto You, and make our abode with You." O sweet Love ! into the word of Thy promise I bring my desires. Thou hast verily said that Thy Father will give the Holy Spirit to them that ask Him. O Sweet Love ! I beseech of Thee, by the love wherewith Thou didst overcome the wrath of God, which Thou didst transform into a divine Paradise, that Thou transform the wrath in my soul by the same great love, that I may become

obedient, and that my soul may eternally love Thee!
Transform Thou my will into Thine own; lead
Thou Thine obedience into my disobedience, that
I may become obedient unto Thee. . . . O my
noble vine, give Thou Thy branch sap, that I may
grow and flourish in Thine essence, by Thy power
and nourishment. . . . O sweet Love, art Thou
not my Light? Lighten Thou my poor soul during
her doleful imprisonment in flesh and blood. Lead
her always by the right way. Break Thou the will
of the Evil One, and lead Thou my body through
the course of this world, through the chamber of
death, into Thy death and peace, that it may, at the
last day, arise in Thee out of Thy death, and live
eternally in Thee. Teach Thou me what I should
do, be Thou my willing, my knowing, and my doing,
and let me go nowhere without Thee. I devote
myself utterly unto Thee. Amen.

118. PHINEAS FLETCHER

I

ME Lord? can'st Thou mispend
  One word, misplace one look on me?
Call'st me Thy Love, Thy Friend?
  Can this poor soul the object be
Of these love-glances, those life-kindling eyes?
What? I the Centre of Thy arm's embraces?
  Of all Thy labour I the prize?
  Love never mocks, Truth never lies.
Oh how I quake: Hope fear, fear hope displaces:
I would, but cannot hope: such wondrous love
  amazes.

II

See, I am black as night,
See I am darkness : dark as hell.
Lord Thou more fair than light ;
Heav'ns Sun Thy shadow ; can Sunns dwell
With Shades ? 'twixt light, and darkness what
commerce ?
True : thou art darkness, I Thy light : my ray
Thy mists, and hellish foggs shall pierce.
With me, black soul, with me converse.
I make the Foul December Flowry May,
Turn thou thy night to me : I'le turn thy night
to day.

III

See Lord, see I am dead :
Tomb'd in myself : myself my grave.
A drudge : so born, so bred :
Myself even to myself a slave.
Thou Freedom, Life : can Life, and Liberty
Love bondage, death ? Thy Freedom I : I tyed
To loose thy bonds ; be bound to me :
My Yoke shall ease, my bonds shall free.
Dead soul, thy Spring of life, my dying side :
There dye with me to live : to live in thee I dyed.

119. FRANCIS QUARLES

E V'N like two little bank-dividing brooks,
That wash the pebbles with their wanton streams,
And having rang'd and search'd a thousand nooks,
Meet both at length in silver-breasted Thames,
Where in a greater current they conjoin :
So I my best-beloved's am ; so he is mine.

His Love and Tenderness

Ev'n so we met; and after long pursuit,
    Ev'n so we joyn'd; we both became entire;
No need for either to renew a suit,
    For I was flax and he was flames of fire:
        Our firm-united souls did more than twine;
So I my best-beloved's am; so he is mine.

If all those glitt'ring Monarchs that command
    The servile quarters of this earthly ball,
Should tender, in exchange, their shares of land,
    I would not change my fortunes for them all:
        Their wealth is but a counter to my coin:
The world's but theirs; but my beloved's mine.

Nay, more; If the fair Thespian Ladies all
    Should heap together their diviner treasure:
That treasure should be deem'd a price too small
    To buy a minute's lease of half my pleasure;
        'Tis not the sacred wealth of all the nine
Can buy my heart from him, or his, from being mine.

Nor Time, nor Place, nor Chance, nor Death can bow
    My least desires unto the least remove;
He's firmly mine by oath; I his by vow;
    He's mine by faith; and I am his by love;
        He's mine by water; I am his by wine;
Thus I my best-beloved's am; thus he is mine.

He is my Altar; I, his holy Place;
    I am his guest; and he, my living food;
I'm his by penitence; he mine by grace;
    I'm his by purchase; he is mine, by bloud;
        He's my supporting elm; and I his vine;
Thus I my best-beloved's am; thus he is mine.

He gives me wealth; I give him all my vows
    I give him songs; he gives me length of dayes;
With wreaths of grace he crowns my conqu'ring
      brows,
    And I his temples with a crown of Praise,
      Which he accepts as an everlasting signe,
That I my best-beloved's am; that he is mine.

120. SAMUEL RUTHERFORD

HANG on our Lord, and He will fill you with
a sense of His love, as He has so often filled me.
Your feast is not far off. Hunger on; for there is
food already in your hunger for Christ. Never go
away from Him, but continue to fash Him; and if
He delays, yet come not away, albeit you should
aswoon at His feet.

121. ARTHUR EDWARD WAITE

I CAME into the world for love of Thee,
    I left Thee at Thy bidding;
I put off my white robes and shining crown
And came into this world for love of Thee.

I have lived in the grey light for love of Thee,
    In mean and darken'd houses:
The scarlet fruits of knowledge and of sin
Have stain'd me with their juice for love of Thee.

I could not choose but sin for love of Thee,
    From Thee so sadly parted;
I could not choose but put away my sin
And purge and scourge those stains for love of Thee.

His Love and Tenderness

My soul is sick with life for love of Thee,
  Nothing can ease or fill me :
Restore me, past the frozen baths of death,
My crown and robes, desired for love of Thee :

And take me to Thyself for love of Thee ;
  My loss or gain counts little,
But Thou must need me since I need Thee so,
Crying through day and night for love of Thee !

16

The Comforter

Come unto me, all ye that labour and are heavy laden, and I will give you rest.—Matthew 11:28

122. MINUCIUS FELIX

WE who bear wisdom not in our dress but in our mind, we do not speak great things, but we live them ; we boast that we have attained what they (the philosophers) sought for with the utmost eagerness, and have not been able to find. . . . How beautiful is the spectacle to God when a Christian does battle with pain ; when he is drawn up against threats, and punishments, and tortures ; when, mocking the noise of death, he treads under-foot the horror of the executioner ; when he raises up his liberty against kings and princes, and yields to God alone, whose he is ; when, triumphant and victorious, he tramples upon the very man who has pronounced sentence against him ! Yet boys and young women among us treat with contempt crosses, and tortures, wild beasts, and all the bugbears of punishment, with the inspired patience of suffering.

The Comforter

I HEARD the voice of Jesus say,
   " Come unto Me and rest ;
Lay down, thou weary one, lay down
   Thy head upon My breast : "
I came to Jesus as I was,
   Weary and worn and sad ;
I found in Him a resting-place,
   And He has made me glad.

I heard the voice of Jesus say,
   " Behold I freely give
The living water ; thirsty one,
   Stoop down, and drink, and live : "

I came to Jesus, and I drank
   Of that life-giving stream ;
My thirst was quenched, my soul revived,
   And now I live in Him.

I heard the voice of Jesus say,
   " I am this dark world's Light ;
Look unto Me, thy morn shall rise,
   And all thy day be bright : "
I looked to Jesus, and I found
   In Him my Star, my Sun ;
And in that Light of life I'll walk,
   Till travelling days are done.

17

His Silence

He answered her not a word.—Matthew 15:23

124. PHILLIPS BROOKS

TURN to the record of one of the silences of Him whose silences must have been most significant because of the richness of His nature and the deep importance of all His relations to mankind. One day a Canaanitish woman came running after Jesus with the cry, " O Lord, thou Son of David, my daughter is grievously vexed with a devil ! " We hear the sharp agony pierce the keen, trembling air. The poor woman's whole soul is in her words. She cries to Him in whom alone seems any chance of help ; then, almost frightened with her cry, she pauses. The thing is done. Her heart has told its story. The face of Christ has touched and stirred her misery into self-consciousness, and out of the cloud this lightning of her cry has flashed. The thing is done, and she waits tremblingly for the result. Can we not almost hear her heart beat as she listens ? What will He say ? And then see what does happen. " He answered her not a word." Bowed down before Him there, waiting to hear whether He was blaming her or blessing her, think of the dismay with which her soul must have been filled as slowly the moments passed by and she became

His Silence

aware that He was doing neither. The sense of His silence standing over her, how bewildering, how terrible, how worse than any blame it must have been! But, behold! I think that I can see her slowly lift her eyes. She cannot bear this suspense. She must look this awful silence in the face. Her eyes find out the face of Christ, and then she feels Him behind, within, His silence. She knows Him not clearly but certainly. He is there, and she has found Him. The disciples come and upbraid her, but she does not stir. She will know what this silence means before she goes. She knows that it means something gracious; and so she listens and listens till at last the silence is broken and she hears Him say, " O woman, great is thy faith : be it unto thee even as thou wilt." Then she goes away satisfied, and finds her daughter whole.

18

His Humility

So also Christ glorified not himself.—Hebrews 5:5

125. FENELON

IT is Jesus who gives us this lesson of meekness and humility : no other being could have taught it without our revolting at it. In all others we find imperfection, and our pride would not fail to take advantage of it. It was necessary that he should himself teach us ; and he has condescended to teach us by his example. What high authority is this ! We have only to be silent and adore, to admire and to imitate.

The Son of God has descended upon the earth, and taken upon himself a mortal body, and expired upon the cross, that he might teach us humility. Who shall not be humble now ? Surely not the sinner who has merited so often, by his ingratitude, God's severest punishments. Humility is the source of all true greatness : pride is ever impatient, ready to be offended. He who thinks nothing is due to him, never thinks himself ill-treated ; true meekness is not mere temperament, for this is only softness or weakness. To be *meek* to others, we must renounce self. The Saviour adds, *lowly of heart ;* this is a humility to which the will entirely consents, because it is the will of God and for his glory.

126. SAINT TERESA

I WAS once considering what the reason was why our Lord loved humility in us so much, when I suddenly remembered that He is essentially the Supreme Truth, and that humility is just our walking in the truth. For it is a very great truth that we have no good in us, but only misery and nothingness, and he who does not understand this walks in lies : but he who understands this the best is the most pleasing to the Supreme Truth. May God grant us this favour, sisters, never to be without the humbling knowledge of ourselves.

O Sovereign Virtues ! O Ladies of all the creatures ! O Empresses of the whole world ! Whoever hath you may go forth and fight boldly with all hell at once. Let your soldiers not fear, for victory is already theirs. They only fear to displease God. They constantly beseech Him to maintain all the virtues in them. It is true these virtues have this property, to hide themselves from him who possesses them, so that he never sees them in himself, nor thinks that he can ever possess a single one of them. Other men see all the virtues in him, but he so values them that he still pursues them, and seeks them as something never to be attained by such as he is. And Humility is one of them, and is Queen and Empress and Sovereign over them all. In fine, one act of true humility in the sight of God is of more worth than all the knowledge sacred and profane, in the whole world.

115

127. STALKER

AFTER one of His miracles was performed, " He charged them straitly that no man should know it." This is the sequel to many a work of wonder in His life. " See thou tell no man," He said to a leper whom He had cleansed. " See that no man know it," He said to two blind men whose sight He had restored. He straitly charged those, as a rule, out of whom He had cast devils not to make Him known.

Such notices abound in the Gospels ; yet I am not sure that I have ever seen the true explanation of them given. All kinds of elaborate explanations have been attempted. In one case, for example, it is said that He forbade the man who had been healed to mention his cure, lest it should do him harm by puffing him up ; in another, because his testimony would have had no weight ; in a third, because it was not yet time to acknowledge Himself to be the Messiah ; and so on. Such are the suggestions made by learned men, and there may be some truth in them all. But they are too elaborate and recondite ; the real explanation lies on the surface. It is simply that, while so great a worker, He disliked to have His good deeds made known. St. Matthew puts this so plainly that it ought not to have been overlooked. After mentioning an occasion when, after healing great multitudes, He charged them that they should not make Him known, the evangelist adds that this was in fulfilment of a prophecy which said, " He shall not strive nor cry, neither shall any one hear His voice in the street." It is one of the penalties of public work for God that it comes to be talked about, and vulgar people make a sensation of it. We are well acquainted with this at the present day, when nothing is allowed to remain private, and, if a man does anything in the least out of the common, the minutest details of his life are dragged out and exposed to the public eye. But this is contrary to the very genius of goodness, and exposes even those occupied with the holiest work to the temptation of playing for the praise of men instead of acting humbly in the eye of God. Jesus detested it. He would have been hidden if He could; and it was a heavy cross to Him that the more He pressed people to say nothing about Him, the more widely did they spread His fame.

128. JOHN BUNYAN

HE that is down needs fear no fall;
   He that is low, no pride;
He that is humble, ever shall
   Have God to be his guide.
I am content with what I have,
   Little be it, or much:
And, Lord, contentment still I crave,
   Because Thou savest such.

19

Compassion and Sympathy

He was moved with compassion.
—Matthew 9:36

129. MATHESON

" I HAVE compassion on the multitude, because they have now been with me three days, and have nothing to eat : and if I send them away fasting to their own houses, they will faint by the way."— Mark viii, 2, 3.

The compassion here displayed by the Son of Man is a pity for the common wants of men. It is their *common* wants that here impress Him. . . .

O Thou Son of Man, in Thy religion alone is there hope for those who toil. Thou alone of all masters hast sympathy with the needs of the common day, with the wants of the passing hour. To all other masters the needs of the common day are ignoble, the wants of the passing hour are sin. The religions of men have no sympathy with man *as* man ; they call on him to leave the world, they frown upon his struggles for the perishable bread. But Thou hast compassion on the prosaic toilers of life. Thou hast compassion on those who are fasting by the way, and who have no spiritual vision to break their fast. Thou hast compassion on the crowd in which each man is alone— alone with his solitary battle, alone with his poverty and care. Thou hast taken up the cross of them that labour, and hast claimed it for Thine own. Thou hast identified Thine interest with the cry of struggling millions :

" Give us this day our daily bread."

130. MARTIN

APPARENTLY it was while He was being nailed to the Cross that Jesus prayed, *Father, forgive them ; for they know not what they do.* The imperfect tense introducing the prayer suggests that the words were repeated with every blow of the hammer upon His hands and feet. And the plea He advanced was that His enemies had no idea how much pain they were causing Him. The implication of the plea was that if they had known they would not have inflicted it. His penetrative searching of men's hearts led Him to despair of no man, and to the very last Jesus refused to believe that the innermost heart of anyone could be hopelessly cruel.

131. UNDERHILL

I COME in the little things,
Saith the Lord :
Not borne on morning wings
Of majesty, but I have set My Feet
Amidst the delicate and bladed wheat
That springs triumphant in the furrowed sod.
There do I dwell, in weakness and in power ;
Not broken or divided, saith our God !
In your strait garden plot I come to flower :
About your porch My Vine
Meek, fruitful, doth entwine ;
Waits, at the threshold, Love's appointed hour.

I come in the little things,
Saith the Lord :
Yea ! on the lancing wings
Of eager birds, the softly pattering feet
Of furred and gentle beasts, I come to meet
Your hard and wayward heart.   In brown bright eyes
That peep from out the brake, I stand confest.
On every nest
Where feathery Patience is content to brood
And leaves her pleasure for the high emprise
Of motherhood—
There doth My Godhead rest.

I come in the little things,
Saith the Lord :
My starry wings
I do forsake,
Love's highway of humility to take :
Meekly I fit my stature to your need.
In beggar's part
About your gates I shall not cease to plead—
As man, to speak with man—
Till by such art
I shall achieve My Immemorial Plan,
Pass the low lintel of the human heart.

20

The Good Shepherd

I am the good shepherd.—John 10:14

132. LONGFELLOW

SHEPHERD! that with Thine amorous, sylvan song
Hast broken the slumber which encompassed me,—
That mad'st Thy crook from the accursèd tree,
On which Thy powerful arms were stretched so long!
Lead me to mercy's ever-flowing fountains;
For Thou my Shepherd, Guard, and Guide shalt be;
I will obey Thy voice, and wait to see
Thy feet all beautiful upon the mountains.
Hear, Shepherd!—Thou for Thy flock art dying,
O, wash away these scarlet sins, for Thou
Rejoicest at the contrite sinner's vow.
O, wait!—to Thee my weary soul is crying,—
Wait for me!—Yet why ask it, when I see,
With feet nailed to the cross, Thou'rt waiting still
      for me!

133. CHRISTINA ROSSETTI

O SHEPHERD with the bleeding Feet,
  Good Shepherd with the pleading Voice,
    What seekest Thou from hill to hill?
Sweet were the valley pastures, sweet
    The sound of flocks that bleat their joys,
      And eat and drink at will.
Is one worth seeking, when Thou hast of Thine
                Ninety and nine?

134. 23rd PSALM

THE Lord's my shepherd, I'll not want,
He makes me down to lie
In pastures green : He leadeth me
The quiet waters by.

My soul He doth restore again ;
And me to walk doth make
Within the paths of righteousness
Ev'n for His own name's sake.

Yea, though I walk in death's dark vale,
Yet will I fear none ill :
For Thou art with me ; and Thy rod
And staff me comfort still.

My table Thou hast furnished
In presence of my foes ;
My head Thou dost with oil anoint,
And my cup overflows.

Goodness and mercy all my life
Shall surely follow me :
And in God's house for evermore
My dwelling-place shall be.

135. RICHARD ROBERTS

CHRISTIAN art made the first faltering attempts
to represent Jesus that still survive, in the Cata-
combs, in the second and third centuries, doubtless
working upon a still older tradition.   He is frequently

The Good Shepherd

represented as "the Good Shepherd—a beautiful, graceful figure," as Dean Stanley has said. This fact is altogether suggestive of the freshness and bloom which the early Christians discerned in the world after the coming of Jesus. Before He came the world had grown old and grey and weary; the pallor of death was upon its face. Judaism was at its last gasp; Greek philosophy was no more than a ruin of its great past; Pan, great Pan, was sick unto death. But the coming of Jesus revitalized this old decadent world; and a new joy and light entered into it. The exuberance and spring of men newly regenerate in a world in which Hope had been raised from the dead, found expression in the fresh joyful young Shepherd of the Catacomb drawings. All this, mark, in the Catacombs, where the young Church lay in hiding, where its martyrs were laid to rest. So strong was the new hope that Jesus had awakened that the gloom of the Catacombs, with all their memorials of bitter persecution, failed to dispel it. And on those walls it graved, in its drawings of Jesus, a witness of its own faith and life which remains to this day.

136. MATTHEW ARNOLD

THE infant Church! of love she felt the tide
 Stream on her from her Lord's yet recent grave.
And then she smiled; and in the Catacombs,
With eye suffused but heart inspired true,
On those walls subterranean, where she hid
Her head 'mid ignominy, death, and tombs,
She her Good Shepherd's hasty image drew—
And on His shoulders, not a lamb, a kid.

137. ALEX. SMELLIE

SHEPHERD He is in the morning hours, leading me forth to the duties and temptations of the day and Himself going before me. As I gird and prepare myself for the activities and the thousand perils of my life, I would be sure that He is with me. I dare not journey out to them alone. For apart from Him I can do nothing.

Shepherd in the hot noonday, too, when the sun is beating fiercely down. He conducts me then to green pastures and along the banks of the waters of quietness. As I ply my daily task with busy feet, I often would come aside to be with Him, to ponder His word, to listen to the restoring whisper of His Spirit. It is the secret of abiding and prevailing peace.

And Shepherd when the night falls and it is growing dark. I recall Sir Noel Paton's picture of *Lux in Tenebrae*, the girl who walks through the Valley of the Shadow with her hand clasped in Christ's hand. Trust is conquering terror on her face, and she grows confident that no enemy will vanquish her. So may it be with me, what time I enter the narrow ravine and breast the chilling floods.

The King of Love my Shepherd is. Can I say it; this *my*, this pronoun of possession ? If I can, humbly and heartily, then assuredly in life and death and eternity I shall not want. For I am persuaded that nothing can separate me from the love of God, which is in Christ my Lord. His Shepherdhood is no transient endowment, no generous impulse, no passing mood ; it is from everlasting to everlasting.

21

Friend and Brother

Friend of sinners.—Matthew 11:19

138. CLIFFORD

HIS standard of human life is the highest yet conceived, and brotherhood is its central and abiding element. He gives a religion which takes up and absorbs all the truths in other religions, including the law and the prophets, and He adds the factors which make it ultimate, and will in due course, render it universal; and in every line of it it is the religion of brotherhood; and its unique characteristic and strong commendation is, that He who founds it, *is* Himself what He taught. He achieved the life He prescribed. He was the Brother every man should be. Action preceded and led the way for speech. He did, and then, said. The " Mountain Sermon " astonished those who heard it, partly because of its contents, but also because in fact it was backed by His deeds, was autobiographic and charged with the mighty forces of His personality. The Beatitudes were lived first; and then fell from His lips in their native simplicity and beauty. The seemingly impossible ethics He preached as principles of living were counsels He had followed. He had loved His enemies; prayed for those who despitefully used Him; and enjoyed the blessing of those who were persecuted for the sake of the right and the true and the good ; displaced anxiety by trust, and low aims by the most determined search for the Kingdom of God. He is the Supreme Authority on brotherhood because He lived the brother's life ; not only without a solitary flaw, but with a splendid fulness and strength. So we sit at His feet with unlimited confidence, and bow to His authority with glad reverence and unstinted homage.

139. A. W. W. DALE

MY own brother's death in 1883 was the beginning of all the physical suffering of later years. Although we had not lived together since we were boys, my house had been his home from the time that our own home was broken up—his home, I mean, when he was away from Cambridge. He had been a kind of son as well as a brother to me. His brilliant success at Cambridge and the power he was gaining there had given me more pleasure than any small achievements of my own. He was my only brother that had lived beyond infancy or early childhood, and I never had a sister. Half my life seemed rent away. I was conscious of the most violent disturbance of the heart. For the first time I learnt what is involved in Christ's having become our Brother. I shrink indeed from what seems to me—it is not so to many others —an irreverent familiarity in addressing Him as Brother : He may call me by that name in His great condescension, but I shrink from calling Him so ; and yet the revelation in my sorrow of what brotherhood means remains a wonder and a glory.

Friend and Brother

140. BROWNING

OUR wars are wars of life, and wounds of love,
  With intellect spears and longwinged arrows of
thought,
Mutual in one another's wrath, all renewing
We live as One Man. For contracting our infinite
  senses
We behold multitude ; or expanding, we behold as
  One,
As one man all the Universal Family ; and that man
We call Jesus the Christ, and He in us, and we in Him,
Live in perfect harmony in Eden the land of life,
Giving, receiving, and forgiving each other's tres-
  passes."

141. BLAKE

JESUS said, " Wouldst thou love one who never
  died
For thee, or ever die for one who had not died for thee ?
And if God dieth not for Man and giveth not Himself
Eternally for Man, Man could not exist ; for Man
  is Love
As God is Love : every kindness to another is a little
  Death
In the Divine Image, nor can Man exist but by
  Brotherhood."

He who would see the Divinity must see Him in
  His Children.
One first, in friendship and love ; then a Divine
  Family, and in the midst
Jesus will appear ; and so he who wishes to see a
  Vision, a perfect Whole
Must see it in its Minute Particulars.

142. MAZZINI

HE bestowed upon the human race that sublime formula of *brotherhood* . . . the lips of patriots will cease to utter the word *foreigner* as a term of reproach, which, in men calling themselves brothers, is a blasphemy against the Cross of Christ.

143. ABBOT MARMION

THIS commandment of the love of our brethren is the supreme wish of Christ: it is so much His desire that He makes of it, not a counsel, but a commandment, *His* commandment, and He makes the fulfilment of it the infallible sign by which His disciples shall be recognized. . . . It is a sign all can understand, none other is given: no one can be mistaken as to it: the supernatural love you have for one another will be the unequivocal proof that you truly belong to Me. And, in fact, in the first centuries, the pagans recognized the Christians by this sign: " See," they would say, " how they love one another."

144. STALKER

FRIENDSHIP can sometimes show its strength as much by the readiness with which it accepts benefits as by the freedom with which it gives them. It proves by this its confidence in the love on the other side. Jesus gave such a proof of the depth of His friendship for St. John when, hanging on the cross, He asked the beloved disciple to adopt Mary as his own mother. Never was there a more delicate

expression given to friendship. Jesus did not ask
him if he would ; He took his devotion for granted ;
and this trust was the greatest honour that could have
been conferred on the disciple.

145. GEORGE MACDONALD

I MISSED him when the sun began to bend ;
I found him not when I had lost his rim ;
With many tears I went in search of him,
Climbing high mountains which did still ascend,
And gave me echoes when I called my friend ;
Through cities vast and charnel-houses grim,
And high cathedrals where the light was dim,
Through books and arts and works without an end,
But found him not—the friend whom I had lost.
And yet I found him—as I found the lark,
A sound in fields I heard but could not mark ;
I found him nearest when I missed Him most ;
I found him in my heart, a life in frost,
A light I knew not till my soul was dark.

22

Lover of Little Children

Suffer little children, and forbid them not, to come unto me : for of such is the kingdom of heaven.
— Matthew 19:14

146. LAURENCE HOUSMAN

IT was in fair Bethlehem,
  Where Love first lay,
That in the street on merry feet,
  He heard the children play.
And all the running sound was sweet,
  And plain as plain could be :
" Jesus, suffer little feet
  To come to Thee ! "

It was in fair Bethlehem,
  They came a merry crowd,
They stopped before the stable door
  And knocked thereon aloud :
" Oh, open, open ! " cried they then,
  " As wide as wide can be !
Heart of Jesus, suffer us
  To come to Thee."

It was in fair Bethlehem,
  That Love spake low :
" Oh, come to-night ! " He called to them,
  " And I will not say no ! "

Lover of Little Children

"To-night, to-night!" they all entreat,
    "As soon as soon may be!"
Jesus, suffer little feet
    To come to Thee!"

It was in fair Bethlehem,
    That night the children died:
They came to play where Jesus lay,
    And Mary's arms were wide.
"Oh, open, open!" cried they then,
    "As wide as wide can be!"
Heart of childhood, suffer us
    To come to Thee!"

147. WATSON

EVERY reader of the Gospels has marked the sympathy of Jesus with children. How He watched their games! How angry He was with His disciples for belittling them! How He used to warn men, whatever they did, never to hurt a little child! How grateful were children's praises when all others had turned against Him! One is apt to admire the beautiful sentiment, and to forget that children were more to Jesus than helpless gentle creatures to be loved and protected. They were His chief parable of the Kingdom of Heaven. As a type of character the Kingdom was like unto a little child, and the greatest in the Kingdom would be the most child-like. According to Jesus, a well-conditioned child illustrates better than anything else on earth the distinctive features of Christian character.

Because he does not assert nor aggrandise himself.
Because he has no memory for injuries, and no room
in his heart for a grudge. Because he has no previous
opinions, and is not ashamed to confess his ignorance.
Because he can imagine, and has the key of another
world, entering in through the ivory gate and living
amid the things unseen and eternal. The new society
of Jesus was a magnificent imagination, and he who
entered it must lay aside the world standards and
ideals of character, and become as a little child.

148. THOMPSON

LITTLE Jesus, wast Thou shy
Once, and just so small as I ?
And what did it feel like to be
Out of Heaven and just like me ?
Thou canst not have forgotten all
That it feels like to be small :
And Thou know'st I cannot pray
To Thee in my father's way—
When Thou wast so little, say,
Couldst Thou talk Thy Father's way ?—
So, a little Child, come down
And hear a child's tongue like Thy own ;
Take me by the hand and walk
And listen to my baby talk.
To Thy Father show my prayer
(He will look, Thou art so fair,)
And say : ' O Father, I, Thy Son,
Bring the prayer of a little one,'
And He will smile, that children's tongue
Has not changed since Thou wast young.

Lover of Little Children

149. OAKLEY

O HOLY Child of Bethlehem
By Heavenly host adored.
O Wondrous Child of Bethlehem
Earth's dear and gracious Lord.

*   *   *   *   *   *

Our youth to keep, our lives to spend,
We offer at thy feet;
O bind us, till our years shall end
In loving service meet.

150. STORRS

FOR childhood, at least, the new age dawned
when He, whom men thought a Celestial Person,
came according to their apprehension, from the
Heavens to the Earth, not in the fulness of power
and supremacy, but amid the very humblest conditions
which ever invest a human birth. That was, for
the world, the coronation of childhood; and from
that time, not only the cruel abandonment of it by
parents has been made impossible, but the shelter of
its weakness, the culture of its delicate but prophesy-
ing power, have been chief ends in all the societies
into which the inspiration of Jesus has entered.

151. TENNYSON II

HERE was a boy—I am sure that some of
our children would die
But for the voice of Love, and the smile,
and the comforting eye—
Here was a boy in the ward, every bone
seem'd out of its place—
Caught in a mill and crush'd—it was all
but a hopeless case:

And he handled him gently enough ; but
    his voice and his face were not kind,
And it was but a hopeless case, he had
    seen it and made up his mind,
And he said to me roughly, ' The lad will
    need little more of your care.'
' All the more need,' I told him, ' to seek
    the Lord Jesus in prayer ;
They are all his children here, and I pray
    for them all as my own : '
But he turn'd to me, ' Ay, good woman,
    can prayer set a broken bone ? '
Then he muttered half to himself, but I
    know that I heard him say
' All very well—but the good Lord Jesus
    has had his day.'

III

Had ? has it come ? It has only dawn'd.
    It will come by and by.
O how could I serve in the wards if the
    hope of the world were a lie ?
How could I bear with the sights and the
    loathsome smells of disease
But that He said ' Ye do it to me, when
    ye do it to these ' ?

152. DIDON

TO be the last, the servant of all, to be humble, to
recognize the vanity of one's own reason, know-
ledge, strength, will, virtue, genius, activity, ambi-
tions, interests, pleasures, and glory—in a word, to
confess one's own nothingness ; that is the condition
to enter and to be great in the Kingdom of Heaven.

Lover of Little Children

God only hears the humble and the needy, the hungry ones who cry to Him with a true feeling of their wretchedness. This was the special teaching of Jesus, and He reminds the Twelve of it by showing them a child, as the symbol of weakness, sincerity, and lowliness.

The innocence and docility of the child moved His compassion, for His sympathy was always aroused by helplessness and purity. He took him in His arms and said :

Whosoever shall receive one of such children, in My name, receiveth Me, and whosoever shall receive Me, receiveth not Me alone, but Him that sent Me.

153. STALKER

HIS own love of children, and the divine words He spoke about them, if they cannot be said to have created the love of parents for their children, have at all events immensely deepened and refined it. The love of heathen mothers and fathers for their offspring is a rude and animal propensity in comparison with the love for children which reigns in our Christian homes. He lifted childhood up, as He raised so many other weak and despised things, and set it in the midst. If the patter of little feet on the stairs and the sound of little voices in the house are music to us, and if the pressure of little fingers and the touches of little lips can make us thrill with gratitude and prayer, we owe this sunshine of life to Jesus Christ. By saying, " Suffer the little children to come unto Me," He converted the home into a church, and parents into His ministers ; and it may be doubted whether He has not by this means won to Himself as many disciples in the course of the Christian ages as even by the institution of the Church itself. Perhaps the lesson of mothers speaking of Jesus, and the examples of Christian fathers, have done as much for the success of Christianity as the sermons of eloquent preachers or the worship of assembled congregations. Not once or twice, at all events, has the religion of Christ, when driven out of the Church, which had been turned by faithless ministers and worldly members into a synagogue of Satan, found an asylum in the home; and there have been few of the great teachers of Christendom who have not derived their deepest convictions from the impressions made by their earliest domestic environment.

154. CHARLES KINGSLEY

JESUS, He loves one and all,
Jesus, He loves children small,
Their souls are waiting round His feet
On High, before His mercy-seat.

While He wandered here below
Children small to Him did go,
At His feet they knelt and prayed,
On their heads His hands He laid.

Came a Spirit on them then,
Better than of mighty men.
A Spirit faithful, pure and mild,
A Spirit fit for King and child.

Oh! that Spirit give to me,
Jesu Lord, where'er I be!

23

At Prayer

He continued all night in prayer.—Luke 6:12

155. A. DE VERE

THEREFORE when thou wouldst pray, or dost
thine alms,
Blow not a trump before thee : hypocrites
Do thus, vaingloriously ; the common streets
Boast of their largess, echoing their psalms.
On such the laud of men, like unctuous balms,
Falls with sweet savour. Impious counterfeits !
Prating of heaven, for earth their bosom beats !
Grasping at weeds, they lose immortal palms !
God needs not iteration nor vain cries :
That man communion with his God might share
Below, Christ gave the ordinance of prayer :
Vague ambages, and witless ecstasies,
Avail not : ere a voice to prayer be given
The heart should rise on wings of love to heaven.

156. MARTIN

ONE evening, Jesus called to Him Peter, James,
and John and asked them to go with Him to the
mountain for prayer. Amid the lengthening shadows
the little party set out, traversing open glades wet
with dew, and entering after a time woods of pine,
dry-pathed with the myriad dust of ages. Probably

there was a moon and a clear sky or the climbing
path would have been too dark for safety. Presently
the trees became scantier and the moonlight fuller,
and the travellers reached a rocky platform high
up on the mountain's side. Above them they caught
a glimpse of the snow-helmet of Hermon, cold beneath
the sky, while the ceaseless trumpets of many waters
descending from the heights proclaimed the majesty
of God. The lights in distant Cæsarea were dropping
out. In the near south gleamed the wide waters of
Merom broken at one end into reedy marsh. Farther
south, hidden by the hills, lay Capernaum by the
Lake, where Mary dwelt in the little stone house
Jesus had built for her with His own hands and at
His own expense. And, again, farther still in the
dark night, He could picture Nazareth lying, His
boyhood's home, a place of dreams, of endless romance,
and of memories exquisitely tender.

It was now the hour of sleep, and no unusual thing
for the Lord and His apostles to take their rest upon
the ground in the open air. But He had come to
pray, if, by the Father's loving kindness, He might
confirm His own trembling purpose of suffering, and
lift the incubus of disappointment from the hearts of
His friends. So He knelt and for awhile the three
disciples knelt with Him, until weary and heavy with
sleep they wrapped their outer cloaks about them and
lay down in sweet forgetfulness. Hour after hour,
while they slept, and while the moon moved across
the sky, while stars rose and other stars set, and the
night air froze the evening dew, Jesus was wrapped
in silent prayer. For such long continued devotion
I fear I have little ability. We Westerns seldom have,
but the Eastern Saint, even to-day, does sometimes

achieve the night-long vigil. And our Lord often opened the gates of the secret garden, and passed along its paths deeper and farther than any of us ever travel. While we seldom get much beyond the entrance, He knew all its alleys and fair-bordered walks.

On Hermon He sought to prepare for Calvary and to carry His chief disciples with Him in this preparation. Doubtless He came to ask for strength, but, I think, yet more He came not seeking a gift so much as bringing one. And as He gave Himself fully and utterly to do the will of the Father, the Divine joy of giving filled Him. He left behind the lower stretches of the garden and passed along its uplands, where the paths die into the timeless amplitudes of the spirit, and a man may have perfect commingling with Heaven, and join those just men who already have been made perfect.

157. STALKER

JESUS appears to have devoted Himself specially to prayer at times when His life was unusually full of work and excitement. His was a very busy life; there were nearly always many coming and going about Him. Sometimes, however, there was such a congestion of thronging objects that He had scarcely time to eat. But even then He found time to pray. Indeed, these appear to have been with Him seasons of more prolonged prayer than usual. Thus we read : " So much the more went there a fame abroad of Him, and great multitudes came together to hear and to be healed by Him of their infirmities ; but He withdrew Himself into the wilderness and prayed."

Many in our day know what this congestion of

occupation is : they are swept off their feet with their engagements and can scarcely find time to eat. We make this a reason for not praying; Jesus made it a reason for praying. Is there any doubt which is the better course ? Many of the wisest have in this respect done as Jesus did. When Luther had a specially busy and exciting day, he allowed himself longer time than usual for prayer beforehand. A wise man once said that he was too busy to be in a hurry ; he meant that, if he allowed himself to become hurried, he could not do all that he had to do. There is nothing like prayer for producing this calm self-possession. When the dust of business so fills your room that it threatens to choke you, sprinkle it with the water of prayer, and then you can cleanse it out with comfort and expedition.

158. TENNYSON

MORE things are wrought by prayer
　　Than this world dreams of. Wherefore, let thy voice
Rise like a fountain for me night and day.
For what are men better than sheep or goats
That nourish a blind life within the brain,
If, knowing God, they lift not hands of prayer
Both for themselves and those who call them friend ?
For so the whole round earth is every way
Bound by gold chains about the feet of God.

159. FORSYTH

IT should be remembered, that human personality is not a ready-made thing, but it has to grow by moral exercise, and chiefly in the Kingdom of God, by prayer. The living soul has to grow into moral personality. And this should not be ignored in connection with the moral psychology of Christ. He no more than we came into the world with a completed personality—which would be not so much a miracle but a magic and a prodigy.

160. FATHER JOHN

ON rising from your bed, say : " In the Name of the Father, the Son, and the Holy Ghost, I begin this new day, when I awake I am still with Thee ; and I shall be satisfied when I awake with Thy righteousness, and with Thy whole image." While washing, say : " Purge me from the sins of the night, and I shall be clean. Wash Thou me, and I shall be whiter than snow." When putting on your clean linen, say : " Create in me a clean heart, O Lord, and clothe me with the fine linen, which is the righteousness of the saints." When you break your fast, think of the length of Christ's fast, and in His Name eat your morning meal with gladness of heart. Drinking water, or tea, or sweet mead, think of the true quenchings of the thirst of the heart. If you wish to walk or drive, or go in a boat somewhere, first pray to the Lord to keep this your going out and coming in. If you see and hear a storm, think of the sea of passions in your own and in other men's hearts. If you are a scholar or an official, or an officer, or a painter, or a manufacturer, or a mechanic, remember that the science of sciences to you is to be a new creature in Christ Jesus. And every day, and in every place, work at the new creation which you yourself are. Working with all your might at your proper and peculiar calling—work out your own salvation in every part of every day.

24

As a Worker

I must work the works of him that sent me.
—John 9:4

161. STALKER

THERE is endless significance in the fact that
Jesus was born in the cottage of a working man
and spent the greater part of His life doing the work
of a village carpenter. It is impossible to believe
that this happened by chance ; for the minutest
circumstances of the life of Christ must have been
ordered by God. The Jews expected the Messiah
to be a prince ; but God decreed that He should
be born a working man. And so Jesus built the
cottages of the villagers of Nazareth, constructed the
waggon of the farmer, and mended perhaps the play-
thing of the child.

This sheds immortal honour upon work. The
Greeks and the Romans despised manual labour,
accounting it only fit for slaves ; and this pagan notion
easily slips back into the minds of men. But the
example of the Son of Man will always protect the
dignity of honest labour ; and the heart of the artisan
will sing at his work as he remembers that Jesus of
Nazareth stood at the bench and handled the tools of
the carpenter.

Although the commonest work well done is honour-
able, every kind of work is not of equal honour.
There are some callings in which a man can contribute

far more directly and amply than in others to the welfare of his fellow-creatures, and these stand highest in the scale of honour.

It was on this principle that Jesus acted when He quitted the bench of the carpenter to devote Himself to preaching and healing. Than these two there are no callings more honourable, the one ministering directly to the soul and the other to the body. By adopting them, however, Jesus stamped a fresh dignity on the work both of the preacher and of the physician; and, ever since, many in both professions have gone about their duties with intenser ardour and enjoyment because they have been conscious of walking in His footsteps.

162. WALTER SMITH

WERE it table, trunk or stool
Fashioned by His hand and tool,
The Carpenter of Nazareth
Who Heaven and earth doth rule,

'Twere something just to view
Handiwork He deigned to do;
'Twould shed on all our daily Tasks
A glory ever new.

For His work by axe and saw
Would be all without a flaw,
Like His patience upon Calvary
To magnify the Law.

Very dear the Cross of shame
Where He took the sinner's blame,
And the tomb wherein the Saviour lay,
Until the third day came;

Yet He bore the self-same load,
And He went the same high road,
When the Carpenter of Nazareth
Made common things for God.

163. MARTIN

I TAKE up the teaching of Jesus and at once I am impressed with the severity of His mind—a mind which would be an impossibility in a dishonest workman. What an edge there is upon His sayings! What a fine scorn, as He describes I fear too many of us feckless make-it-do people! The patch on an old garment, the misuse of old wine skins, the building of a house without proper foundations, the lazy hopefulness concerning a half-filled lamp, the loins ungirt—all these scorns of Jesus, and, with them, the strenuous note that bids us brace ourselves for work in the house after a day's hard toil in the field, or courageously take up a cross day by day — all these, I say, are not the thoughts of a man who would use green timber for seasoned, or daub with badly-tempered mortar, or be too careless to use a plumbline. No: just as there is no haste in His words, no saying of His we have to unsay for Him, so we nay be sure in those days of His artisan life there were no loose touches of the hammer and chisel as He wrought in stone or wood, no unfinished edges that might tear the user's hand. And just because He was a workman not needing to be ashamed, He was qualified to speak of the things that concerned God. Through the long year's of His builder's toil this maker of earthly houses learnt how to build also houses not made with hands, in that City which hath foundations whose architect and builder is God.

As a Worker

But beyond all the healthy reaction of His work was the superb escape of His spirit. His mind was in no sense caged by His calling. It had a far-flung reach. He had both tactics and strategy. He could confine Himself for the time to the quest of the lost sheep of the house of Israel, while yet looking for His Gospel to be preached in all the world and to the end of Time. He lived and wrought at common tasks in an unshadowed consciousness of God ; and from His tools and His designs, His workshop and His quarry there came gifts that gave ballast to the thought-ships He set sailing upon the Infinite Sea.

164. WATSON

NO one has seriously denied that Jesus was an optimist, although it has been hinted that He was a dreamer, and no one can object to the optimism of Jesus, for it was in spite of circumstances. He was born of a peasant woman : in early age He worked for His bread : as a Prophet He depended on alms ; during the great three years He knew not where to lay His head. But the bareness and hardship of His life never embittered His soul, neither do they stiffen Him into Stoicism. A sweet contentment possessed Him, and He lives as child in His Father's house. This poorest of men warns His disciples against carking care and vain anxiety ; He persuades them to a simple faith in the Divine Providence. They are to " Take no thought for the morrow, for the morrow will take thought for the things of itself." " Sufficient unto the day is the evil thereof." They are to " behold the fowls of the air," and to " take no thought for meat or drink"; to "consider the lilies of the field," and to " take no thought for raiment." Jesus met the grinding poverty of a Galilean peasant's life with one inexhaustible consolation,—" Your Heavenly Father knoweth that ye have need of all these things."

The severity of Jesus' circumstances was added to their poverty, since this Man, who lived only for others, was the victim of the most varied injury. He was exiled as soon as He was born ; His townsmen would have killed Him ; His brethren counted Him mad ; the city of His mighty works did not believe ; the multitudes He had helped forsook Him; the professional representatives of religion set themselves against Jesus, and pursued this holiest of men with ingenious slanders ; He was a " Samaritan " (or heretic), and " had a devil " ; He was a " gluttonous man and a wine bibber," and kept disreputable company ; He was a blasphemer and deceiver. A huge conspiracy encompassed Him, and laboured for His death ; one of His intimates betrayed Him ; the priests of God produced false witnesses against Him ; the people He loved clamoured for His death ; the Roman power He had respected denied Him justice ; He was sent to the vilest death. During this long ordeal His serenity was never disturbed ; He was never angry save with sin. He never lost control of Himself or became the slave of circumstances. His bequest to the disciples was Peace, and He spake of Joy in the upper room. He was so lifted above the turmoil of this life, that Pilate was amazed ; and, amid the agony of the Cross, He prayed for His enemies. Nothing has so embittered men as utter poverty or social injustice. Jesus endured both, and maintained the radiant brightness of His soul. His was optimism set in the very environment of pessimism.

25

The Prince of Peace

Blessed are the peacemakers.—Matthew 5:9

165. GIOVANNI PAPINI

JESUS commands us to invert the relations that now prevail amongst men. When man shall love what he hates to-day and hate to-day what he loves, he will be a different being and life will become the opposite to what it now is. And as life to-day is made up of evil and despair, the new life, being its opposite in all things, will be goodness and happiness. For the first time bliss will be ours; the Kingdom of Heaven will begin on earth. We shall find Eden once more, and for all eternity; that Eden which was lost because the first human beings sought the difference between good and evil. But with the absolute love, that is equal to that of the Father, good and evil will no longer exist. Evil is overcome, destroyed by good. Eden was love—love between God and man; between man and woman. The love of every man for all men will be the new earthly Paradise, the Paradise regained. In this sense Christ leads Adam back to the gates of Eden and teaches him how to re-enter the garden and dwell therein for ever.

The sons of Adam have not believed the Lord's word. They have repeated His precepts without obeying them; and man, because of his spiritual deafness, still groans in an earthly hell which, from century to century, becomes more infernal. And these evils must continue until the pains become so unbearable that within the hearts of the damned themselves there will be born the hatred of hate, until, in the frenzy of their despair, the very dying themselves shall rebel and be filled with love for them who strike them down. Then at last out of the all-encompassing gloom of suffering there shall shine forth the pure radiance of a miraculous springtide.

166. NAVILLE

IN the interests of religion men have used both sword and fire. On the employment of sword and fire, here is the express teaching of Christ. A Samaritan village refuses to receive Him ; the disciples ask, " Lord, wilt Thou that we command fire to come down from heaven and consume them ? " The Master rebukes them, and says unto them, " Ye know not what manner of spirit ye are of." (Luke ix, 54, 55.) When you read the history of religious persecutions, when you stand with horror face to face with racks, tortures, and the stakes of the inquisition, above those impious flames, above that criminal smoke, listen then to the Master's words, " Ye know not what manner of spirit ye are of." And higher still, in the calm serenity of the sky, above the word of condemnation, listen to the word of infinite mercy, " Father, forgive them ; for they know not what they do." (Luke xxiii, 34.)

They knew not what they did, but we know. We know that they hindered for centuries the normal development of Christian civilization ; we know that they forged the most powerful weapons of which the enemies of religious liberty make use to-day. That is what Jesus thought of the employment of fire ; let us see what He thought of the sword.

At the moment of His arrest, one of His disciples draws his sword to defend Him. " Put up again thy sword into his place : for all they that take the sword shall perish with the sword." (Matt. xxvi, 52.) There you have the repudiation of every measure of violence. There are two things in this word,— a command : " Put up again thy sword into his place " ; and a menace : " They that take the sword shall perish with the sword."

167. BLUNTSCHLI

IN point of fact many Christian ideas shine forth before the foundation of International Law. Christianity sees in God the Father of mankind, and in men the children of God. The unity of the human race, and the brotherhood of all peoples, are herein recognized in their principle. The Christian religion humbles the haughtiness of the ancient self-complacency, and demands humility ; it lays its hand on egotism at its roots, and requires its renunciation ; it reckons self-sacrifice for men grander than any lordship over them. It thus removes the impediments which were in the way of any ancient Law of Nations. Its highest commandment is the love of mankind, and it carries this up even to the point of love for enemies. It works to liberate and enfranchise, as it purifies men, and unites them in reconciliation with God. It announces the Message of Peace. It becomes then a thing not remote to transport these ideas and commandments into the language of Law and to transform them into fundamental propositions of a humane Law of Nations, which recognizes all peoples, as free members of the great human family, which concerns itself for the World's peace, and which even in time of war demands respect for the rights of humanity.

168. LIDDON

CHRIST is the predestined point of unity in which earth and heaven, Jew and Gentile, meet and are one. Christ's Death is the triumph of peace in the spiritual world. Peace with God is secured through the taking away of the law of condemnation by the dying Christ, Who nails it to His Cross and openly triumphs over the powers of darkness. Peace among men is secured, because the Cross is the centre of the regenerated world, as of the moral universe. Divided races, religions, nationalities, classes, meet beneath the Cross ; they embrace as brethren ; they are fused into one vast society which is held together by an Indwelling Presence, reflected in the general sense of boundless indebtedness to a transcendent Love.

26

The Transfiguration

He was transfigured before them.—Mark 9:2

169. RUSKIN

WE are afraid to harbour in our own hearts, or
to utter in the hearing of others, any thought
of our Lord as hungering, tired, or sorrowful, or
having a human soul, a human will, and affected by
the events of human life as a finite creature is : and
yet one-half of the efficacy of His atonement and the
whole of the efficacy of His example depend on His
having been this to the full. Consider therefore the
Transfiguration as it relates to the human feelings of
our Lord. It was the first definite preparation for
His death. . . . What other hill could it have
been than the southward slope of that goodly moun-
tain, Hermon, which is, indeed, the centre of all the
promised land, from the entering in of Hamath to
the river of Egypt ; the mount of fruitfulness, from
which the springs of Jordan descended to the valleys
of Israel. Along its mighty forest avenues, until
the grass grew fair with the mountain lilies, His feet
dashed with the dew of Hermon, He must have gone
to pray His first recorded prayer about death ; and
from the steep of it, before He knelt, could see, to
the south, all the dwelling-places of the people that
had sat in darkness, and seen the great light, the

land of Zabulon and of Naphthali, Galilee of the
Gentiles : could see even with His human sight,
the gleam of that lake by Capernaum and Chorazin,
and many a place loved by Him and vainly ministered
to, whose house was now left unto them desolate ;
and, chief of all, far in the utmost blue, the hills above
Nazareth, sloping down to His old home ; hills on
which the stones yet lay loose that had been taken
up to cast at Him, when He left them for ever.
" And as He prayed two men stood by Him."

Among the many ways in which we miss the help
and hold of Scripture, there is none more subtle
than our habit of supposing that, even as man, Christ
was free from the fear of death.   How could He then
have been tempted as we are ?—since among all
the trials of the earth none spring from the dust more
terrible than that of fear.   It had to be borne by
Him. . . . and the presence of it is surely marked for
us enough by the rising of those two at His side.

170. PHILLIPS BROOKS

IN all this story I think there is a graphic parable of
that truth concerning human life which I have tried
to state.   Man is surprised at his own weakness.
He tries his strength and fails.   How the whole
history of humankind is like that scene which took
place at the foot of Tabor while Jesus was being
transfigured on the top.   You remember how, in
Raphael's great painting of Christ's Transfiguration,
the whole story is depicted.   Up above Christ is
hovering in glory, lifted from earth and clothed
in light and accompanied on each side by His saints.
Down below, in the same picture, the father holds

his frantic child, and the helpless disciples are gazing in despair at the struggles which their charms have wholly failed to touch. It is the peace of divine strength above ; it is the tumult and dismay of human feebleness below. But what keeps the great picture from being a mere painted mockery is that the puzzled disciples in the foreground are pointing the distressed parents of the child up to the mountain where the form of Christ is seen. They have begun to get hold of the idea that what they could not do He could do. So they are on the way to the faith which He described to them when they came to Him with their perplexity.

171. TRENCH

FEW the homages and small
That the guilty earth at all
Was permitted to accord
To her King and hidden Lord.
Dear to us for this account
Is the glory of the Mount,
When bright beams of light did spring
Thro' the sackcloth covering.
Rays of glory found their way
Thro' the garment of decay,
With which, as with a cloak, He had
His divinest splendour clad.

172. MARTIN

IS it wonderful that the exaltation of Jesus in His praying should have magnetised into visibility that higher hidden world which is always over us and around, or that the love of Jesus for the three apostles, love which is ever an interpenetration of soul with soul, should have broken their sleep with shafts of that glory and voices of that speech, which in Himself were an infinite and a flawless thing ? No names were spoken ; no one said to the apostles, this is Elijah, this Moses ; but intuitions leaped into the minds of all three, that the greatest of the lawgivers and the greatest of the prophets were with them then. Sleep was utterly gone ; their blood flowed in racing tumults as they looked upon the illumined Face of Jesus. The mists that had crept up the hillsides from thick woods of pine and cedar became luminous with a kindred beauty, as when in the old Hebrew story the Glory of God rested upon the tabernacle in the Wilderness. And in each man's inmost soul came a conviction as with a voice that pealed from God, *This is My Son, My Chosen : hear ye Him.*

Day was lighting a beacon fire upon the mountain top as the three with their Lord descended through the woods. The shadows vanished. The hill on which Cæsarea was built stood up from the plain. In the marble halls of Philip's Temple an altar fire burnt leapingly to the Majesty of Rome. From that broad place of waters before the red cliff came the smoke of incense to the god Pan. But a power mightier than Rome and cleaner than Greece had been revealed in a human form. And for all time this had been made clear that the divinest thing in the world is not power to compel the reluctant obedience of men, nor even skill to weave the gossamer beauty of mythology out of our human instinct for the supernatural, but faithfulness to truth, love of love, obedience to the things of the spirit, blending in a devotion which can make of Life itself one supreme offering.

The Transfiguration

IT is when I have lifted up mine eyes that I am impressed with the solitary majesty of the Son of Man; it is in the elevation of my own moral view that I see Him to be what He is—the King of kings. When my moral view was not lofty I thought of Him as of other men; I would have built for Moses and Elias tabernacles by His side. But when the transfiguration glory touched me I awoke to *His* glory—His solitary, unrivalled glory. I saw Him to be the chief among ten thousand, and fairer than the children of men. Moses and Elias faded from the mountain's brow, and *He* stood alone in peerless, unapproachable splendour; I saw no man there save Jesus only. I never knew before that it was so great a thing to be good, for I had not felt before the struggle between the old life and the new. It was only when, like the disciples on the mount, I had fallen prostrate in the struggle to be holy that I learned how really heroic it was to keep the conscience pure. It was from the depth of my conscious abasement that I lifted up mine eyes with longing to the hills of holiness. The Son of Man became to me more than all the sons of men—the first, the last, the only one, the altogether lovely. The strength of Elias paled before Him. I felt that to conquer by fire was easier than to conquer by love, that to shed the blood of enemies required less strength than to shed one's own, and I lifted up mine eyes in reverence to behold Jesus only.

27

Entry into Jerusalem

*They drew nigh unto Jerusalem. . . . And the
multitudes that went before, and that followed, cried,
saying, Hosanna to the Son of David: Blessed is he that
cometh in the name of the Lord ; Hosanna in the
highest.*—Matthew 21:9

174. GIOVANNI PAPINI

WITH the noisy onrush of a torrent that has
burst its bounds, the procession approached
the deaf, mysterious and hostile city. These peasants
and provincials were advancing amidst waving branches,
a moving image of the forests, as if they would bring
within the city's walls, into the fetid, narrow
lanes, something of the country and of liberty. The
boldest had cut palm, olive and myrtle branches and
long fronds of willow by the wayside, as had they
been preparing for the Feast of Tabernacles ; and
these they waved in the air as they chanted the im-
passioned words of the psalms, their eyes fixed upon
the shining face of Him who was come in God's
name.

And now the first Christian legion has reached the
gates of Jerusalem, and the voices raised in praise
never cease crying : " Blessed be the King that
cometh in the name of the Lord ; peace in heaven
and glory in the highest ! " These cries reach the
ears of the Pharisees who are come forth, severe and

dignified, to ascertain for themselves the cause of all this seditious uproar. Their wise ears are shocked by these cries, and their suspicious hearts are sore troubled. Some of them, drawing their robes of office more closely round them, shout to Jesus, saying : " Master, rebuke thy disciples. Dost thou not know that such words may be spoken only to the Lord, or to him who will come in His name ? "

But, passing on, Jesus answered : " I tell you that if these should hold their peace, the stones would immediately cry out."

The immovable, voiceless stones out of which, as John declares, God might have raised up " children unto Abraham "; the scorching stones of the desert that Jesus would not turn into bread to please His enemy ; the hostile stones of the roadway that were twice gathered to cast at Him ; even the deaf stones of Jerusalem would have been more responsive and more sensitive than the hearts of the Pharisees.

By that retort Jesus proclaimed Himself the Christ. It was a declaration of war ; and indeed hardly had the new King entered His city when His enemies gave the signal to attack.

175. HENRY MILMAN

RIDE on, ride on in majesty !
Hark ! all the tribes " Hosanna " cry :
O Saviour meek, pursue Thy road,
With palms and scattered garments strowed.

Ride on, ride on in majesty !
In lowly pomp ride on to die !
O Christ, Thy triumphs now begin
Oe'r captive death and conquered sin.

Ride on, ride on in majesty !
In lowly pomp ride on to die !
Bow Thy meek head to mortal pain !
Then take, O God, Thy power, and reign !

176. HENRY VAUGHAN

COME, drop your branches, strew the way,
    Plants of the day !
Whom sufferings make most green and gay.
The King of grief, the man of sorrow
Weeping still, like the wet morrow,
Your shades and freshness comes to borrow.

Put on, put on your best array ;
Let the joyed road make holiday,
And flowers, that into fields do stray,
Or secret groves, keep the highway.

Trees, flowers, and herbs ; birds, beasts, and stones,
That since man fell, expect with groans
To see the Lamb, come, all at once,
Lift up your heads and leave your moans !
    For here comes he
    Whose death will be
Man's life, and your full liberty.

Hark ! how the children shrill and high
    " Hosanna " cry ;
Their joys provoke the distant sky,
Where thrones and seraphims reply ;
And their own angels shine and sing
    In a bright ring :
    Such young, sweet mirth
    Makes heaven and earth
Join in a joyful symphony.

28

The Last Supper

This do in remembrance of me.—Luke 22:19

177. A KEMPIS

" COME unto me all ye that labour and are heavy laden, and I will refresh you " (Matt. xi, 28), saith the Lord.

" The bread which I will give is my flesh, which I will give for the life of the world." (John vi, 51.)

" Take ye and eat; this is my body which is given for you " (Matt. xxvi, 26), " do this in remembrance of me." (I Cor. xi, 24.)

" He that eateth my flesh and drinketh my blood, dwelleth in me, and I in him."

" The words which I have spoken unto you are spirit and life." (John vi, 56, 63.)

These are thy words, O Christ, the everlasting truth, though not spoken all at one time, nor written in one place.

Because therefore they are thine and true, they are all thankfully and faithfully to be received by me.

They are thine, and thou hast pronounced them: and they are mine also, because thou hast spoken them for my salvation.

I cheerfully receive them from thy mouth, that they may be the more deeply implanted in my heart.

They arouse me, those most gracious words, so full of sweetness and of love ; but mine own offences do dishearten me, and an impure conscience driveth me back from the receiving of so great mysteries.

The sweetness of thy words doth encourage me, but the multitude of my sins weigheth me down. . . .

O the admirable and hidden grace of this sacrament, which only the faithful ones of Christ do know. But the unbelieving and such as are slaves unto sin cannot have experience thereof !

In this sacrament spiritual grace is conferred, and the strength which was lost is restored in the soul, and the beauty which by sin had been disfigured again returneth.

This grace is sometimes so great, that out of the fulness of devotion here given, not the mind only, but the weak body also, feeleth great increase of strength bestowed on it.

Rejoice, O my soul, and give thanks unto God, for so noble a gift, and so precious a consolation, left unto thee in this vale of tears.

For as often as thou callest to mind this mystery, and receivest the body of Christ, so often dost thou go over the work of thy redemption, and art made partaker of all the merits of Christ.

For the love of Christ is never diminished, and the greatness of His propitiation is never exhausted.

Therefore thou oughtest to dispose thyself here-unto by a constant fresh renewing of thy mind, and to weigh with attentive consideration the great mystery of salvation.

So great, so new, and so joyful ought it to seem unto thee, when thou comest to these holy mysteries, as if on this same day Christ first descending into the womb of the virgin were become man, or hanging on the cross did this day suffer and die for the salvation of mankind.

178. NAVILLE

WHEN the soul is seriously awakened to a sense of its sin, Jesus brings it pardon. This work of forgiveness is, by Himself, connected especially with His death. On a certain day, when addressing some Greeks who had drawn near unto Him, He announced His approaching end. For a moment that prospect troubled Him, but He said, " For this cause came I unto this hour." Foreseeing the death on the cross, He then said, " And I, if I be lifted up from the earth, will draw all men unto Me ? " (John xii, 27–32.) In this manner He has pointed to His death as to the most important event of His life, and the most powerful means of His action upon the world. He has indicated this not only in words, but also by an action. When a man feels himself nearing his end, if he preserves his lucidity of mind, his last recommendations express either the dominant idea of his life, or that which he considers in that solemn moment as the most important. Now, we have in the life of Jesus Christ an act like this. Knowing that He was taking his last repast with His disciples, " He took bread, and gave thanks, and brake it, and gave unto them, saying, ' This is My body which is given for you '; afterwards He took the cup, saying, ' This cup is the new testament in My blood, which is shed for you ' " (Luke xxii, 19, 20.) In this manner was instituted the Lord's Supper, which is in the larger Christian Churches the habitual

centre of worship, and in all Churches the most
solemn act of worship. Hence it follows that by an
effect of a precise will of Jesus, expressed in the most
touching manner, the dominant idea which must be
connected with His work as the Saviour is the idea
of His voluntary death for the salvation of men.
This is a fact which results with certainty from the
writings of the New Testament, consulted merely
as historical documents.

179. PRINCESS ELIZABETH

HE was the Word and spake it,
He took the bread and brake it
And that which He did make it
I do receive and take it.

180. SYDNEY DOBELL

"Good father,
Which of the angels do they miss in heaven?
Ofttimes at mass I press him close, and tremble
To the sweet voices, lest at 'in excelsis'
He should remember, and go back."

181. SAMUEL RUTHERFORD

I URGE upon you . . . a nearer communion with
Christ and a growing communion. There are
curtains to be drawn by in Christ that we never saw,
and new foldings of love in Him. I despair that

The Last Supper

ever I shall win to the far end of that love, there are so many plies in it; therefore dig deep, and sweat, and labour, and take pains for Him, and set by so much time in the day for Him as you can He will be won with labour.

Neither need we fear crosses, or sigh, or be sad for anything that is on this side of heaven, if we have Christ.

O, that we could put our treasure in Christ's hand, and give Him our gold to keep, and our crown.

Lay all your loads and your weights by faith upon Christ. Ease yourself, and let Him bear all. He can, He does, He will bear you.

I am in this house of my pilgrimage every way in good case; Christ is most kind and loving to my soul: it pleaseth Him to feast with His unseen consolations a stranger, and an exiled prisoner: and I would not exchange my Lord Jesus, with all the comfort out of heaven; His yoke is easy, and His burden light. This is His truth I now suffer for; for He hath sealed it with His blessed presence.

Therefore I commend Christ to you as the Staff of your old age: let Him have now the rest of your days; and think not much of a storm upon the ship that Christ saileth in; there shall no passenger fall overboard; but the crazed ship and the sea-sick passenger shall come to land safe.

I am in as sweet communion with Christ as a poor sinner can be; and am only pained that He hath much beauty and fairness, and I little love; He great power and mercy, and I little faith; He much light, and I bleared eyes.

163

182. DIGBY MACKWORTH DOLBEN

TELL us, tell us, holy shepherds,
What at Bethlehem you saw.—
'Very God of Very God
Asleep amid the straw.'

Tell us, tell us, all ye faithful,
What this morning came to pass
At the awful elevation
In the Canon of the Mass.—
'Very God of Very God,
By whom the worlds were made,
In silence and in helplessness
Upon the altar laid."

Tell us, tell us, wondrous Jesu,
What has drawn Thee from above
To the manger and the altar.—
All the silence answers—Love.

29

The Betrayal

Judas Iscariot, who betrayed him.
— Matthew 10:4

183. ST. MATTHEW

JUDAS his betrayer saw he was condemned, and repented : he brought back the thirty silver pieces to the high priests and elders, saying, " I did wrong in betraying innocent blood." " What does that matter to us ? " they said ; " it is your affair, not ours ! " Then he flung down the silver pieces in the temple and went off and hung himself.

184. DIDON

A TERRIBLE conflict was raging within one of the apostles. On this very day, when they were pressing the more closely around their Master, with souls darkened by the thought of his death, one of the Twelve, Judas Iscariot, the man who was entrusted with the scanty purse of the community, was planning to betray his Master. We cannot understand how such an idea could have sprung up in this man's mind if he had faith in the Son of God ; or if he had remained shut out from his confidence and love how he could have lived for two years in intimate communion with Jesus.

The man who has long resisted God grows hardened and debased. He is no more touched or captivated by the divine inspiration, but grows docile and malleable to the influence of the evil spirit. Evil becomes incarnate in him, possesses him, makes a slave of him, and, once under its tyranny, there is no crime which he may not conceive and which he has not the terrible power of carrying into execution. He hates goodness and he hates God.

This is the psychological law of the mystery of iniquity buried in the conscience of Judas. Throughout the two years of his intimacy with Jesus, the traitor must have been hardening himself against the Spirit of the Master. While the faithful disciples were being raised to a higher life, growing gentler, transforming themselves by casting off the errors, vices, and faults of their nature, race, and religion ; while they were entering by degrees into the Kingdom of God through faith, docility, humility, and disregard of all earthly things, he, the false apostle, growing stubborn in his own nature, must have become more and more fixed in his earthly instincts, and in those narrow tendencies natural to his surroundings, which Jesus came to combat. Ostensibly, he shared in the generous feelings of his companions, but in reality he only sought after his own wretched interests. He must have been compelled to have constant recourse to hypocrisy, and, no doubt, pretended to watch zealously over the simple material administration that the community demanded. Perhaps, like others, he had embraced the idea of a worldly kingdom in which his cupidity would be satiated. Such an hypothesis will explain his persistence in living in the train of a Master in whom he refused to believe, and among companions in whose love and worship he did not share.

185. DE QUINCEY

THE miscalculation . . . of Judas Iscariot . . . did not hinge at all upon political oversight, but upon a total spiritual blindness; in which blindness, however, he went no farther than at that time did probably most of his brethren. Upon *them*, quite as little as upon *him*, had yet dawned the true grandeur of the Christian scheme. In this only he outran his brethren—that, sharing in their blindness, he greatly exceeded them in presumption. All alike had imputed to their Master views utterly irreconcilable with the grandeur of his new and heavenly religion.

It was no religion at all which they, previously to the crucifixion, supposed to be the object of Christ's teaching; it was a mere preparation for a pitiably vulgar scheme of earthly aggrandizement. But whilst the other apostles had simply failed to comprehend their Master, Judas has presumptuously assumed that he *did* comprehend Him; and understood His purposes better than Christ Himself. His object was audacious in a high degree, but (according to the theory which I am explaining) for that very reason not treacherous at all. The more that he was liable to the approach of audacity, the less can he be suspected of perfidy. He supposed himself executing the very innermost purposes of Christ. . . .

His hope was, that, when at length actually arrested

by the Jewish authorities, Christ would no longer vacillate ; he would be forced into giving the signal to the populace of Jerusalem, who would then rise unanimously, for the double purpose of placing Christ at the head of an insurrectionary movement, and of throwing off the Roman yoke. As regards the worldly prospects of this scheme, it is by no means improbable that Iscariot was right. It seems, indeed, altogether impossible that he, who (as treasurer of the apostolic fraternity) had, in all likelihood, the most worldly wisdom, and was best acquainted with the temper of the times, could have made any gross blunder as to the wishes and secret designs of the populace in Jerusalem.

186. SHAKESPEARE

SO Judas kissed his Master,
And cried, " All hail ! " whenas he meant all harm.

187. STALKER

THE world has agreed to regard Judas as the chief of sinners ; but, in so judging, it has exceeded its prerogative. Man is not competent to judge his brother. The master passion of Judas was a base one ; Dante may be right in considering treachery the worst of crimes ; and the supreme excellence of Christ affixes an unparalleled stigma to the injury inflicted on Him. But the motives of action are too hidden, and the .history of every deed is too complicated, to justify us in saying who is the worst of men. . . .

The Betrayal

Two things it is our duty to do in regard to Judas : first, not so to palliate his sin as to blunt the healthy, natural abhorrence of it ; and, secondly, not to think of him as a sinner apart and alone, with a nature so different from our own that to us he can be no example. But for the rest, there is only one verdict which is at once righteous, dignified and safe ; and it is contained in the declaration of St. Peter, that he " went to his own place."

188. ANONYMOUS

STILL, as of old
Man by himself is priced.
For thirty pieces Judas sold
Himself, not Christ.

30

Gethsemane

My soul is exceeding sorrowful, even unto death.
—Matthew 26:38

189. JAMES MONTGOMERY

GO to dark Gethsemane,
Ye that feel the tempter's power.
Your Redeemer's conflict see,
Watch with Him one bitter hour.

190. JOHN TAULER

O MY soul, and all ye who love God, come, and
let us follow now Christ Jesus with sorrow of heart
and inward devotion, and with tears and pity, into
the garden. Let us contemplate with the eyes of
our heart Jesus, that is our Saviour, the Lamb without
spot, how he bore therein all our sins; how heavily,
all alone, he trod the wine-press, that like the grape
that is pressed with all care he too might be pressed
in the wine-press of his Passion, and might pour
upon us richly, and give us to drink, the red wine of
his precious Blood, so as to make us drunk with his
love. . . . See how he lieth with his face upon
the ground, in much anguish of spirit, covered with
a bloody sweat, forsaken even by his Father as well

as by all men. There he lieth, I say, and prayeth, not as God, not as a just man, but as it were a public malefactor, as some dreadful sinner, as if he were not worthy to be heard by his Father, or at least as if he were ashamed to lift up his eyes to heaven.

191. FAIRBAIRN

IN the dark eventide before the final agony the souls of the disciples were clothed in darkness, but the soul of the Master walked in light. They were as men that dreamed ; He was as the one wakeful being in a world of dreamful sleepers, and His wakefulness was more than the world's sleep. Their talk seems like the cheery and heedless prattle of a child at the knees of a man whose heart grief has cloven in twain, or like the babbling of a summer brook in a sky dark with thunder-gloom and gathering storm. Yet as to the Master these figures are impertinent. The sorrow that filled His soul did not quench His sympathy ; the clouds that enfolded His spirit did not shut from those who had clustered round Him the sunshine of His love. If they live with touching, almost tragic, unconsciousness of the fate He sees approaching with inevitable step and awful form, He, living at the same moment, as it were, in the present and in the future, with suffering in idea translated into utmost reality, thinks of His thoughtless disciples, and with forward-looking care seeks to arm them against the evil day. And so here emerges one of His divinest qualities, illustrated in action at every moment of His closing sufferings. Sorrow is often selfish, loves to be indulged, to sit blind and deaf to the world and duty, ministered unto, but not ministering. But here is suffering, the greatest ever known, the deepest, intensest that ever strained a heart, yet He who bears it, and is being borne by it to death, broods over His unsuspecting children, thinks of their agony when His shall have reached its climax and done its work, thinks of their misery when He is laid, the smitten Shepherd, in the tomb of Joseph, and they, the scattered flock, shall have fled every man to his own. Were there nothing else, this sublime thoughtfulness, this conquest of the sorrow that conquered not Him, but His life, would speak Him in a real sense Divine.

It is, then, in His last sorrows that Christ seems most Christly. " Though He were a son, yet learned He obedience by the things which He suffered," and through His sufferings He was " made perfect " as " the Captain of our salvation." (Heb. v, 8 ; ii, 10.) His sorrows have been the great interpreter of Christ to man ; in them lie the source and secret of His power. They have in a real sense redeemed man, and were, in a sense no less real, universal, doing for the race what the discipline of suffering is designed to do for the individual.

And the sorrow of Christ has had as beneficial a mission for humanity as personal sorrow for the individual. It has so revealed God to man, and so bound man to God, as to be his salvation.

192. ANONYMOUS (1400 A.D.)

THOU bare the cross and took thy gait
Out of Jerûsalem's city-gate ;
All thy footsteps sweet and good
Were seen through shedding of thy blood ;

172

Gethsemane

Thou met with women of Bethlehem
And also of Jerusalem,
And all wept for thine agony;
To them thou saidest openly:
Now weep ye not for this my woe,
But for your children weep also;
For them ye may lament full sore.
And your salt tears for them down pour;
For they shall have great torment hard
An hundred winters here-afterward.
Those steps of thine give us pardon
When forth we go with devotion
On pilgrimage on horse or foot,
Of all our sins be they our boot!

31

Trial and Crucifixion

*He is despised and rejected of men ; a man of sorrows,
and acquainted with grief.*—Isaiah 53:3

*Pilate saith unto them, What shall I do then with
Jesus which is called Christ. They all say unto him,
Let him be crucified.*—Matthew 27:22

193. GEORGE HERBERT

AH, how they scourge Me ! yet My tendernesse
Doubles each lash : and yet their bitternesse
Windes up My grief to a mysteriousnesse :
        Was ever grief like Mine ?

And now I am deliver'd unto death ;
Which each one calls for so with utmost breath,
That he before Me well-nigh suffereth :
        Was ever grief like Mine ?

The souldiers leade Me to the common hall :
There they deride Me, they abuse Me all ;
Yet for twelve heav'nly legions I could call :
        Was ever grief like Mine ?

Then with a scarlet robe they Me aray,
Which shews My bloud to be the onely way
And cordial left to repair man's decay :
        Was ever grief like Mine ?

Then on My head a crown of thorns I wear ;
For these are all the grapes Sion doth bear,
Though I My vine planted and wat'red there :
        Was ever grief like Mine ?

Trial and Crucifixion

Then with the reed they gave to Me before
They strike My head, the rock from whence all store
Of heav'nly blessings issue evermore :
           Was ever grief like Mine ?

They bow their knees to Me, and cry, " Hail, King ! "
Whatever scoffes or scornfulnesse can bring,
I am the flooer, the sink, where they it fling :
           Was ever grief like Mine ?

The souldiers also spit upon that face
Which angels did desire to have the grace,
And prophets, once to see, but found no place
           Was ever grief like Mine ?

Thus trimmëd forth they bring Me to the rout,
Who " Crucifie Him ! " crie with one strong shout.
God holds His peace at man, and Man cries out :
           Was ever grief like Mine ?

They leade Me in once more, and putting then
Mine own clothes on, they leade Me out agein.
Whom devils flie, thus is He toss'd of men :
           Was ever grief like Mine ?

O, all ye who pass by, behold and see :
Man stole the fruit, but I must climb the tree—
The tree of life to all but only Me :
           Was ever grief like Mine ?

*   *   *   *

But, O My God, My God ! why leav'st Thou Me
The Sonne, in Whom Thou dost delight to be ?
My God, My God——
           Never was grief like Mine.

194. MILMAN

BOUND upon th' accursed tree,
Faint and bleeding, who is He?
By the eyes so pale and dim,
Streaming blood and writhing limb,
By the flesh with scourges torn,
By the crown of twisted thorn,
By the side so deeply pierced,
By the baffled, burning thirst,
By the drooping death-dew'd brow,
Son of Man! 'tis Thou! 'tis Thou!

Bound upon th' accursed tree,
Dread and awful, who is He?
By the sun at noon-day pale,
Shivering rocks, and rending veil,
By earth that trembles at His doom,
By yonder saints who burst their tomb,
By Eden, promised 'ere He died
To the felon at His side—
Lord, our suppliant knees we bow,
Son of God! 'tis Thou! 'tis Thou!

195. E. BARRETT BROWNING

THE Saviour looked on Peter. Ay, no word,
No gesture of reproach; the heavens serene,
Though heavy with armed justice, did not lean
Their thunders that way; the forsaken Lord
Looked only on the traitor. None record
What that look was, none guess; for those who
have seen
Wronged lovers loving through a death-pang keen,
Or pale-cheeked martyrs smiling to a sword,

Trial and Crucifixion

Have missed Jehovah at the judgment-call.
And Peter, from the height of blasphemy,—
    "I never knew this Man,"—did quail and fall
As knowing straight that God, and turned free
And went out speechless from the face of all,
And filled the silence, weeping bitterly.

196. THOMAS HARDY

"MAN, you too, aren't you, one of these rough
    followers of the criminal?
All hanging hereabout to gather how He's going to
    bear
Examination in the hall."   She flung disdainful
    glances on
The shabby figure standing at the fire with others
    there,
        Who warmed them by its flare.

"No indeed, my skipping maiden: I know nothing
    of the trial here,
Or criminal, if so He be.—I chanced to come this way,
And the fire shone out into the dawn, and morning
    airs are cold now;
I, too, was drawn in part by charms I see before me
    play,
        That I see not every day."

"Ha, ha!" then laughed the constables who also
    stood to warm themselves,
The while another maiden scrutinized his features
    hard,

177

As the blaze threw into contrast every line and knot
    that wrinkled them,
Exclaiming, " Why, last night when He was brought
    in by the guard,
        You were with Him in the yard ! "

" Nay, nay, you teasing wench, I say ! You know
    you speak mistakenly.
Cannot a tired pedestrian who has footed it afar
Here on his way from northern parts, engrossed in
    humble marketings,
Come in and rest awhile, although judicial doings are
        Afoot by morning star ? "

" O, come, come ! laughed the constables. " Why,
    man, you speak the dialect
He uses in His answers ; you can hear Him up the
    stairs.
So own it. We shan't hurt ye. There He's speaking
    now ! His syllables
Are those you sound yourself when you are talking
    unawares,
        As this pretty girl declares."

" And you shudder when His chain clinks ! " she
    rejoined. " O, yes, I noticed it.
" And you winced, too, when those cuffs they gave
    Him echoed to us here.
They'll soon be coming down, and you may then
    have to defend yourself
Unless you hold your tongue, or go away and keep
    you clear
        When He's led to judgment near ! "

Trial and Crucifixion

197. SPURGEON

THE hill of comfort is the hill of Calvary; the house of consolation is built with the wood of the cross; the temple of heavenly blessing is founded upon the riven rock, riven by the spear which pierced His side. No scene in sacred history ever gladdens the soul like Calvary's tragedy.

" Is it not strange, the darkest hour
    That ever dawned on sinful earth,
Should touch the heart with softer power,
    For comfort, than an angel's mirth?
That to the Cross the mourner's eye should turn,
Sooner than where the stars of Bethlehem burn? "

Light springs from the midday-midnight of Golgotha, and every herb of the field blooms sweetly beneath the shadow of the once accursed tree. In that place of thirst, grace hath dug a fountain which ever gusheth with waters pure as crystal, each drop capable of alleviating the woes of mankind. You who have had your seasons of conflict, will confess that it was not at Olivet that you ever found comfort, not on the hill of Sinai, nor on Tabor; but Gethsemane, Gabbatha, and Golgotha have been a means of comfort to you. The bitter herbs of Gethsemane have often taken away the bitters of your life; the scourge of Gabbatha has often scourged away your cares, and the groans of Calvary have put all other groans to flight. Thus Calvary yields us comfort rare and rich. We never should have known Christ's love in all its heights and depths if He had not died; nor could we guess the Father's deep affection if He had not given His Son to die. The common mercies we enjoy all sing of love, just as the sea-shell, when we put it to our ears, whispers of the deep sea whence it came ; but if we desire to hear the ocean itself, we must not look at every-day blessings, but at the transactions of the crucifixion. He who would know love, let him retire to Calvary and see the Man of sorrows die.

198. LAURENCE HOUSMAN

WHEN shame and darkness covered Him and thee,
　　What didst thou see,
O thou great penitent of Calvary,
　　That thou couldst beg this boon as thy reward
　　For suffering ?—" When Thou comest to Thy
　　　　Kingdom, Lord,
　　Remember me ! "

In that most darkest hour,
　　Of hatred born,
When Satan's power
　　Showed Love held up to scorn,
　　　　What way
　　　　To thee came strength to pray ?
" Lord, when Thy Kingdom cometh unto Thee,
Remember me ! "

199. WATSON

WITHOUT His Cross Jesus had been poorer in the world this day, and might have been unloved. It was suffering that wrought in Him that beauty of holiness, sweetness of patience, wealth of sympathy, and grace of compassion, which constitute

His divine attraction, and are seating Him on His throne. Once, when the cloud fell on Him, He cried, " Father, save Me from this hour " ; when the cloud lifted Jesus saw of the travail of His soul— " I, if I be lifted up from the earth, will draw all men unto Me." In the upper room Jesus was cast down for an instant ; then Iscariot went out to arrange for the arrest, and Jesus revived at the sight of the Cross : " Now is the Son of Man glorified." Two disciples are speaking of the great tragedy as they walk to Emmaus, when the risen Lord joins them and reads the riddle of His Life. It was not a disaster : it was a design. " Ought not Christ to have suffered these things, and to enter into His glory ? " The Perfection of Jesus was the fruit of the Cross.

200. SAMUEL RUTHERFORD

O, PITY for evermore that there should be such an one as Christ Jesus, so boundless, so bottomless, and so incomparable, in infinite excellency, and sweetness, and so few to take Him ! O, ye poor dry and dead souls, why will ye not come hither with your toom vessels and your empty souls to this huge, and fair, and deep, and sweet well of life, and fill all your toom vessels.

O, that Christ should be so large in sweetness and worth, and we so narrow, pinched, so ebb, and so void of all happiness, and yet men will not take Him ! they lose their love miserably, who will not bestow it upon this lovely One.

Ye will not get leave to steal quietly to heaven, in Christ's company, without a conflict and a cross.

I find crosses Christ's carved work that He marketh out for us, and that with crosses He figureth and portrayeth us to His own image, cutting away pieces of our ill and corruption. Lord cut, Lord carve, Lord wound, Lord do anything that may perfect Thy Father's image in us, and make us meet for glory.

O, what owe I to the file, to the hammer, to the furnace of my Lord Jesus!

Why should I start at the plough of my Lord, that maketh deep furrows on my soul? I know He is no idle husbandman, He purposeth a crop.

Crosses are proclaimed as common accidents to all the saints, and in them standeth a part of our communion with Christ.

How sweet a thing were it for us to learn to make our burdens light by framing our hearts to the burden, and making our Lord's will a law.

It is not the sunny side of Christ that we must look to, and we must not forsake Him for want of that; but must set our face against what may befall us, in following on, till He and we be through the briers and bushes on the dry ground. Our soft nature would be borne through the troubles of this miserable life in Christ's arms. And it is His wisdom, who knoweth our mould, that His bairns go wet-shod and cold-footed to heaven.

201. HENRY NUTCOMBE OXENHAM

VICTIM of love, in manhood's prime
Thou wilt ascend the Cross to die;
Why hangs the Child before His time
Stretched on that bed of agony?

"No thorn-wreath crowns My boyish brow,
No scourge has dealt its cruel smart,

Trial and Crucifixion

In hands and feet no nail-prints show,
    No spear is planted in My heart.

" They have not set Me for a sign,
    Hung bare beneath the sunless sky ;
Nor mixed the draught of gall and wine
    To mock My dying agony.

" The livelong night, the livelong day,
    My child, I travail for thy good,
And for thy sake I hang alway
    Self-crucified upon the Rood.

" To witness to the living Truth,
    To keep thee pure from sin's alloy,
I cloud the sunshine of My youth ;
    The Man must suffer in the Boy.

" Visions of unrepented sin,
    The forfeit crown, the eternal loss,
Lie deep My sorrowing soul within,
    And nail My Body to the Cross.

" The livelong night, the livelong day,
    A Child upon that Cross I rest ;
All night I for My children pray,
    All day I woo them to My breast.

" Long years of toil and pain are Mine,
    Ere I be lifted up to die,
Where cold the Paschal moonbeams shine
    At noon on darkened Calvary.

" Then will the thorn-wreath pierce My brow
    The nails will fix Me to the tree ;
But I shall hang as I do now,
    Self-crucified for love of thee ! "

202. R. ROLLE

THE passion of Jesu Christ confounds the fiend : it destroys his deceits and his snares : it slackens fleshly temptations : it clarifies the mind to covet only Jesu Christ's love. Fasten in thine heart the memory of His passion : I wot nothing, that shall so inwardly take thine heart to covet God's love, and to desire the joy of heaven, and to despise vanities of this world, as stedfast thinking on the hurts and the wounds, and on the death of Jesu Christ. It will raise thy thought above earthly pleasure, and set thine heart burning in Christ's love, and purchase into thy soul delightability and savour of heaven.

203. JOHN TAULER

THERE stood by the Cross of Jesus his Mother. Whence came thy strength ? Of a certainty, thy body was not of steel or stone, that this day thou couldst be pierced so many times by the sword of sorrow, and crucified so many times and wounded together with thy Son, nevertheless thou didst *stand* there firm both in body and soul. Peradventure those strong and rough nails held thee also fast upon the Cross of thy Son, so that thou couldst not fall. But far more strongly did thy mighty love, love stronger than death itself, bear thee up, so that thou couldst not fall. Thou stoodest, therefore, the immovable column of the faith, the lioness that hath never been conquered, and that feareth no attack or threat when her little ones have been taken from her. Thou hadst no fear for the fury of the Jews, the neighing of

the horses, the noise of arms, for thou wert ready
to die with thy Son. Nor couldst thou deny him,
as Peter had done, or fly, like the other apostles, or
doubt, like the disciples, or suffer any scandal, like
not a few, for well thou knewest whom thou hadst
conceived, and brought forth, and how.

Therefore thou stoodest by his Cross, and didst
adore his Godhead in spirit. Truly thou stoodest
like some strong tower, in which the king, who had
set forth on a long journey, had hidden the precious
treasure of faith. Thou stoodest, I say, by the tree
of the Cross, in order to co-operate by thy bitter pain
in man's redemption, by looking on the fruit of life.

204. RACHEL ANNAND TAYLOR

I SAW the Son of God go by
  Crowned with the crown of Thorn.
" Was It not finished, Lord ? " I said,
  " And all the anguish borne ? "

He turned on me His awful eyes :
  " Hast thou not understood ?
Lo ! Every soul is Calvary,
  And every sin a Rood."

205. EVELYN UNDERHILL

COME, dear Heart !
  The fields are white to harvest ; come and see
As in a glass the timeless mystery
Of Love, whereby we feed
On God, our bread indeed.

Torn by the sickles, see Him share the smart
Of travailing Creation : maimed, despised,
Yet by His lovers the more dearly prized
Because for us He lays His beauty down—
Last toll paid by Perfection for our loss !
Trace on these fields His everlasting Cross,
And o'er the stricken sheaves the Immortal Victim's
    crown.

206. NEWMAN

IT is the death of the Eternal Word of God made
flesh, which is our great lesson how to think and
how to speak of this world. His Cross has put its
due value upon everything which we see, upon all
fortunes, all advantages, all ranks, all dignities, all
pleasures ; upon the lust of the flesh, and the lust
of the eyes, and the pride of life. It has set a price
upon the excitements, the rivalries, the hopes, the
fears, the desires, the efforts, the triumphs of mortal
man. It has given a meaning to the various, shifting
course, the trials, the temptations, the sufferings, of
his earthly state. It has brought together and made
consistent all that seemed discordant and aimless.
It has taught us how to live, how to use this world,
what to expect, what to desire, what to hope. It is
the tone into which all the strains of this world's
music are ultimately to be resolved.

Look around, and see what the world presents of
high and low. Go to the court of princes. See the
treasure and skill of all nations brought together to
honour a child of man. Observe the prostration
of the many before the few. Consider the form and

Trial and Crucifixion

ceremonial, the pomp, the state, the circumstance; and the vainglory. Do you wish to know the worth of it all? Look at the Cross of Christ.

Go to the political world: see nation jealous of nation, trade rivalling trade, armies and fleets matched against each other. Survey the various ranks of the community, its parties and their contests, the strivings of the ambitious, the intrigues of the crafty. What is the end of all this turmoil? the grave. What is the measure? The Cross.

Go, again, to the world of intellect and science: consider the wonderful discoveries which the human mind is making, the variety of arts to which its discoveries give rise, the all but miracles by which it shows its power; and next, the pride and confidence of reason, and the absorbing devotion of thought to transitory objects, which is the consequence. Would you form a right judgment of all this? look at the Cross.

Again: look at misery, look at poverty and destitution, look at oppression and captivity; go where food is scanty, and lodging unhealthy. Consider pain and suffering, diseases long or violent, all that is frightful and revolting. Would you know how to rate all these? Gaze upon the Cross.

Thus in the Cross, and Him who hung upon it, all things meet; all things subserve it, all things need it. It is their centre and their interpretation. For He was lifted up upon it, that He might draw all men and all things unto Him.

The great and awful doctrine of the Cross of Christ may fitly be called, in the language of figure, the *heart* of religion. The heart may be considered as the seat of life; it is the principle of motion, heat, and activity; from it the blood goes to and fro to the extreme parts of the body. It sustains the man in his powers and faculties; it enables the brain to think; and when it is touched, man dies. And in like manner the sacred doctrine of Christ's atoning Sacrifice is the vital principle on which the Christian lives, and without which Christianity is not. Without it no other doctrine is held profitably; to believe in Christ's divinity, or in His manhood, or in the Holy Trinity, or in a judgment to come, or in the resurrection of the dead, is an untrue belief, not Christian faith, unless we receive also the doctrine of Christ's sacrifice.

32

His Resurrection

The Lord is risen indeed.—Luke 24:34

207. ST. PAUL

MOREOVER, brethren, I declare unto you the gospel which I preached unto you, which also ye have received, and wherein ye stand;

By which also ye are saved, if ye keep in memory what I preached unto you, unless ye have believed in vain.

For I delivered unto you first of all that which I also received, how that Christ died for our sins according to the scriptures.

And that He was buried, and that He rose again the third day according to the scriptures:

And that He was seen of Cephas, then of the twelve:

After that, He was seen of above five hundred brethren at once; of whom the greater part remain unto this present, but some are fallen asleep.

After that, He was seen of James: then of all the apostles.

And last of all He was seen of me also, as of one born out of due time.

For I am the least of the apostles, that am not meet to be called an apostle, because I persecuted the church of God.

But by the grace of God I am what I am;
and His grace which was bestowed upon me was
not in vain; but I laboured more abundantly than
they all: yet not I, but the grace of God which was
with me.

208. JOSEPHUS

ABOUT this time lived Jesus, a wise man, if
it be proper to call him a man; for he was a
doer of wonderful works,—a teacher of such men as
receive the truth with pleasure. He drew over to
him both many of the Jews and many of the Greeks.
He was the Christ. And when Pilate, at the instiga-
tion of the principal men among us, had condemned
him to the cross, those who had loved him at first
did not forsake him. For he appeared to them alive
again on the third day; the divine prophets having
foretold these and many other wonderful things
concerning him. And the sect of Christians, so
named after him, are not extinct to this day.

209. CHRISTINA ROSSETTI

THERE is nothing more that they can do
For all their rage and boast;
Caiaphas with his blaspheming crew,
  Herod with his host.

Pontius Pilate in his judgment-hall
  Judging their Judge and his,
Or he who led them all and passed them all,
  Arch-Judas with his kiss.

His Resurrection

The sepulchre made sure with ponderous stone,
    Seal that same stone, O priest;
It may be thou shalt block the Holy One
    From rising in the east:

Set a watch about the sepulchre
    To watch on pain of death;
They must hold fast the stone if One should stir
    And shake it from beneath.

210. ALICE MEYNELL

ALL night had shout of men and cry
    Of woeful women filled his way;
Until that noon of sombre sky
    On Friday, clamour and display
Smote him; no solitude had he,
No silence, since Gethsemane.

Public was Death; but Power, but Might,
    But Life again, but Victory,
Were hushed within the dead of night,
    The shuttered dark, the secrecy.
And all alone, alone, alone
He rose again behind the stone.

211. DIDON

THE story of a great man ends at his grave. He enters by death into an invisible world which is closed against us. We see him no more; we hear him no more. All that survives of him, besides his memory, is his disciples, his teachings, his institutions, his works, and the secret working of his immortal spirit. But just as the birth of Jesus bears no resemblance to ours, so neither does his death resemble our death.

The body, which he had given up to all the suffering and torments of crucifixion, is now for ever freed from the laws of suffering and corruption. It cannot change, it cannot suffer. It acquires a sort of spirituality. Matter, with its grossness and denseness, troubles it no more ; it is possessed of a subtlety which can penetrate matter. It is no longer controlled by laws of gravitation, no longer limited by space ; it is as swift and agile as the will which moves it and whose perfect instrument it is. It becomes palpable and visible at pleasure ; it appears and disappears as it chooses. As the soul assumes the form of its ideas, so the body of Jesus assumes the form which best becomes it, without interfering with the essentials of its nature and identity. Yet it has retained its wounds to be the glorious and ineffaceable marks of its earthly struggles, and even in his heavenly Kingdom to witness to his victory over sin, and his infinite love towards mankind.

212. MARY ELIZABETH COLERIDGE

GOOD FRIDAY in my heart ! Fear and affright !
My thoughts are the Disciples when they fled,
My words the words that priest and soldier said,
My deed the spear to desecrate the dead.
And day, Thy death therein, is changed to night.

Then Easter in my heart sends up the sun.
My thoughts are Mary, when she turned to see.
My words are Peter, answering, " Lov'st thou Me ? "
My deeds are all Thine own drawn close to Thee,
And night and day, since Thou dost rise, are one.

His Resurrection

213. ANONYMOUS

ONE place alone had ceased to hold its prey,
   A form had pressed it, and was there no more ;
The garments of the grave beside it lay
   Where once they wrapped Him on the rocky floor.

He only with returning footsteps broke
   The eternal calm wherewith the tomb was bound ;
Among the sleeping dead alone He woke,
     And blessed with outstretched hands the hosts
      around.
Well is it that such blessing hovers here,
   To soothe each sad survivor of the throng,
Who haunt the portals of the solemn sphere,
   And pour their woe the loaded air along.

214. LACORDAIRE

HIS tomb is now the centre of the religious world ;
Mussulmans, Greeks, Protestants, Catholics,
guard it. All, gathered together from the four winds
of heaven, agree to venerate the inanimate stone upon
which the mangled body of Christ for three days and
nights reposed. A hundred battles have been fought
around it ; the destinies of the world have a score
of times changed their aspect there ; but defeat or
victory has ever borne to it the homage of nations,
and so many struggles have but served to glorify
that fragile tomb where all come to prostrate them-
selves. If Catholics alone had guarded it, it would
have been an ordinary protection, like all the rest
that is measured by the sword ; it was more fitting
to the designs of God that Jerusalem " should be
trodden under foot of nations," as the Gospel had

foretold, and that the Holy Sepulchre, held up by a thousand hands, should appear amidst all the events as the indicative sign that no religious establishment is thenceforth possible save on condition of participating in Christ by something at least of His blood, His doctrine and His memory.

215. GOETHE

CHRIST is arisen,
 Joy to thee, mortal!
Out of his prison,
 Forth from its portal!
Christ is not sleeping,
 Seek Him no longer;
Strong was his keeping,
 Jesus was stronger.

Christ is arisen,
 Seek Him not here;
Lonely his prison,
Empty his bier;
Vain his entombing,
 Spices and lawn,
Vain the perfuming,
 Jesus is gone.

Christ is arisen,
 Joy to thee, mortal!
Empty his prison,
 Broken its portal
Rising, He giveth
 His shroud to the sod;
Risen, He liveth,
 And liveth to God.

His Resurrection

216. COWPER

IT happened, on a solemn eventide,
  Soon after he that was our surety died,
Two bosom friends, each pensively inclined,
The scene of all those sorrows left behind,
Sought their own village, busied, as they went,
In musings worthy of the great event :
They spake of him they loved, of him whose life,
Though blameless, had incurred perpetual strife,
Whose deeds had left, in spite of hostile arts,
A deep memorial graven on their hearts.
The recollection, like a vein of ore,
The farther traced, enriched them still the more;
They thought him, and they justly thought him, one
Sent to do more than He appeared t'have done ;
To exalt a people, and to place them high
Above all else, and wondered he should die.
Ere yet they brought their journey to an end,
A Stranger joined them, courteous as a friend,
And asked them, with a kind engaging air,
What their affliction was, and begged a share.
Informed, he gathered up the broken thread,
And, truth and wisdom gracing all he said,
Explained, illustrated, and searched so well
The tender theme, on which they chose to dwell,
That reaching home, " The night," they said, " is near,
We must not now be parted, sojourn here."
The new acquaintance soon became a guest,
And, made so welcome at their simple feast,
He blessed the bread, but vanished at the word,
And left them both exclaiming, " 'Twas the Lord !
Did not our hearts feel all he deigned to say,
Did they not burn within us by the way ? "

217. MATHESON

WE often mistake Christ for the gardener— attribute to mere physical beauty what comes from faith alone. . . . It is from the things beyond the earth that earth beauty flows. The voice which thou hearest in the garden is the voice of the Lord. That which uplifts thee in the flower is just what the gardener has not planted. It is the life below the stem, the mystery beneath the root. It is the sense of a presence which has escaped the eye, of a power which has eluded the botanist. It is the feeling that the gardener has planted something which he has not seen—a seed from the life eternal, a blossom from the breast of God.

Oh, Thou, whose Easter morning shines in many disguises, help me to recognize Thee everywhere. Let me not ascribe to the gardener the work that is done by Thee. I often speak of the noble lives led by men who do not know Thee ; teach me that Thou knowest *them*. Tell me that Thy presence is wider than our creed, Thy temple bigger than our sanctuary, Thy love larger than our law. Convince me that Thou enfoldest that which does not enfold *Thee*. Let me learn that Thou art the one " excellent name in all the earth." Men call their excellent things by other names ; they take Thee to be the gardener. Hasten the time when they shall take the gardener to be Thee ; they shall be nearer to the truth of things. Hasten the time when " in the *flesh* they shall see God " —see Him in the forms of earth, see Him in the duties of the hour, see Him in the paths of life, see Him in the progress of the day. Make Thyself known to them in the breaking of the earthly bread ; in the planting of the earthly flower let them gaze on *Thee*.

His Resurrection

218. RUSKIN

I SUPPOSE there is no event in the whole life of Christ to which, in hours of doubt or fear, men turn with more anxious thirst to know the close facts of it, or with more earnest and passionate dwelling upon every syllable of its recorded narrative, than Christ's showing Himself to His disciples at the Lake of Galilee. There is something pre-eminently open, natural, full fronting your disbelief, in this manifestation. The others, recorded after the Resurrection, were sudden, phantom-like, occurring to men in profound sorrow and wearied agitation of heart; not, it might seem, safe judges of what they saw. But the agitation was now over. They had gone back to their daily work, thinking still their business lay net-wards, unmeshed from the literal rope and drag. 'Simon Peter saith unto them, I go a-fishing. They say unto him, We also go with thee.' True words enough, and having far echo beyond those Galilean hills. That night they caught nothing; but when the morning came, in the clear light of it, behold ! a figure stood on the shore. They were not thinking of anything but their fruitless hauls. They had no guess who it was. It asked them simply if they had caught anything. They say, No; and it tells them to cast again. And John shades his eyes from the morning sun with his hands to look who it is ; and though the glistening of the sea, too, dazzles him, he makes out who it is at last; and poor Simon, not to be outrun this time, tightens his fisher's coat about him, and dashes in over the nets. One would have liked to see him swim those hundred yards, and stagger to his knees upon the beach.

Well, the others get to the beach, too, in time, in such slow way as men in general do get in this world to its true shore, much impeded by that wonderful ' dragging the net with fishes ' ; but they get there— seven of them in all ; first the Denier, and then the slowest believer, and then the quickest believer and then the two throne-seekers, and two more, we know not who.

They sit down on the shore, face to face with Him, and eat their broiled fish as He bids. And then to Peter, all dripping still, shivering, and amazed, staring at Christ in the sun, on the other side of the coal- fire—thinking a little perhaps of what happened by another coal-fire, when it was colder, and having had no word changed with him by his Master since that look of His—to him so amazed, comes the question, ' Simon, lovest thou Me ? ' Try to feel that a little ; and think of it till it is true to you.

219. BAUR

WHAT the Resurrection was in itself, lies beyond the sphere of historical inquiry. Historical contemplation has only to keep itself to this point : that for the faith of the disciples the Resurrection of Jesus became the most fixed and incontrovertible certainty. In this faith Christianity first secured the firm foundation of its historical development. What for all the succeeding history is the indispensable basis is not so much the fact itself of the Resurrection of Jesus, as, rather, the faith in that fact. . . . No psychological analysis can enter into the interior spiritual process through which, in the consciousness of the disciples, their faithlessness in presence of the death of Jesus was changed into their conviction of

His Resurrection

His Resurrection. . . . We can therefore only continue to stand by this : that for them, whatever the intervening means may have been, the Resurrection of Jesus became to their consciousness a matter of fact, and possessed for them all the reality of a historical fact.

220. A. W. W. DALE

THE late Dr. Dale was writing an Easter sermon, and when half way through, the thought of the risen Lord broke in upon him as it had never done before. " Christ is alive," I said to myself : " alive ! " and then I paused :—" alive ! " and then I paused again ; " alive ! Can that really be true ? living as really as I myself am ? " I got up and walked about repeating, " Christ is living ! Christ is living ! " At first it seemed strange and hardly true, but at last it came upon me as a burst of sudden glory ; yes, Christ is living. It was to me a new discovery. I thought that all along I had believed it ; but not until that moment did I feel sure about it. I then said, " My people shall know it ; I shall preach about it again and again until they believe it as I do now." For months afterwards, and in every sermon, the Living Christ was his one great theme ; and there and then began the custom of singing in Carr's Lane on every Sunday morning an Easter hymn. When first I attended service there I was surprised to hear on a November morning the hymn given out " Christ is risen : Hallelujah ! " I mentioned it to Dr. Dale afterwards and he said : " I want my people to get hold of the glorious fact that Christ is alive, and to rejoice over it ; and Sunday, you know, is the day on which Christ left the dead."

221. NICOLL

THE proof of the Resurrection is the living Church of Jesus Christ. The life of the Church proves the life of the Saviour. When Jesus Christ died, His disciples, as might be expected, were plunged in profound despair. When the Shepherd was smitten, the flock was scattered abroad. But no long time had passed before a great revolution took place. They were at first in despair, in spite of all that He had said. His enemies were quicker to discern the meaning of His prophecies than His disciples, and their fears were stronger than His disciples' hopes. No collapse could be imagined more complete than that which took place at the entombment of the Saviour; but in a little time all was changed. The men who before had been cowards, slow of heart to believe, were completely transformed. They became brave and strong, and full of the most resolved faith. It was not that their outward circumstances had changed. They were sheep in the midst of wolves, and the beginning of their conflict with the world might have been expected to disappoint rather than encourage them; but instead of that, they have a new faith in the power of Jesus Christ—a faith which transforms them and makes them men. What explains this? Something must have happened in the interval to account for so marvellous a transformation. Nothing can explain it, save the Resurrection of Jesus Christ. That Resurrection breathed into them new faith, and hope, and strength, by virtue of which they faced fearlessly the most formidable odds, and most determined enemies. That is the explanation of Paul. It has never been denied, even by the extremest scepticism, that the First Epistle to the Corinthians was written within thirty-five years after the death of Christ. In that Epistle the whole gospel is built on the risen Christ. Jesus had broken the fetters of the tomb—the Lord had risen indeed ; and in the strength of that risen Lord His disciples were henceforth to fight.

222. LAURENCE HOUSMAN

SPRING comes with silent rush of leaf
　　Across the earth, and cries,
" Lo, Love is risen ! "　But doubting Grief
　　Returns, " If with mine eyes

" I may not see the marks, nor reach
　　My hand into His side,
　I will not hear your lips that preach
　　Love raised and-glorified.

" Except by all the wounds that brake
　　His heart, and marred His brow
Most grievously for sorrow's sake,
　　How shall I know Him now ? "

Love came, and said, " Reach hither, Grief,
　　Thy hand into My side :
Oh, slow of heart to win belief,
　　Seeing that for grief I died.

" Lo, all the griefs of which I died
　　Rise with Me from the dead ! "
Then Grief drew near, and touched the side,
　　And touched the wounds that bled.

And cried, " My God, O blessèd sign,
   O Body raised, made whole,
Now do I know that Thou art mine,
   Upholder of my soul ! "

223. ARTHUR SHEARLY CRIPPS

PILATE and Caiaphas
   They have brought this thing to pass—
That a Christ the Father gave,
Should be guest within a grave.

Church and State have willed to last
This tyranny not over-past ;
His dark southern Brows around
They a wreath of briars have bound,
In His dark despised Hands
Writ in sores their writing stands.

By strait starlit ways I creep,
Caring while the careless sleep,
Bearing balms, and flow'rs to crown
That poor Head the stone holds down,
Through some crack or crevice dim
I would reach my sweets to Him.

Easter suns they rise and set,
But that stone is steadfast yet :
Past my lifting 'tis but I
When 'tis lifted would be nigh.
I believe, whate'er they say,
The sun shall dance on Easter Day,
And I that through thick twilight grope
With balms of faith, and flow'rs of hope,
Shall lift mine eyes and see that stone
Stir and shake, if not be gone.

His Resurrection

SOME folk as can afford,
So I've heard say,
Set up a sort of cross
Right in the garden way
To mind 'em of the Lord.

But I, when I do see
Thik apple tree
An' stoopin' limb
All spread wi' moss,
I think of Him
And how He talks wi' me.

I think of God
And how He trod
That garden long ago;
He walked, I reckon, to and fro
And then sat down
Upon the groun'
Or some low limb
What suited Him
Such as you see
On many a tree,
And on thik very one
Where I at set o' sun
Do sit and talk wi' He.

And mornings too, I rise and come
An' sit down where the branch be low;
A bird do sing, a bee do hum,
The flowers in the border blow.

And all my heart's so glad and clear
As pools when mists do disappear;
As pools a-laughing in the light
When mornin' air is swep' an' bright,
As pools be when the sun do peer;
So's my heart's cheer
When He be near.

He never pushed the garden door,
He left no footmark on the floor;
I never heard 'Un stir nor tread
And yet His hand do bless my head,
And when 'tis time for work to start
I takes Him with me in my heart.

And when I die, pray God I see
At very last thik apple tree
An' stoopin' limb,
And think of Him
And all He been to me.

225. GARVIE

WHAT the Resurrection means is that the work
of Jesus the Christ our Lord was not ended at
death, and is not merely continued by a posthumous
tradition and influence, but that He Himself, and
no other, in the fulness of His real divine-human
personality works on. As it is not an activity of
which there are any sensible tokens, but only spiritual
evidence, we may say that it is by His Spirit or
the Spirit of God that He still teaches, succours,
comforts, saves, and blesses men. The record of
His earthly ministry is invaluable as indicating so

clearly the content and character of His person and
work, that it can serve as a test of every historical
movement which claims to be inspired by Him.
While His activity is freed from the conditions and
limitations of the earthly life, its purpose is the same
as was that of His ministry among men in the days
of His flesh. It is through His Church that the
sensible manifestation of His presence and Power
is now made; hence it is His body, His necessary
complement, as He is Himself in and by it com-
pleting His vocation (Eph. i, 23). But it can serve
as His body only as it is realizing that He, the Head,
is diffusing His own life through all the members of
that body.

226. C. F. GELLERT

JESUS lives! Thy terrors now
  Can, O Death, no more appal us;
Jesus lives! By this we know
Thou, O Grave, canst not enthral us.
        Hallelujah.

Jesus lives! Henceforth is death
  But the gate to life immortal;
This shall calm our trembling breath
When we pass its gloomy portal.
        Hallelujah.

227. NAVILLE

THE apostles believed in the resurrection of their
  Master, and this belief was one of the forces of
their ministry. On this point all Christendom
shares in the faith of the apostles. In our day the

representatives of the various Christian Churches, who met one Easter Sunday in the Church of the Holy Sepulchre in Jerusalem, bore witness, by the fact of their meeting, to the faith which united them, at the same time that they bore witness, alas ! by their unhappy quarrels, to the divisions which separated them. After considering all the difficulties to which the accounts of the resurrection may give rise, one must, if he be sincere, come to the conclusion reached by a learned living theologian, M. Reuss of Strasbourg : " There remains this incontestable fact, that the Church which has lasted eighteen centuries was built on this foundation."

These are the facts upon which my study is based. If there exists a single historical verity ; if it is certain that Cæsar crossed the Rubicon, and that Bonaparte died at St. Helena, it is certain that the message " Christ is risen " has been proclaimed by Christendom, from the day when Peter the boatman harangued the crowds in Jerusalem to our times, when this message is sent back by all the echoes of the globe. That is a fact. Men may seek to explain it in various ways ; but who can contradict it with seriousness and sincerity ? No one. And who can deny that the message of the resurrection is one that has consoled many hearts, and raised heavenward many eyes sadly cast downward towards the earth ? Assuredly no one.

228. ST. PAUL

WHAT is sown is mortal,
What rises is immortal ;
Sown inglorious,
   it rises in glory.

His Resurrection

Sown in weakness,
    it rises in power ;
Sown an animate body,
    it rises a spiritual body.
As there is an animate body,
    so there is a spiritual body . . .
For this perishing body must be
    invested with the imperishable
And this mortal body invested with immortality
    and when this mortal body has been invested with
    immortality then the saying of Scripture will be
    realized.

Death is swallowed up in Victory,
O Death, where is your Victory ?
O Death, where is your Sting ?

The victory is ours, thank God ! He makes it
    ours by our Lord Jesus Christ.

33

The Ascension

While he blessed them, he was parted from them. and carried up into heaven.—Luke 24:51

229. CAMPBELL

THE fact is that we do not know anything about the ultimate relation of matter to spirit. Matter is the language of spirit. Living our lives as we do under the conditions of a three-dimensional world our bodies are our means of expression and of communication one with another. But if once we could be freed from the limitations of our three-dimensional experience of life many things which now appear to us impossible or at least abnormal would become normal and reasonable. After the resurrection our Lord was a being no longer subject to physical limitations but used His physical body for a time as the very best kind of language He could employ wherewith to assure those who loved Him that He had triumphed over sin and death and in spirit was with them evermore. The ascension was not the carrying up of a physical body to another plane of existence above the sky but its withdrawal into and assimilation to its spiritual background, like the melting of a white cloud into the fathomless blue of the firmament out of which it arose. The whole story is literally and exactly true.

The Ascension

WE were not by when Jesus came,
　　But round us far and near
We see His trophies, and His name
　　In choral echoes hear.
In a fair ground our lot is cast,
As in the solemn week that past.
While some might doubt, but all adored
Ere the whole widowed Church had seen her Risen
　　Lord.

231. H. C. G. MOULE

THE return of the Lord Jesus bodily for a season to
His people on earth, was much, unspeakably much,
but it was not all; the Resurrection was the avenue
to the Ascension. Or, to put it otherwise and perhaps
in a safer way, as the blessed Death is seen in its
comfort and glory only in the light of the Resurrection,
so the Resurrection is fully seen in all its precious import
only in the light of the Ascension. The Risen One is
hastening on to His true place, the place of Rev. v.
(where we are permitted to see the Ascension, as it were,
from its heavenly side); He is going to be the Lamb
upon the throne. The finished work of His Death
and Rising, what was it but the beginning of His
continuing work of Intercession? Let us not forget
this in all our daily contemplation of, and intercourse
with, our Lord; in our life in and on Him, who is at
once our pardon, our power, and our holiness. After
all, we are not so much to look back as to look up, on
Him who was crucified for us and rose again.

Thus the Ascension is, in deepest spiritual truth,

the sum and crown of the work of Jesus Christ.
Looking at it through the lens of Scripture, we see,
gathered into one, the rays of the Cross and of the
Resurrection, the atoning Work once and for ever
done, and the ceaseless Result, in the power of the
Lord's endless life, ever flowing out, flowing down,
from Him who, as our Mediator and as our Head,
ever liveth to make intercession for us; to receive
for us, to give to us.

232. MICHAELANGELO

IF Christ was only six hours crucified,
After few years of toil and misery,
Which for mankind He suffered willingly,
While heaven was won for ever when He died—
Why should He still be shown on every side,
Painted and preached, in nought but agony,
Whose pains were light matched with His victory,
When the world's power to harm Him was defied?
Why rather speak and write not of the realm
He rules in heaven, and soon will bring below,
Unto the praise and glory of His name?
Ah, foolish crowd! The world's thick vapours whelm
Your eyes, unworthy of that glorious show,
Blind to His splendour, bent upon His shame.

233. EDWIN ARNOLD

BUT now Thou art in the Shadowless Land,
Behind the light of the setting Sun;
And the worst is forgotten which Evil planned,
And the best which Love's glory could win is won.

The Ascension

234. VAUGHAN

LORD JESUS! with what sweetness and delights,
  Sure, holy hopes, high joys, and quick'ning flights,
Dost Thou feed Thine! O Thou! the Hand that
  lifts
To Him, Who gives all good and perfect gifts,
Thy glorious, bright Ascension—though remov'd
So many ages from me—is so prov'd
And by Thy Spirit seal'd to me, that I
Feel me a sharer in Thy victory.
        I soar and rise
        Up to the skies,
            Leaving the world their day,
        And in my flight
        For the true light
            Go seeking all the way.
I greet Thy sepulchre, salute Thy grave,
That blest enclosure, where the angels gave
The first glad tidings of Thy early light,
And resurrection from the earth and night.
I see that morning in Thy convert's tears,
Fresh as the dew, which but this dawning wears.
I smell her spices; and her ointment yields
As rich a scent as the now primros'd fields:
The Day-star smiles, and light, with Thee deceas'd,
Now shines in all the chambers of the East.

*   *   *   *   *

With these fair thoughts I move in this fair place,
And the last steps of my mild Master trace;
I see Him leading out His chosen train
All sad with tears; which like warm summer rain
In silent drops steal from their holy eyes,
Fix'd lately on the Cross, now on the skies.

And now, eternal Jesus, Thou dost heave
Thy blessed hands to bless these Thou dost leave;
The Cloud doth now receive Thee, and their sight
Having lost Thee, behold two men in white!
Two and no more: "What two attest, is true,"
Was Thine own answer to the stubborn Jew.
Come then, Thou faithful Witness! come, dear Lord,
Upon the clouds again to judge this world!

235. MARTIN

FOR us who are to be younger brothers to this
Firstborn from the Dead and who may see the
apex of the truth of His Resurrection in the story
we have now considered, the Ascension casts a beauty
about the world beyond the hues of sunshine, pointing
the direction of the noblest Art, and giving impulse
to the Sciences that concern the physical and moral
welfare of men. It teaches us,

> that a twofold world
> Must go to a perfect cosmos. Natural things
> And Spiritual,—who separates those two
> In art, in morals, or the Social drift,
> Tears up the bond of nature.

It opens to us a vision of the End for which Man
was made, when all things of sense and time shall lie
beneath his feet, when his earthly home shall have
been outgrown, and a new earth and a new heaven
be needed as his appropriate environment, and when,
in entering upon that higher state, he shall not so
much leave behind the lower, in which too often
now he seems imprisoned, as carry with him the best
it is able to contribute to the fulness of his life. Thus
the Ascension is the symbol of the measure of man's

life, of the gathering into himself of the very essence of his sense-conditioned activities. It is the pellucid spring of that joy which rises in the heart when our faith and hope are in God, for it shews us that the things which are to come, and which here we can but dimly discern, are yet not foreign to our nature, but infinitely friendly, at once surpassing imagination, and yet also of the very spirit to which we already belong.

236. BROWNING

EARTH breaks up, time drops away,
In flows heaven, with its new day
Of endless life, when He who trod,
Very Man and very God,
This Earth in weakness, shame and pain,
Dying the death whose signs remain
Up yonder on the accursed tree—
Shall come again, no more to be
Of Captivity the thrall,
But the One God, all in all,
King of kings, and Lord of lords,
As His servant John received the words,
" I died, and live for evermore ! "

237. ST. JULIANA

NOW sitteth not the Son on earth in wilderness, but He sitteth in His noblest seat, which He made in Heaven most to His pleasing. Now standeth not the Son afore the Father as a servant afore the Lord dreadingly, meanly clad, in part naked ; but He standeth afore the Father even-right, richly clad in blissful largeness, with a Crown upon His head of Precious Richness. For it was shewed that *we be His*

Crown ; which Crown is the joy of the Father, the Worship of the Son, the satisfying of the Holy Ghost, and endless marvellous Bliss afore the Father on the left side, as a labourer, but He sitteth on his Father's right hand, in endless rest and peace. (But it is not meant that the Son sitteth on the right hand, side by side, as one man sitteth by another in this life —for there is no such sitting, as by my sight, in the Trinity—but He sitteth on His Father's right hand —that is to say : in the highest nobleness of the Father's joy.) Now is the Spouse, God's Son, in peace with his loved Wife, which is the Fair Maiden of endless joy. Now sitteth the Son, from God and Man, in His City in rest and peace : which (City) His Father hath adight to Him of His endless purpose ; and the Father in the Son ; and the Holy Ghost in the Father and in the Son.

238. ALEXANDER WHYTE

OUR Lord carried up to His Father's house a human heart, a human character, which was and is and will for ever be a new wonder in Heaven. He carried up all His human nature with Him, with all the stamp and impress of His divine nature upon it : all His human meekness and humility and lowliness of mind ; all His human love and pity and compassionateness ; all His human sympathy and approachableness and affableness. And like Him, if we are found at last in Him and like Him, we also shall carry to the same place the same things that He carried, and they are the only things we possess here that are worth carrying so far ; even as they are the only things that will be admitted there. And there is no fear but that all these things will be both admitted and welcomed there, as well as all those who shall possess them. For all these things are nothing else but the divine nature here and now partaken of by us, and then to all eternity to be possessed by us. And he who possesses these things in Christ and in himself; he who has while here put on the whole express image of God in Christ he will be immortal with the same immortality as the God-Man Himself; and will be for ever blessed with the same blessedness as the God-Man Himself.

239. FRANCIS THOMPSON

O CAPTAIN of the wars, whence won Ye so
   great scars?
    In what fight did Ye smite, and what manner
    was the foe?
Was it on a day of rout they compassed Thee about,
   Or gat Ye these adornings when Ye wrought their
    overthrow?

'Twas on a day of rout they girded Me about,
   They wounded all My Brow, and they smote Me
    through the side:
My hand held no sword when I met their armed horde,
   And the conqueror fell down, and the Conquered
    bruised his pride.

What is this, unheard before, that the Unarmed make
   war,
   And the Slain hath the gain, and the Victor hath
    the rout?
What wars, then, are these, and what the enemies,
   Strange Chief, with the scars of Thy conquest
    trenched about?

" The Prince I drave forth held the Mount of the
North,

  Girt with the guards of flame that roll round the
  pole.

I drave him with My wars from all his fortress-stars,

  And the sea of death divided that My march
  might strike its goal.

" In the keep of Northern Guard, many a great
dæmonian sword

  Burns as it turns round the Mount occult, apart :

There is given him power and place still for some
certain days,

  And his name would turn the Sun's blood back
  upon its heart."

What is *Thy* Name ? Oh, show !—" My Name ye
may not know ;

  'Tis a going forth with banners, and a baring of
  much swords ;

But my titles that are high, are they not upon My
thigh ?

  ' King of Kings ! ' are the words, ' Lord of
  Lords ! '

  It is written ' King of Kings, Lord of Lords.' "

240. NEWMAN

WHAT a time must that forty days have been,
during which, while He taught them, all
His past teaching must have risen in their minds,
and their thoughts then must have recurred in over-
powering contrast to their thoughts now. His
manner of life, His ministry, His discourses, His

parables, His miracles, His meekness, gravity, incomprehensible majesty, the mystery of His grief and joy ; the agony, the scourge, the cross, the crown of thorns, the spear, the tomb ; their despair, their unbelief, their perplexity, their amazement, their sudden transport, their triumph,—all this was in their minds ; and surely not the least at that awful hour, when He led His breathless followers out to Bethany, on the fortieth day. " He led them out as far as to Bethany, and He lifted up His hands, and blessed them. And it came to pass, while He blessed them, He was parted from them, and carried up into heaven."

Christ is already in that place of peace, which is all in all. He is on the right hand of God. He is hidden in the brightness of the radiance which issues from the everlasting throne. He is in the very abyss of peace, where there is no voice of tumult or distress, but a deep stillness,—stillness, that greatest and most awful of all goods which we can fancy,—that most perfect of joys, the utter, profound, ineffable tranquillity of the Divine Essence. He has entered into His rest.

O how great a good will it be, if, when this troublesome life is over, we in our turn also enter into that same rest, if the time shall one day come, when we shall enter into His tabernacle above, and hide ourselves under the shadow of His wings ; if we shall be in the number of those blessed dead who die in the Lord, and rest from their labour. Here we are tossing upon the sea, and the wind is contrary. All through the day we are tried and tempted in various ways. We cannot think, speak, or act, but infirmity and sin are at hand. But in the unseen world where

Christ has entered, all is peace. There is the eternal throne and a rainbow round about it, like unto an emerald ; and in the midst of the throne the Lamb that has been slain, and has redeemed many people by His blood. " There is no more death, neither sorrow nor crying, neither any more pain ; for the former things are passed away." Nor any more sin ; nor any more guilt ; no more remorse ; no more punishment ; no more penitence ; no more trial ; no infirmity to depress us ; no affection to mislead us ; no passion to transport us ; no prejudice to blind us ; no sloth, no pride, no envy, no strife ; but the light of God's countenance, and a pure river of water of life, clear as crystal, proceeding out of the throne. That is our *home ;* here we are but on pilgrimage, and Christ is calling us home. He calls us to His many mansions, which He has prepared. And the Spirit and the Bride call us too, and all things will be ready for us by the time of our coming. " Seeing then that we have a great High Priest that has passed into the heavens, Jesus the Son of God, let us hold fast our profession " ; seeing we have " so great a cloud of witnesses, let us lay aside every weight " ; " let us labour to enter into our rest " ; " let us come boldly unto the Throne of Grace, that we may obtain mercy, and find grace to help in time of need."

34

Saviour of Mankind

He was wounded for our transgressions, he was bruised for our iniquities: the chastisement of our peace was upon him; and with his stripes we are healed.—Isaiah 53:5

We have heard him ourselves, and know that this is indeed the Christ, the Saviour of the World.
—John 4:42

241. ST. PETER

FORASMUCH as ye know that ye were not redeemed with corruptible things, as silver and gold, from your vain conversation received by tradition from your fathers;

But with the precious blood of Christ, as of a lamb without blemish and without spot:

Who verily was foreordained before the foundation of the world, but was manifest in these last times for you,

Who by him do believe in God, that raised him up from the dead, and gave him glory; that your faith and hope might be in God.

Seeing ye have purified your souls in obeying the truth through the Spirit unto unfeigned love of the brethren, see that ye love one another with a pure heart fervently:

Being born again, not of corruptible seed, but of incorruptible, by the word of God, which liveth and abideth for ever.

242. TERESA GERTRUDE

WE must now turn to consider our Lord in His relations with sinners, and, as we write, our heart grows full and we would fain lay down our pen, and in the silence of prayer contemplate the loveliness of Jesus in this, its most winning form. Besides the sick and infirm upon whom our Lord bestowed His miraculous cures, many of them being, as we may well infer from the Gospel narrative, sinners in a more particular sense than other men, a separate and distinct class of persons stands forth, as though especially chosen by the Holy Spirit to afford an illustration of the mercifulness and tenderness with which the Son of God dealt with souls held captive by sin. Truly chief among these may be named that dear Magdalen, whose passionate grief, whose agonizing love, and whose spirit of abiding reparation, are as precious to our hearts as they are familiar to our contemplation. . . .

She knew of His presence at a banquet in the house of a certain Pharisee, but she could not bear to wait till He came forth. She felt impelled to enter and cast herself at His feet, and disclose to Him the love and the sorrow He had poured into her breaking heart. Tears—precious tears—coursed down her cheeks when she stood behind at His feet, and began with those tears to bathe them, and with those long tresses, that as a veil fell around her, to wipe them dry again. More than this, she dared to imprint on His sacred feet her warm yet most chaste kisses, and to anoint them with the precious ointment she had brought. Will He not shrink from the contamination of the sinner's lips? Will He not instinctively withdraw Himself from the touch of her hands? Did He not know what manner of woman this was that touched Him—how great a sinner she had been? Who knew it all so well as He did? Who could tell, as He could do, the number and the heinousness of her sins, and the foulness of their dye? And yet, it is the Pharisee who despises her—who could not abide her presence, much less her contact. Whilst Jesus, Infinite Purity and Sanctity and Truth, looks upon her with the ineffable tenderness of His Sacred Heart, and loves her even in her unworthiness.

243. FULLERTON

ON a sudden, like a flash of lightning from the sky, my soul returned to me. I was free, the iron fetter was broken in pieces, my prison door was open, I leaped for joy of heart. The Name, the precious Name of Jesus, was like Ithuriel's spear, bringing back my soul to its right and proper state. I was a man again, and, what is more, a believer. The garden in which I stood became an Eden to me, and the spot was most solemnly consecrated in my most grateful memory. Then did I give to my Well-Beloved a song touching my Well-Beloved. Then did I cast my burden on the Lord. I could have riven the very firmament to get at Him, to cast myself at His feet, and lie there bathed in the tears of joy and love. Never since the day of my conversion had I known so much of Him, never had my spirit leaped with such unutterable delight. Scorn, tumult, and war seemed less than nothing for His sake. I girded up my loins to run before His chariot and shout forth His glory.

244. DOLBEN

I ASKED for Peace—
My sins arose,
And bound me close,
I could not find release.

I asked for Truth—
My doubts came in,
And with their din
They wearied all my youth.

I asked for Love—
My lovers failed,
And griefs assailed
Around, beneath, above.

I asked for Thee—
And Thou didst come
To take me home
Within Thy Heart to be.

245. CAIRNS

WHAT is Christian experience but the secret history of the affection of the soul for an ever-present Saviour? Take this away, and it becomes a dark orb, a science of optics to the blind, a world of harmony to the deaf, a tale buried in the hearts of the dumb. The first glad word of the sinner when he falls upon the Cross is, None but Christ; and this is the last of the most experienced saint. This goes with him through life with all its changes and developments of character. He outgrows his childhood and youth, forgetting many things as things behind. He forsakes the books which once he loved, the studies from which he was inseparable ; the earthly objects, it may be, no longer able in the light of conscience to retain his affection. His path is upward, and the tread of time urges him into scenes that are ever new. But time cannot antiquate his attachment to his Saviour. Distance cannot make it fade, nay, brightens it, as it draws him to the lonely isle or pathless desert to make that Saviour known. As it kindled in the soul of the stripling, it burns more ardently in the breast of the patriarch.

246. DORA GREENWELL

HE did not come to judge the world, He did not come to blame ;
He did not only come to seek—it was to save He came :
And when we call Him Saviour, then we call Him by His name.

247. GEORGE HERBERT

THOUSANDS of things do Thee employ
In ruling all
This spacious globe : angels must have their joy,
Devils their rod, the sea his shore,
The winds their stint ; and yet when I did call,
Thou heard'st my call and more.

248. DAVID LIVINGSTONE

FOR my own part, I have never ceased to rejoice that God has appointed me to such an office. People talk of the sacrifice I have made in spending so much of my life in Africa. Can that be called a sacrifice which is simply paid back as a small part of a great debt owing to our God, which we can never repay ? Is that a sacrifice which brings its own blest reward in healthful activity, the consciousness of doing good, peace of mind, and a bright hope of a glorious destiny hereafter ? Away with the word in such a view, and with such a thought ! It is emphatically no sacrifice. Say rather it is a privilege. Anxiety, sickness, suffering, or danger, now and then, with a foregoing of the common conveniences and charities of this life, may make us pause, and cause the spirit to waver, and the soul to sink ; but let this be only for a moment. All these are nothing when compared with the glory which shall hereafter be revealed in, and for, us. I never made a sacrifice. Of this we ought not to talk, when we remember the great sacrifice which He made who left His Father's throne on high to give Himself for us ; " who being the brightness of that Father's glory, and the express image of his person, and upholding all things by the word of his power, when he had by himself purged our sins, sat down on the right hand of the Majesty on high."

249. GOETHE

THERE is in the four Gospels, which are thoroughly genuine, the reflection of a greatness which emanated from the person of Jesus, and which was of as divine a kind as ever was seen upon earth. If I am asked whether it is in my nature to pay Him devout reverence, I say—certainly ! I bow before Him as the divine manifestation of the highest principle of morality.

250. CHRISTINA ROSSETTI

THEN is it nothing to thee? Open, see
Who stands to plead with thee.
Open, lest I should pass thee by, and thou
One day entreat My Face
And howl for grace,
And I be deaf as thou art now.
Open to Me.

251. DALE

NOTHING is more intensely real than the sense
of guilt; it is as real as the eternal distinction
between right and wrong in which it is rooted. And
nothing is more intensely real than the sense of release
from guilt which comes from the discovery and assur-
ance of the remission of sins. The evil things which
a man has done cannot be undone; but when they
have been forgiven through Christ, the iron chain
which so bound him to them as to make the guilt
of them eternally his has been broken; before God
and his own conscience he is no longer guilty of
them. This is the Christian mystery of justification,
which, according to Paul—and his words have been
confirmed in the experience of millions of Christian
men—is " the power of God unto salvation to every
one that believeth." It changes darkness into light;
despair into victorious hope; prostration into buoyancy
and vigour. It is one of the supreme motives to
Christian living, and it makes Christian living possible.
The man who has received this great deliverance is
no longer a convict, painfully observing all prison
rules with the hope of shortening his sentence, but
a child in the home of God.

There are experiences of another kind by which the faith of a Christian man is verified. Of these one of the most decisive and most wonderful is the consciousness that through Christ he has passed into the eternal and Divine order. He belongs to two worlds, he is just as certain that he is environed by things unseen and eternal as that he is environed by things seen and temporal. In the power of the life given to him in the new birth he has entered into the kingdom of God. He is conscious that that Diviner region is now the native land of his soul. It is there that he finds perfect rest and perfect freedom. It is a relief to escape to its eternal peace and glory from the agitations and vicissitudes, the sorrows and successes, of this transitory world. It is not always that he is vividly conscious of belonging to that eternal order; this supreme blessedness is reserved for the great hours of life; but he knows that it lies about him always, and that at any moment the great apocalypse may come. And even when it is hidden, its " powers " continue to act upon him, as the light and heat of the sun pass through the clouds by which the burning splendour is softened and concealed.

252. L. P. JACKS

WHOEVER sets out to follow Christ will have to follow him a long way and to follow him into some dark places. The path we have to follow is a narrow one. It runs all the time on the edge of a precipitous mystery, sometimes taking you up to the sunlit heights and the Mount of Transfiguration, and sometimes taking you down into the fires of suffering and into the shadows of death. Following Christ means that when you find these dizzy things before you, these dark things in your path, you go through them and not round them. Have you a good head? Have you a stout heart? Are you loyal to the leader in front? Easy enough when the road runs by the shining shores of the Lake of Galilee, but not so easy when it turns into the Garden of Gethsemane and becomes the Via Dolorosa.

There are those who think they have followed Christ when they have obeyed the precepts of the Sermon on the Mount, loved their neighbour as themselves and done unto others as they would that others should do to them. To follow as far as that is to go a long way, much longer indeed than most of us can claim to have gone. But to stop there is to stop in the middle, to miss the end of the journey, to come short of the point of arrival, where the key lies to the meaning and value of all that has gone before. We are too apt to rest in the thought that to follow Christ is merely to follow a teacher or a reformer, so that enough has been done when we have repeated his doctrine of Fatherhood and brother-hood, voted for his precepts, and practised as much of them as we can, or perhaps only as much as we find convenient. Let there be no mistake as to the in-adequacy of all that, whether presented in a simple form or any other. To follow Christ is to follow a victor in life's battle, a conqueror over suffering and death, through the completeness of his loyalty to the Great Companion. Hence the power which makes his teaching live; hence the driving force which makes his Gospel effective for the regeneration of society.

253. ANATOLIUS

JESUS, Deliverer !
  Come Thou to me :
Soothe Thou my voyaging
    Over Life's sea.
Thou, when the storm of Death
    Roars, sweeping by,
Whisper, O Truth of Truth
    —" Peace ! It is I."

254. FRANCES HAVERGAL

ONLY a few minutes before Frances Havergal died, while she was, as it were, lying before " the golden gates," she sang clearly though faintly, to a tune which she had herself composed, the first verse of the hymn—

Jesus, I will trust Thee, trust Thee with my soul ;
Guilty, lost, and helpless, Thou can'st make me whole.
There is none in heaven, or on earth, like Thee :
Thou hast died for sinners ; therefore, Lord, for me.

255. R. H. BENSON

I CANNOT live alone another hour ;
  Jesu, be Thou my Life !
I have not power to strive ; be Thou my Power
  In every strife !
I can do nothing—hope, nor love, nor fear,
  But only fail and fall.
Be Thou my soul and self, O Jesu dear,
  My God and all !

256. DR. SUTTON

*L**ORD**, wherefore diddest thou suffer thyself to be
sold ?*
That I might deliver thee from servitude . . .
Wherefore diddest thou sweat blood ?
To wash away the spots of thy sin . . .
Why wouldest thou be bound ? . . .
To loose the bands of thy sins.
Why wert thou denied of Peter ?
To confess thee before my Father . . .
Why wouldest thou be accused ?
To absolve thee.
Why wouldest thou be spitted on ?
To wipe away thy foulness.
Why wouldest thou be whipped ?
That thou mightest be freed from stripes.
Why wouldest thou be lifted up upon the Cross ?
That thou mightest be lifted up to heaven . . .
Why were thine arms stretched out ?
To imbrace thee, O fainting Soul.
Why was thy side opened ?
To receive thee in.
Why didst thou die amidst two thieves ?
That thou mightest live in the midst of angels.

257. ALEXANDER WHYTE

BUT the best way to see what it is to be born
of the Spirit is to look at Jesus Christ Himself.
Look well at the Preacher of that night, if you would
understand His sermon. Look well at the Teacher
of that night, for He is the best explanation and
illustration of His own lesson. Do not look at

Nicodemus, nor even at John, no, nor even at Paul.
Look well at them also. But look first and last at
Jesus Christ. *That* is what it is to be born of the
Spirit. *That* is what it is to be born again. *That*
is what it is to have a spiritual mind. You know to
your cost, and to the cost of all who come near you,
what it is to be born of the flesh. But look well
and look long at Jesus Christ if you would fall in love
with the new birth. Look at Him at all times and
in all places; and as you look at Him, it is a law of
the new birth that you will become like Him. No
man can keep looking all his days at Jesus
Christ without in the end becoming wholly like
Him.

258. BROWNING

THEREFORE to whom turn I but to Thee,
the ineffable Name?
   Builder and maker, Thou, of houses not made
     with hands!
What, have fear of change from Thee who art ever
     the same?
   Doubt that thy power can fill the heart that thy
     power expands?
There shall never be one lost good! What was shall
     live as before;
   The evil is null, is nought, is silence implying
     sound;
What was good shall be good, with, for evil, so much
     good more;
   On the earth the broken arcs; in the heaven, a
     perfect round.

Saviour of Mankind

259. ROBERT HERRICK

CHRIST took our nature on Him, not that He
    'Bove all things loved it, for the purity :
No, but He dressed Him with our human trim,
Because our flesh stood most in need of Him.

260. LAURENCE HOUSMAN

LORD, let this house be swept and garnished first !
    For fear lest sin do there look in,
Let me shut fast the windows : lest Thou thirst,
Make some pure inner well of waters burst :
    For no sweet water can man's delving win—
Earth is so curst !
Also bar up the door : Thou wilt do well
To dwell, whilst with us, anchorite in Thy cell.

Christ said, " Let be : leave wide
    All ports to grief !
Here when I knock I will not be denied
The common lot of all that here abide ;
    Were I so blinded, I were blind in chief :
    How should I see to bring the blind relief ? "

Wilt Thou so make Thy dwelling ? Then I fear
Man, after this, shall dread to enter here :
For all the inner courts will be so bright,
He shall be dazzled with excess of light,
    And turn, and flee !
" But from his birth I will array him right,
And lay the temple open for his sight,
    And say to help him, as I bid him see :
      This is for thee ! ' "

261. TENNYSON

LATE, late, so late! and dark the night and chill!
Late, late, so late! but we can enter still.
Too late, too late! ye cannot enter now.

No light had we: for that we do repent;
And learning this, the bridegroom will relent.
To late, too late! ye cannot enter now.

No light: so late! and dark and chill the night!
O let us in, that we may find the light!
Too late, too late! ye cannot enter now.

Have we not heard the bridegroom is so sweet?
O let us in, though late, to kiss His feet!
No, no, too late! ye cannot enter now.

262. MARTIN

AND the Passion of Christ, once an event in time,
now a heavenly reality, streams upon me and
through me, as I am joined to my Lord by faith.
All that He once was He ever is. All that He is
I may become, for *He that is joined to the Lord is
one Spirit*. The dynamic of the Cross is the Christ
who died and lives for evermore. In Him I grow
towards Holiness. And—here is a great wonder
too—in me He grows towards the World. Through
all elect souls whom He indwells does the Saviour
draw near to the unreconciled. It is not a doctrine
nor a formula that redeems the sinful. We are never
saved until we meet our Saviour. But we may meet
Him in His priests, in James and John and in all
those who belong to the Holy Society of Faith,
of which Christ is Head and King.

263. ADAM DE SAINT VICTOR

NOW that the sun is gleaming bright,
Implore we, bending low,
That He, the Uncreated Light,
May guide us as we go.

264. FORSYTH

WHAT I have in Christ is not an impression,
but a life change ; not an impression which
might evaporate, but a faith of central personal
change. I do not merely feel changes ; I am changed.
Another becomes my moral life. He has done
more than deeply influence me. He has possessed
me. I am not His loyal subject, but His absolute
property.

265. BACON

MEDICINE receives great honour from the works
of our Saviour, who was Physician both of
soul and body, and made the latter the perpetual
subject of His miracles, as the soul was the constant
subject of His doctrine.

266. SADHU SUNDAR SINGH

CHRIST is my Saviour. He is my life. He is
everything to me in heaven and earth. Once
while travelling in a sandy region I was tired and
thirsty. Standing on the top of a mound I looked
for water. The sight of a lake at a distance brought
joy to me, for now I hoped to quench my thirst.
I walked toward it for a long time, but I could never

reach it. Afterwards I found out that it was a mirage, only a mere appearance of water caused by the refracted rays of the sun. In reality there was none. In a like manner I was moving about the world in search of the water of life. The things of this world—wealth, position, honour and luxury—looked like a lake by drinking of whose waters I hoped to quench my spiritual thirst. But I could never find a drop of water to quench the thirst of my heart. I was dying of thirst. When my spiritual eyes were opened I saw the rivers of living water flowing from His pierced side. I drank of it and was satisfied. Thirst was no more. Ever since I have always drunk of that water of life, and have never been athirst in the sandy desert of this world. My heart is full of praise.

His presence gives me a Peace which passeth all understanding, no matter in what circumstances I am placed. Amidst persecution I have found peace, joy and happiness. Nothing can take away the joy I have found in my Saviour. In home He was there. In prison He was there. In Him the prison was transformed into Heaven, and the cross into a source of blessing. To follow Him and bear His cross is so sweet and precious that, if I find no cross to bear in Heaven, I shall plead before Him to send me as His missionary, if need be to Hell, so that there at least I may have the opportunity to bear His cross. His presence will change even Hell into Heaven.

Now I have no desire for wealth, position and honour. Nor do I desire even Heaven. But I need Him who has made my heart Heaven. His infinite love has expelled the love of all other things. Many Christians cannot realize His precious, life-giving

presence, because for them Christ lives in their heads
or in their Bibles, not in their hearts. Only when
a man gives his heart shall he find Him. The hear
is the throne for the King of Kings. The capital oi
Heaven is the heart where that King reigns.

267. LEWES BAILY

BUT I from my soul, humbly with Emmanuites,
intreat thee, O sweet Jesus, to abide with me
because it draweth toward night. For the night of
temptation, the night of tribulation, yea, my last
long night of death approacheth. O blessed Saviour,
stay with me therefore now and ever. And if thy
presence go not home with me, carry me not from
hence. Go with me, and live with me, and let
neither death nor life separate me from thee. Drive
me from myself, draw me unto thee. Let me be sick,
but sound in thee ; and in my weaknesse let thy
strength appear. . . . Set me as a seal upon thine
heart, and let thy seal be settled upon mine ; that
I may be out of love with all, that I may be onely in
love with thee.

268. ROBERT BURNS

FAIN would I say, ' Forgive my foul offence ! '
Fain promise never more to disobey ;
But, should my Author health again dispense,
  Again I might desert fair virtue's way ;
Again in folly's path might go astray ;
  Again exalt the brute and sink the man ;
Then how should I for heavenly mercy pray,
  Who act so counter heavenly mercy's plan ?
Who sin so oft have mourned, yet to temptation ran ?

269. JOHN NEWTON

IN evil long I took delight,
　Unawed by shame or fear,
Till a new object struck my sight,
　And stopped my wild career :
I saw One hanging on a tree
　In agonies and blood,
Who fixed His languid eyes on me,
　As near His cross I stood.

Sure never till my latest breath
　Can I forget that look :
It seemed to charge me with His death,
　Though not a word He spoke :
My conscience felt and owned the guilt,
　And plunged me in despair ;
I saw my sins His Blood had spilt,
　And helped to nail Him there.

Alas ! I knew not what I did !
　But now my tears are vain :
Where shall my trembling soul be hid ?
　For I the Lord have slain !
A second look He gave, which said,
　' I freely all forgive ;
This Blood is for thy ransom paid ;
　I die, that thou mayst live.'

Thus, while His death my sin displays
　In all its blackest hue,
Such is the mystery of grace,
　It seals my pardon too.

With pleasing grief, and mournful joy,
    My spirit now is filled,
That I should such a life destroy,
    Yet live by Him I killed !

270. PASTOR HSI

IT is related of the well known Chinese Christian Pastor Hsi, that one day a New Testament was given to him, and he went to his room to read it. He was so fascinated that he fell on his knees, still reading. Then as he read he became aware of a strange mystical power around him. It was a sense of the over-powering presence of Christ. Suddenly in a moment of transcendent faith he exclaimed " He has enthralled me, and I am His for ever."

271. ST. THOMAS AQUINAS

THE Word of God proceeding forth,
    Yet leaving not the Father's side,
And going to His work on earth,
    Had reached at length life's eventide.

By a disciple to be given
    To rivals for His blood athirst
Himself the very bread of Heaven
    He gave to His disciples first.

In birth man's fellow man was He,
    His meat while sitting at the board,
He died his ransomer to be,
    He reigns to be his great reward.

272. BROWNING

STILL, as I say, though you've found Salvation,
  If I should choose to cry, as now, " shares ! "—
    See if the best of you bars me my return
  Because I prefer for my expounder
Of the laws of the feast, the feast's own Founder

273. R. ROLLE

JESU, in me thy love inspire,
  That nothing but thee may I seek
In thy love set my soul afire
  May thy love make me mild and meek.

Jesu, my joy and my loving
  Jesu, my comfort clear !
Jesu, my God ! Jesu, my king !
  Jesu, withouten peer !

Jesu, my dear and my one joy !
  Delight thou art to sing !
Jesu, my mirth and my melody !
  Into thy love me bring.

Jesu, Jesu, my honey sweet,
  My heart, my comforting !
Jesu, my woes do thou down beat,
  And to thy bliss me bring.

Jesu, with thy love wound my thought,
  And lift my heart to thee ;
Jesu, my soul that thou dear bought
  Thy lover make to be.

Now, Jesu, Lord, give thou me grace,
  If so it be thy will,
That I may come into thy place
  And dwell aye with thee still.

274. ANONYMOUS

O MOST sweetest spouse of my soul, Christ Jesu;
Desiring heartily evermore for to be with thee in
mind and will, and to let no earthly thing be so nigh
mine heart as thee, Christ Jesu ;—

And that I dread not for to die, for to go to thee,
Christ Jesu ;—

And that I may evermore say to thee with glad
cheer, My Lord, my God, my sovereign Saviour,
Christ Jesu ;—

I beseech thee heartily to take me, a sinner, unto
thy great mercy and grace. For I love thee with all
mine heart, with all my mind, and with all my might ;
and nothing so much in earth, nor above the earth
as I do thee, my sweet Lord, Christ Jesu.

And, for that I have not loved thee nor worshipped
thee above all things, as my Lord, my God, and my
Saviour, Christ Jesu ;—

I beseech thee, with meekness and contrite heart,
for mercy and for forgiveness of my great unkindness,
for the great love that thou shewedst for me and all
mankind, what time thou offeredst thy glorious body,
God and man, unto the cross, there to be crucified and

wounded ; and unto thy glorious heart a sharp spear, whence ran out plenteously blood and water for the redemption and salvation of me and all mankind.

And thus having remembrance stedfastly in my heart, Christ Jesu ;—

I doubt not but that thou wilt be full nigh me, and comfort me both bodily and ghostly with thy glorious presence ; And at the last bring me unto thine everlasting bliss, the which shall never have end.

275. NEWMAN

BLESSED are they who give the flower of thei days, and their strength of soul and body to Him blessed are they who in their youth turn to Him who gave His life for them, and would fain give it to them and implant it in them, that they may live for ever. Blessed are they who resolve—come good, come evil, come sunshine, come tempest, come honour, come dishonour—that He shall be their Lord and Master, their King and God ! They will come to a perfect end, and to peace at the last. They will, with Jacob, confess Him, ere they die, as " the God that fed them all their life long unto that day, the Angel which redeemed them from all evil ; " with Moses, that " as is their day, so shall their strength be " ; and with David, that in " the valley of the shadow of death, they fear no evil, for He is with them, and that His rod and His staff comfort them," for " when they pass through the waters He will be with them, and through the rivers, they shall not overflow them ; when they walk through the fire, they shall not be burnt, neither shall the flame kindle upon them, for He is the Lord their God, the Holy One of Israel, their Saviour."

35

Light of the World

I am the light of the world.—John 8:12

276. PHILLIPS BROOKS

HE says: "I am the Light of the World." A thousand things that means. A thousand subtle, mystic miracles of deep and intricate relationship between Christ and humanity must be enfolded in those words; but over and behind and within all other meanings, it means this,—the essential richness and possibility of humanity and its essential belonging to Divinity. Christ is unspeakably great and glorious in Himself. The glory which He had with His Father "before the world was," of that we can only meditate and wonder; but the glory which He has had since the world was, the glory which He has had in relation to the world, is all bound up with the world's possibilities, has all consisted in the utterance and revelation and fulfilment of capacities which were in the very nature of the world on which His Light has shone.

If the figure of the Light is true, Christ when He comes finds the soul or the world really existent, really having within itself its holiest capabilities, really moving, though dimly and darkly, in spite of all

its hindrances, in its true directions; and what
He does for it is to quicken it through and through,
to sound the bugle of its true life in its ears, to make
it feel the nobleness of movements which have seemed
to it ignoble, the hopefulness of impulses which
have seemed hopeless, to bid it to be itself. The
little lives which do in little ways that which the
life of Jesus does completely, the noble characters of
which we think we have the right to say that they are
the lights of human history, this is true also of them.
They reveal and they inspire. The worthless
becomes full of worth, the insignificant becomes full
of meaning at their touch. They faintly catch the
feeble reflection of His life who is the true Light of
the World, the real illumination and inspiration of
humanity.

277. JAMES CLARENCE MANGAN

CHRIST, as a light,
  Illumine and guide me!
Christ, as a shield, o'ershadow and cover me!
Christ be under me! Christ be over me!
  Christ be beside me
  On left hand and right!
Christ be before me, behind me, about me!
Christ this day be within and without me!

278. TENNYSON

OUR little systems have their day;
  They have their day, and cease to be:
They are but broken lights of Thee,
And Thou, O Lord, art more than they.

Light of the World

279. MATHESON

CHRIST has illuminated the world, not by what He did, but by what He was; His *life* is the Light of Men. We speak of a man's life-work; the work of Jesus was His life itself. When I want to get light from others, I consult their books; when I want to get light from Christ I hang up His picture. It is not what He says that I chiefly treasure. The Sermon on the Mount is grand; but the Preacher is greater. It is good to be told that the pure in heart shall see God; but the vision of heaven in a pure man's face outweighs it all. They tell us that the Easter morning has revealed His glory; rather would I say that His glory has revealed the Easter morning. It is not resurrection that has made Christ; it is Christ that has made resurrection. To those who have seen His beauty, even Olivet can add no certainty; the light of immortality is as bright on His Cross as on His Crown. "I *am* the resurrection," are His own words about Himself —not "I teach," not "I cause," not "I predict," but "I am." He thought it almost superfluous to say "In My Father's house are many mansions"; His life should have been itself our light. "If it were not so, I would have told you."

280. VESPER HYMN OF GREEK CHURCH

HAIL, gladdening Light, of His pure glory pour'd Who is the Immortal Father, Heavenly, Blest, Holiest of Holies, Jesus Christ, our Lord.

Now we are come to the sun's hour of rest,
The lights of evening round us shine,
We hymn the Father, Son, and Holy Spirit Divine.

Worthiest art Thou at all times to be sung
                    With undefilèd tongue,
Son of our God, Giver of life Alone !
Therefore in all the world Thy glories, Lord, they
    own.

281. JOHN BANNISTER TABB

I HAD no God but these,
    The sacerdotal Trees,
And they uplifted me.
" *I hung upon a tree.*"

The sun and moon I saw,
And reverential awe
Subdued me day and night.
" *I am the perfect Light.*"

Within a lifeless Stone—
All other gods unknown—
I sought Divinity.
" *The Corner-Stone am I.*"

For sacrificial feast,
I slaughtered man and beast,
Red recompense to gain.
" *So I, a Lamb, was slain.*"

" *Yea ; such My hungering Grace
That wheresoe'er My face
Is hidden, none may grope
Beyond eternal Hope.*"

Light of the World

282. ILLINGWORTH

WE find, then, that Jesus Christ, as depicted in the pages of the New Testament, threw a totally new light upon the personality of man. He took love as His point of departure, the central principle in our nature, which gathers all its other faculties and functions into one; our absolutely fundamental and universal characteristic. He taught us that virtues and graces are only thorough when they flow from love; and further, that love alone can reconcile the opposite phases of our life—action and passion, doing and suffering, energy and pain, since love inevitably leads to sacrifice, and perfect sacrifice is perfect love. It may be granted that previous teachers had said somewhat kindred things. But Jesus Christ carried His precepts home by practice, as none had ever done before. He lived and died the life and death of love; and men saw, as they had never seen, what human nature meant. Here at last was its true ideal, and its true ideal realized. Now the contents of man's own personality is, as we have seen, the necessary standard by which he judges all things, human or divine; his final court of critical appeal. Consequently one effect of the life of Christ upon our race was to provide us, if the phrase may be allowed, with a new criterion of God. Man had learned that love was the one thing needful, and had looked into the depths of love, as he had never looked before. And thenceforth love became the only category under which he could be content to think of God.

36

Our Example

*I have given you an example, that ye should do as
I have done to you.*—John 8:15

283. LUDOLPHUS DE SAXONIA

ALWAYS and everywhere have Him devoutly
before the eyes of your mind—in His behaviour
and in His ways, as when He is with His disciples
and when He is with sinners, when He speaks and
when He preaches, when He goes forth and when
He sits down, when He sleeps and when He wakes,
when He eats and when He serves others, when
He heals the sick and when He does His other
miracles, setting forth to thyself and thy heart His
ways and His doings, how humbly He bore Himself
among men, how tenderly among His disciples;
how pitiful He was to the poor, to whom He made
Himself like in all things, and who seemed to be
His own special family; how He despised none or
shrank from them, not even from the leper; how He
paid no court to the rich; how free He was from the
cares of the world, and from trouble about the needs
of the body; how patient under insult, and how
gentle in answering, for He sought not to maintain
His cause by keen and bitter words, but with gentle
and humble answer to cure another's malice; what
composure in all His behaviour, what anxiety for

the salvation of souls, for the love of whom He also deigned to die ; how He offered Himself as the pattern of all that is good ; how compassionate He was to the afflicted ; how He condescended to the imperfection of the weak, how He despised not success, how mercifully He received the penitent, how dutiful He was to His parents ; how ready in serving all, according to His own words, " I am among you as He that doth serve " ; how He shunned all display and show, all singularity ; how He avoided all occasions of offence, how temperate in eating and drinking, how modest in appearance, how earnest in prayer, how sober in His watching, how patient of toil and want, how peaceful and calm in all things.

284. SEELEY

LIVING examples are, as a general rule, more potent than those of which we read in books. And it is true that the sight of very humble degrees of Christian humanity in action will do more to kindle the enthusiasm, in most cases, than reading the most impressive scenes in the life of Christ. It cannot, therefore, be said that Christ is the direct source of all humanity. It is handed on like the torch from runner to runner in the race of life. Still it not only existed in Christ in a pre-eminent degree, but the circumstances of his life and death gave him pre-eminent opportunities of displaying it. The story of his life will always remain the one record in which the moral perfection of man stands revealed in its root and its unity, the hidden spring made palpably manifest by which the whole machine is moved.

And as, in the will of God, this unique man was elected
to a unique sorrow, and holds as undisputed a
sovereignty in suffering as in self-devotion, all lesser
examples and lives will for ever hold a subordinate
place, and serve chiefly to reflect light on the central
and original Example. In his wounds all human
sorrows will hide themselves, and all human self-
denials support themselves against his cross.

285. WHITTIER

TO Thee our full humanity,
   Its joys and pains belong;
The wrong of man to man on Thee
   Inflicts a deeper wrong.

   *   *   *   *   *

In simple trust like theirs who heard,
   Beside the Syrian sea,
The gracious calling of the Lord,
Let us, like them, without a word,
   Rise up and follow Thee.

286. EDMUND SPENSER

FROM thence read on the story of His life,
   His humble carriage, His unfaulty ways,
His canker'd foes, His fights, His toil, His strife.
His pains, His poverty, His sharp assays,
Through which He past His miserable days,
Offending none, and doing good to all,
Yet being maliced both of great and small.

Our Example

287. HOUSMAN

THOU the Cross didst bear :
    What bear I ?
Thou the Thorn didst wear :
    What wear I ?
Thou to death didst dare :
    What dare I ?
Thou for me dost care :
    What care I ?

288. ROBERTS

ON a certain Palm Sunday, a service for children
was held in the Cathedral prior to a procession ;
and after speaking to the children awhile, Savonarola
turned to the men and women present and cried,
" Florence, behold ! This is the Lord of the Universe
and would fain be thine. Wilt thou have Him for
thy king ? " And the multitude answered, " Long
live Christ our King ! "

Savonarola has left us for his monument the thought
of Jesus as the great overlord of our corporate life.
In these democratic days there is a growing sense of
the incongruity of conceiving Jesus under terms of
secular monarchy. But what was in Savonarola's
mind is plain. He meant that our legislation shall
be conceived in His spirit, that it shall be enacted
and administered along the lines of His will, and that
our public bodies, from Parliament and Congress
down to the veriest sub-committee of parish councillors
or selectmen, shall sit as it were in His presence.
Let His will be the touchstone of our enactments,
let His principles become the fundamentals of civic

and national life, let His character become the citizen's
ideal. Thus Savonarola, though he be dead, yet
speaketh; and this generation, God knows, needs to
listen to him.

289. ABBOT MARMION

NEVER forget this: Jesus Christ, having taken our
nature, has sanctified all our actions, all our feelings:
His human life was like to ours, and His Divine Heart
is the centre of every virtue. Jesus Christ exercised
every form of human activity; we must not think of
Our Lord as living rapt in ecstasy; on the contrary
He found the motive power of His activity in the
beatific vision of the perfections of His Father;
He willed to glorify His Father by sanctifying in
His Person the forms of activity we ourselves have
to exert. We pray: He passed the nights in prayer;
we work: He toiled in labour till the age of thirty;
we eat: He sat at table with His disciples; we suffer
contradictions on the part of men: He has known
them; did the Pharisees ever leave Him in peace?
We suffer: He has shed tears. He suffered for us,
before us, both in His body and soul, as none other
has ever suffered. We experience joy: His holy
soul felt ineffable joy; we take rest: sleep has like-
wise closed His eyelids. In a word, He has done all
we do. And why has He done all this? Not
only to set us the example, since He is our Head;
but also by all these actions, to merit for us the power
of sanctifying all *our* acts: to give us that grace
which renders our actions pleasing to His Father. This
grace unites us to Him, makes us members of His
body; and in order to grow up in Him, to attain

our perfection as His members, we have but to let
this grace take possession, not only of our being, but
of all our activities.

290. THOMAS CHUBB

IN Christ we have an example of a quiet and peace-
able spirit; of a becoming modesty and sobriety;
just, honest, upright, sincere; and, above all, of a
most gracious and benevolent temper and behaviour.
One who did no wrong, no injury to any man; in
whose mouth was no guile; who went about doing
good, not only by his ministry, but also in curing all
manner of diseases among the people. His life was
a beautiful picture of human nature in its native
purity and simplicity, and showed at once what
excellent creatures men would be when under the
influence and power of that gospel which he preached
unto them.

291. GARVIE

JESUS lived what He taught alike in His religious
experience and His moral character, as well as
the grace of His dealings with men.

His teaching was enforced by His *example*. Those
whom He enjoined to learn of Him were also called
to take His yoke upon them, that is, to serve not
Him, but as He served, to be His yoke-fellows
(Matt. xi, 29–30). What He said and did was not
to set an example but because it was just what it was
most fit should then and there be said and done.
Jesus never assumed the moral pose which some men
do in trying to set an example; in fulfilling His
calling in word and deed He showed what moral

perfection is. On one occasion He is represented as doing something for the sake of example. When He had washed the disciples' feet, He enforced the meaning of His deed in the words : " I have given you an example, that ye also should do as I have done to you " (John xiii, 15). As the deed, however, was one of humble service, there was in it no moral pose, which is often so offensive in those who offer themselves as patterns to their fellows. As the words to Peter show : " If I wash thee not thou hast no part with Me " ; the example was not one merely to be imitated ; it was in itself one may even say sacramental, the channel of the grace that cleansed the disciples from the rivalry and ambition which so endangered their personal relation to Himself. As it was necessary for them, so it was a duty for Him as charged with their training for His work. By its moral quality it was morally efficacious. This is essentially what the moral example of Jesus means. His holy love gains such influence over His disciples, that without conscious imitation they are gradually conformed to His likeness. Literal reproduction of what He said and did is not to follow His example ; but vital participation in His motive, disposition, purpose is. His vocation on the one hand, and His circumstances on the other, were so unlike ours, that such artificial imitation would be a moral absurdity. His perfection, while it humbles, also encourages us, for it is the perfection of the grace that enables us to do what it enjoins ; it is a pattern which does not make us despair, because it is also a power that is sufficient according to our faith for every demand. We may truly use of His example the words of Augustine, *Jube quod vis, Da quod jubes.*

Our Example

292. SABATIER

AT peace with God, Jesus found Himself at peace with the universe. The idea of nature, that formidable screen erected between ourselves and God, destroying hope and quenching prayer, did not exist for Him. Nature—that was the Will of His Father. He submitted to it with confidence and joy, whereas we submit to it with desperate resignation. He did not feel Himself to be an orphan or an exile in the world; He conducted Himself in it with ease and in security, not as a slave, but as a son in the house which the Father filled with His presence. It is the Father that directs all things; He makes His sun to shine upon the evil and the good; He watches over the sparrows; He clothes the lilies of the field; He gives life and food, the body and raiment; He notices the work we have to do, the trials we must bear. He never leaves us to ourselves. His spirit vivifies and fortifies our own. He is at the origin of our life and at the end. We are ever in the Father's hands.

293. JOHN TAULER

O GOOD Jesus, by that immense love which drew thee from thy Father's heart and bosom into the womb of the Virgin unstained; by thy taking on thee our human nature, in which thou becamest my servant, and deliveredst me from everlasting death, draw me out of myself to thee, my God; and may this thy love, O my God, recover for me thy grace, and perfect and increase in me whatever is imperfect in me; may it raise up what is fallen down, restore what hath been destroyed, conform me to thy most holy life and loving conversation; and may it make me one with thee, and enclose me within thee, and engrave on the fleshly tables of my heart, and in all my behaviour, thy holy life with all its virtues, as well as the goodness of thy behaviour. Loosen my spirit, O my God, from all lower things, rule my soul, and, at the same time, work together with my body holy and just works.

294. JACOB BEHMEN

ONLY give thyself utterly to Christ—this is the greatest and the most important thing. Place all at His disposal. If thou possess Him, He will surely teach thee what thou shouldest do and what thou shouldest give up. He will teach thee to speak for Him; He will give thee courage and wisdom as to how thou shouldest behave. Be not anxious as to thy dealings with others, but commit it all to Him. He will assuredly work within thee that which is well-pleasing in His sight.

295. THOMAS EDWARD BROWN

HIGH stretched upon the swinging yard,
I gather in the sheet;
But it is hard
And stiff, and one cries haste.
Then He that is most dear in my regard
Of all the crew gives aidance meet;
But from His hands, and from His feet,
A glory spreads wherewith the night is starred:

Our Example

Moreover of a cup most bitter-sweet
With fragrance as of nard,
And myrrh, and cassia spiced,
He proffers me to taste.
Then I to Him :—'Art Thou the Christ ? '
He saith—' Thou say'st.'

Like to an ox
That staggers 'neath the mortal blow,
She grinds upon the rocks :—
Then straight and low
Leaps forth the levelled line, and in our quarter locks.
The cradle's rigged ; with swerving of the blast
We go,
Our Captain last—
Demands
' Who fired that shot ? ' Each silent stands—
Ah, sweet perplexity !
This too was He.

I have an arbour wherein came a toad
Most hideous to see—
Immediate, seizing staff or goad,
I smote it cruelly.
Then all the place with subtle radiance glowed—
I looked, and it was He !

296. CHARLES DICKENS

CHARLES DICKENS wrote in a letter to his
youngest boy, when leaving home to join his
brother in Australia, " Try to do to others as you
would have them do to you, and do not be discouraged
if they fail sometimes. It is much better for you
that they should fail in obeying the greatest rule

laid down by our Saviour than that you should.
I put a New Testament among your books for the
very same reasons, and with the very same hopes,
that made me write an easy account of it for you,
when you were a little child. Because it is the best
book that ever was, or will be, known in the world ;
and because it teaches you the best lessons by which
any human creature, who tries to be truthful and
faithful to duty, can possibly be guided. As your
brothers have gone away, one by one, I have written
to each such words as I am now writing to you, and
have entreated them all to guide themselves by this
Book, putting aside the interpretations and inventions
of Man. You will remember that you have never
at home been harassed about religious observances,
or mere formalities. I have always been anxious not
to weary my children with such things, before they
are old enough to form opinions respecting them.
You will therefore understand the better that I now
most solemnly impress upon you the truth and beauty
of the Christian Religion, as it came from Christ
Himself, and the impossibility of your going far wrong
if you humbly but heartily respect it."

297. MARY ELIZABETH COLERIDGE

A S Christ the Lord was passing by,
    He came, one night, to a cottage door,
  He came, a poor man, to the poor ;
He had no bed whereon to lie.

He asked in vain for a crust of bread,
    Standing there in the frozen blast.
    The door was locked and bolted fast.
" Only a beggar ! " the poor man said.

Our Example

Christ the Lord went further on,
 Until he came to a palace gate.
 There a king was keeping his state,
In every window the candles shone.

The king beheld Him out in the cold.
 He left his guests in the banquet-hall.
 He bade his servants tend them all.
" I wait on a Guest I know of old."

" 'Tis only a beggar-man ! " they said.
 " Yes," he said ; " it is Christ the Lord."
 He spoke to Him a kindly word,
He gave Him wine and he gave Him bread.

Now Christ is Lord of Heaven and Hell,
 And all the words of Christ are true.
 He touched the cottage, and it grew ;
He touched the palace, and it fell.

The poor man is become a king.
 Never was man so sad as he,
 Sorrow and Sin on the throne make three,
He has no joy in mortal thing.

But the sun streams in at the cottage door
 That stands where once the palace stood,
 And the workman, toiling to earn his food
Was never a king before.

37

The Character of Christ

Whom do men say that I the Son of man am?
—Matthew 16:13

298. ROUSSEAU

I WILL confess to you, that the majesty of the
Scriptures strikes me with admiration, as the purity
of the gospel has its influence on my heart. Peruse the
words of our philosophers, with all their pomp of
diction, how mean, how contemptible are they, com-
pared with the Scriptures! Is it possible that a book,
at once so simple and so sublime, should be merely the
work of man? Is it possible that the sacred personage
whose history it contains should be himself a mere
man? Do we find that he assumed the tone of an
enthusiast or ambitious sectary? What sweetness,
what purity in his manner! What an affecting
gracefulness in his instructions! What sublimity
in his maxims! What profound wisdom in his dis-
courses! What presence of mind, what subtlety,
what fitness, in his replies! How great the command
over his passions! Where is the man, where the
philosopher, who could so live and so die, without
weakness, and without ostentation? When Plato
describes his imaginary righteous man, loaded with all
the punishments of guilt, yet meriting the highest
rewards of virtue, he describes exactly the character
of Jesus Christ: the resemblance is so striking that all
the Church Fathers perceived it. What preposses-

sion, what blindness must it be to compare the son of Sophroniscus to the son of Mary! What an infinite disproportion there is between them! Socrates, dying without pain or ignominy, easily supported his character to the last, and, if this easy death had not crowned his life, it might have been doubted whether Socrates, with all his wisdom, was anything more than a mere sophist. He invented, it is said, the theory of ethics. Others, however, had before put them into practice : he had only to say, therefore, what they had done, and to reduce their examples to precepts. Aristides had been just before Socrates defined justice. Leonidas had given up his life for his country before Socrates declared patriotism to be a duty. The Spartans were a sober people before Socrates recommended sobriety. Before he had even defined virtue Greece abounded in virtuous men. But where could Jesus learn, among his contemporaries, that pure and sublime morality of which he only had given us both precept and example? The greatest wisdom was made known among the most bigoted fanaticism; and the simplicity of the most heroic virtues did honour to the vilest people on earth. The death of Socrates, peacefully philosophising among friends, appears the most agreeable that one could wish : that of Jesus, expiring in agonies, abused, insulted, and accused by a whole nation, is the most horrible that one could fear. Socrates, indeed, in receiving the cup of poison, blessed the weeping executioner who administered it; but Jesus, amidst excruciating tortures, prayed for his merciless tormentors.

" *Yes, if the life and death of Socrates were those of a sage, the life and death of Jesus are those of a God.*"

299. NAPOLEON

I KNOW men; and I tell you that Jesus Christ is not a man. Superficial minds see a resemblance between Christ and the founders of empires, and the gods of other religions. That resemblance does not exist. There is between Christianity and whatever other religions the distance of infinity. . . .

Everything in Christ astonishes me. His spirit overawes me, and his will confounds me. Between him and whoever else in the world there is no possible term of comparison. He is truly a being by himself. His ideas and his sentiments, the truth which he announces, his manner of convincing, are not explained either by human organisation or by the nature of things.

The nearer I approach, the more carefully I examine, everything is above me ; everything remains grand,—of a grandeur which overpowers. His religion is a revelation from an intelligence which certainly is not that of man. There is there a profound originality which has created a series of words and of maxims before unknown. Jesus borrowed nothing from our science. One can absolutely find nowhere, but in him alone, the imitation or the example of his life.

. . . I search in vain in history to find the similar to Jesus Christ, or anything which can approach the gospel. Neither history, nor humanity, nor the ages, nor nature, offer me anything with which I am able to compare it or to explain it. Here everything is extraordinary. The more I consider the gospel, the more I am assured that there is nothing there which is not beyond the march of events, and above the human mind.

The Character of Christ

300. F. PECAUT

TO what height does the character of Jesus Christ rise above the most sublime and yet ever imperfect types of antiquity ! What man ever knew how to offer a more manly resistance to evil ? Who endured vexation and contradiction better than he ? Where is such a development of moral power united with less severity ? Was there ever one seen who made himself heard with such royal authority ? And yet no one ever was so gentle, so humble and kind, as he. What cordial sympathy at the sight of misery, and the spiritual need of his brethren ! and yet, even when his countenance is moistened by tears, it continues to shine in indestructible peace. In his spirit, he lives in the house of his heavenly Father. He never loses sight of the invisible world ; and at the same time reveals a moral and practical sense possessed by no son of the dust. Which is more wonderful—the nobility of his princely greatness spread over his person, or the inimitable simplicity which surrounds his whole appearance ? Pascal had seen this heavenly form when describing it in a manner worthy of the object : Jesus Christ has been humble and patient ; holy, holy, holy before God ; terrible to devils ; without any sin. In what great brilliancy and wonderful magnificence he appears to the eye of the spirit which is open to wisdom ! To shine forth in all his princely splendour of his holiness, it was not necessary that he should appear as a king ; and yet he came with all the splendour of his standing. He was the master of all, because he is really their brother. His moral life is wholly penetrated by God. He represents virtue to me under the form of love and obedience. On our part, we do more than esteem him : we offer him love.

301. CARLYLE

OUR divinest symbol. Higher has the human thought not yet reached. A symbol of quite perennial, infinite character; whose significance will ever demand to be anew inquired into, and anew made manifest.

302. CHANNING

THIS Jesus lived with men : with the consciousness of unutterable majesty, he joined a lowliness, gentleness, humanity, and sympathy which have no example in human history. I ask you to contemplate this wonderful union. In proportion to the superiority of Jesus to all around him, was the intimacy, the brotherly love, with which he bound himself to them. I maintain that this is *a character wholly remote from human conception.* To imagine it to be the production of imposture or enthusiasm, shows a strange unsoundness of mind. I contemplate it with a veneration second only to the profound awe with which I look up to God. It bears no mark of human invention. It was real. It belonged to, and it manifested, the beloved Son of God. . . .

Here I pause ; and indeed I know not what can be added to heighten the wonder, reverence, and love which are due to Jesus. When I consider him, not only as possessed with the consciousness of an unexampled and unbounded majesty, but as recognizing a kindred nature in human beings, and living and dying to raise them to a participation of his divine glories ; and when I see him, under these views, allying himself to men by the tenderest ties, embracing them with a spirit of humanity, which no insult, injury, or pain could for a moment repel or over-power,—I am filled with wonder as well as reverence and love. I feel that this character is not of human invention ; that it was not assumed through fraud, or struck out by enthusiasm ; for it is infinitely above their reach. When I add this character of Jesus to the other evidence of his religion, it gives, to what before seemed so strong, a new and a vast accession of strength : I feel as if I could not be deceived. *The Gospels must be true : they were drawn from a living original ; they were founded on reality.* The character of Jesus is not a fiction : *he was what he claimed to be, and what his followers attested.* Nor is this all. Jesus not only *was, he is still, the Son of God, the Saviour of the world.* He exists now : he has entered that heaven to which he always looked forward on earth. There he lives and reigns. With a clear, calm faith, I see him in that state of glory ; and I confidently expect, at no distant period, to see him face to face. We have, indeed, no absent friend whom we shall so surely meet. Let us, then, my hearers, by imitation of his virtues and obedience to his word, prepare ourselves to join him in those pure mansions, where he is surrounding himself with the good and pure of our race, and will communicate to them for ever his own spirit, power, and joy.

303. STRAUSS

IF in Jesus the union of the self-consciousness with the consciousness of God has been real, and ex-pressed not only in words, but actually revealed in all the conditions of his life, he represents within the religious sphere the highest point, beyond which posterity cannot go ; yea, whom it cannot even equal, inasmuch as every one who hereafter should climb the same height, could only do it with the help of Jesus, who first attained it. As little as humanity will ever be without religion, as little will it be without Christ ; for to have religion without Christ would be as absurd as to enjoy poetry without regard to Homer or Shakespeare. And this Christ, as far as he is inseparable from the highest style of religion, is *historical*, not mythical ; is an *individual*, no mere symbol. To the historical person of Christ belongs all in his life that exhibits his religious perfection, his discourses, his moral action, and his passion. . . . *He remains the highest model of religion within the reach of our thought ; and no perfect piety is possible without his presence in the heart.*

If we ask how Jesus attained that harmony of the soul, we find in the existing records of his life no trace of painful conflicts from which it might have proceeded. . . . In all those great natures which were purified by violent conflict, as Paul, Augustine, Luther, there remained wound-prints for all time, something harsh and sad which adhered to them through life. But in Jesus not a trace of this is found. Jesus appears a beautiful nature from the very start, which had only to unfold itself from within, to become more and more clearly conscious of itself, and more firm in itself, but had no need of returning and beginning another life. . . . In this respect, as already intimated, the highly-gifted Apostle of the Gentiles was not equal to his Master ; and the two great renovators of Christianity in later times, Augustine and Luther, were more Pauline than Christ-like.

The Character of Christ

304. THEODORE PARKER

IN estimating the character of Jesus, it must be remembered that he died at an age when man has not reached his fullest vigour. The great works of creative intellect, the maturest products of man, all the deep and settled plans of reforming the world, come from a period when experience gives a wider field as the basis of hope. Socrates was but an embryo sage till long after the age of Jesus. Poems, and philosophies that live, come at a later date. Now, here we see a young man, but little more than thirty years old, with no advantage of position; the son and companion of rude people; born in a town whose inhabitants were wicked to a proverb; of a nation, above all others distinguished for their superstition, for national pride, exaltation of themselves and contempt for all others; in an age of singular corruption, when the substance of religion had faded out from the mind of its anointed ministers, and sin had spread wide among a people turbulent, oppressed, and down-trodden. A man ridiculed for his lack of knowledge, in this nation of forms, of hypocritical priests, and corrupt people, falls back on simple morality, simple religion, unites in himself the sublimest precepts and divinest practices, thus more than realising the dream of prophets and sages; rises free from all prejudice of his age, nation, or sect; gives free range to the Spirit of God in his breast; sets aside the law, sacred and time-honoured as it was, its forms, its sacrifice, its temple, and its priests; puts away the doctors of the law, subtle, learned, irrefragable, and pours out a doctrine, beautiful as the light, sublime as heaven, and true as God. The

philosophers, the poets, the prophets, the Rabbis—
he rises above them all. Yet Nazareth was no
Athens, where philosophy breathed in the circum-
ambient air : it had neither Porch nor Portico ;
not even a school of the prophets. There is God
in the heart of this youth.

305. COBBE

THE view which seems to be the sole fitting one
for our estimate of the character of Christ, is
that which regards him as the great regenerator of
humanity. *His coming was, to the life of humanity,
what regeneration is to the life of the individual.*
This is not a conclusion doubtfully deduced from
inference from the universal history of our race.
We may dispute all details ; but the grand result
is beyond criticism. The world *has* changed, and
that change is historically traceable to Christ. The
honour, then, which Christ demands of us, must be
in proportion to our estimate of the value of such
regeneration. He is not merely a moral reformer,
inculcating pure ethics ; not merely a religious
reformer, clearing away old theological errors, and
teaching higher ideas of God. These things he was ;
but he might, for all we can tell, have been them
both as fully, and yet have failed to be what he has
actually been to our race. He might have taught
the world better ethics and better theology, and
yet have failed to infuse into it that new life which
has ever since coursed through its arteries and pene-
trated its minutest veins. What Christ has really
done is beyond the kingdom of the intellect and its

theologies; nay, even beyond the kingdom of the conscience, and its recognition of duty. His work has been in that of the heart. He has transformed the law into the gospel. He has changed the bondage of the alien for the liberty of the sons of God. He has glorified virtue into holiness, religion into piety, and duty into love.

306. SCHWEITZER

JESUS as a concrete historical personality remains a stranger to our time, but His spirit, which lies hidden in His words, is known in simplicity, and its influence is direct. Every saying contains in its own way the whole Jesus. The very strangeness and unconditionedness in which He stands before us makes it easier for individuals to find their own personal standpoint in regard to Him. . . .

For that reason it is a good thing that the true historical Jesus should overthrow the modern Jesus, should rise up against the modern spirit and send upon earth, not peace, but a sword. He was not teacher, not a casuist; He was an imperious ruler. It was because He was so in His inmost being that He could think of Himself as the Son of Man. That was only the temporally conditioned expression of the fact that He was an authoritative ruler. The names in which men expressed their recognition of Him as such, Messiah, Son of Man, Son of God, have become for us historical parables. We can find no designation which expresses what He is for us.

He comes to us as One unknown, without a name, as of old, by the lake-side, He came to those men who knew Him not. He speaks to us the same word : " Follow thou me ! " and sets us to the tasks which He has to fulfil for our time. He commands. And to those who obey Him, whether they be wise or simple, He will reveal Himself in the toils, the conflicts, the sufferings which they shall pass through in His fellowship, and, as an ineffable mystery, they shall learn in their own experience Who He is.

38

His Influence

Lo, I am with you alway, even unto the end of the world.—Matthew 28:20

307. CORNELIUS TACITUS

NERO punished, with exquisite torture, a race of men detested for their evil practices, by vulgar appellation commonly called Christians.

The name was derived from Christ, who in the reign of Tiberius, suffered under Pontius Pilate, the procurator of Judea. By that event the sect, of which he was the founder, received a blow, which, for a time, checked the growth of a dangerous superstition; but it revived soon after, and spread with recruited vigor, not only in Judea, the soil that gave it birth, but even in the city of Rome, the common sink into which everything infamous and abominable flows like a torrent from all quarters of the world.

Nero proceeded with his usual artifice. He found a set of profligate wretches, who were induced to confess themselves guilty, and, on the evidence of such men, a number of Christians were convicted, not, indeed, upon clear evidence of their having set the city on fire, but rather on account of their sullen hatred of the whole human race. They were put to death with exquisite cruelty, and to their sufferings Nero added mockery and derision. Some were covered with the skins of wild beasts, and left to be devoured by dogs; others were nailed to the cross; numbers were burnt alive; and many, covered over with inflammable matter, were lighted up, when the day declined, to serve as torches during the night.

For the convenience of seeing this tragic spectacle, the emperor lent his own gardens. He added the sports of the circus, and assisted in person, sometimes driving a curricle, and occasionally mixing with the rabble in his coachman's dress. At length the cruelty of these proceedings filled every breast with compassion. Humanity relented in favour of the Christians. The manners of that people were, no doubt, of a pernicious tendency, and their crimes called for the hand of justice; but it was evident, that they fell a sacrifice, not for the public good, but to glut the rage and cruelty of one man only.

308. LIDDON

THE death-cry of the martyrs must have familiarized the heathen mind with the honour paid to the Redeemer by Christians. Of the worship offered in the Catacombs, of the stern yet tender discipline whereby the early Church stimulated, guided, moulded the heavenward aspirations of her children, paganism knew, could know, nothing. But the bearing and the exclamations of heroic servants of Christ when arraigned before the tribunals of the empire, or when exposed to a death of torture and shame in the amphitheatres, were matters of public notoriety. The dying prayers of St. Stephen expressed the instinct, if they did not provoke the imitation, of many a martyr of later days. What matters it to Blandina of Lyons that her pagan persecutors have first entangled her limbs in the meshes of a large net, and then have exposed her to the fury of a wild bull? She is insensible to pain; she is entranced in a profound communion with Christ. What matters it to that servant-boy in Palestine, Porphyry, that his mangled body is 'committed to a slow fire'? He does but call more earnestly in his death-struggle upon Jesus. Felix, an African Bishop, after a long series of persecutions, has been condemned to be beheaded at Venusium for refusing to give up the sacred books to the proconsul. 'Raising his eyes to heaven, he said with a clear voice—"O Lord God of heaven and earth, Jesus Christ, to Thee do I bend my neck by way of sacrifice, O Thou Who abidest for ever, to Whom belong glory and majesty, world without end, Amen."' Theodotus of Ancyra has been betrayed by the apostate Polychronius, and is joining in a last prayer with the sorrowing Church. 'Lord Jesu Christ,' he cries, 'Thou Hope of the hopeless, grant that I may finish the course of my conflict, and offer the shedding of my blood as a libation and sacrifice, to the relief of all those who suffer for Thee. Do Thou lighten their burden; and still this tempest of persecution, that all who believe in Thee may enjoy rest and quietness'; and afterwards, in the extremity of his torture, he prays thus: 'Lord Jesu Christ, Thou Hope of the hopeless, hear my prayer, and assuage this agony, seeing that for Thy Name's sake I suffer thus.' And when the pain had failed to bend his resolution, and the last sentence had been pronounced by the angry judge, 'O Lord Jesu Christ,' the martyr exclaims, 'Thou Maker of heaven and earth, Who forsakest not them that put their hope in Thee, I give Thee thanks for that Thou hast made me meet to be citizen of Thy heavenly city, and to have a share in Thy kingdom. I give Thee thanks, that Thou has given me strength to conquer the dragon, and to bruise his head. Give rest unto Thy servants, and stay the fierceness of the enemies in my person. Give peace unto Thy Church, and set her free from the tyranny of the devil.'

Or listen to such an extract from an early document as the following :—' Calvisianus, interrupting Euplius, said, " Let Euplius, who hath not in compliance with the edict of the emperors given up the sacred writings, but readeth them to the people, be put to the torture." And while he was being racked, Euplius said, " I Thank Thee, O Christ. Guard Thou me, who for Thee am suffering thus." Calvisianus the consular said, " Cease, Euplius, from this folly. Adore the gods, and thou shalt be set at liberty." Euplius said, " I adore Christ ; I utterly hate the demons. Do what thou wilt : I am a Christian. Long have I desired what now I suffer. Do what thou wilt. Add yet other tortures : I am a Christian." After he had been tortured a long while, the executioners were bidden hold their hands. And Calvisianus said, " Unhappy man, adore the gods. Pay worship to Mars, Apollo, and Aesculapius." Euplius said, " I worship the Father and the Son and the Holy Ghost. I adore the Holy Trinity, beside Whom there is no God. Perish the gods who did not make heaven and earth, and all that is in them. I am a Christian." Calvisianus the Præfect said, " Offer sacrifice, if thou wouldest be set at liberty." Euplius said, " I sacrifice myself only to Christ my God : more than this I cannot do. Thy efforts are to no purpose ; I am a Christian." Calvisianus gave orders that he should be tortured again more severely. And while he was being tortured, Euplius said, " Thanks to Thee, O Christ. Help me, O Christ. For Thee do I suffer thus, O Christ." And he said this repeatedly. And as his strength gradually failed him, he went on repeating these or other exclamations, with his lips only—his voice was gone.'

309. POLYCARP

EIGHTY and six years have I served Him, and He hath done me no wrong, How then can I speak evil of my King who saved me ?

310. CHURCH SERVICE

IN the heavenly kingdom the souls of the Saints are rejoicing who follow'd the footsteps of Christ their Master : and since for love of Him they freely poured forth their life-blood, therefore with Christ they reign for ever and ever.

311. PASCAL

JESUS CHRIST, without worldly riches, without the exterior productions of science, was infinitely great in His sublime order of holiness. He neither published inventions nor possessed kingdoms ; but He was humble, patient, pure before God, terrible to evil spirits, and without spot of sin. Oh, with what illustrious pomp, with what transcendent magnificence did He come attended, to such as beheld with the eyes of the heart, and with those faculties which are the judges and discerners of true wisdom !

It had been needless for our Lord Jesus Christ to have assumed the state of an earthly king, for the illustration of His kingdom of holiness. But how great, how excellent did He appear in the brightness of His proper order !

It is most unreasonable to be scandalised at the mean condition of our Lord, as if it were opposed in the same order and kind to the greatness which He came to display. Let us consider this greatness in His life, in His sufferings, in His solitude, in His death, in the choice of His attendants, in their act of forsaking Him, in the privacy of His resurrection, and in all the other parts of His history ; we shall find it so truly raised and noble, as to leave no ground for our being offended at a meanness which was quite of another order.

312. EUCKEN

HOW came it to pass that this particular point was the fountainhead of so mighty a movement, that old ideals were shattered, and new ones arose, that the whole previous balance of life was upset and previous standards failed to satisfy, that a mighty longing took possession of mankind, a stormy unrest which even now after hundreds of years is not allayed ?

His Influence

THE distinction between B.C. and A.D. is not merely an affair of the calendar. It represents a very important historical circumstance—namely, that a new quality entered into life when Jesus appeared in the world, which has profoundly affected the course of human affairs.

Suppose that useful person, the " man from Mars," were to visit us and to examine our human story during the last twenty centuries. He would find that it is dominated by one figure. The greatest and oldest voluntary society known to history is called by His name ; many of the most significant passages in secular history gather around His person. Many of the greatest achievements of mankind in literature, art, and music either commemorate Him or owe their inspiration to Him. Hardly a single department of our life but has been touched and profoundly modified by Him. In short, it is impossible to understand the history of two millenniums without reference to Him. He is by far the most outstanding figure in the history of the world, and His influence upon the lives and affairs of men is unique and without parallel. And to-day, after so long a time, His name has power to evoke from men large sacrifices and to inspire them to great heroism.

There appears to be a certain ubiquity about the figure of Jesus ; wheresoever we turn, we encounter Him or see His footsteps. There is hardly any literary figure in whose work He does not soon or late appear. Not indeed that He is always welcome ; but He is palpably a figure to be reckoned with. No literature which professes to be true to life can ignore Him; some account has to be taken of Him. He cannot be hid. His challenge seems inevasible.

314. WYKE BAYLISS

THE one central figure that in the splendour of His divine beauty consecrated art for ever was that of Jesus.

315. JAMESON

THE history of our Lord as represented in Art, is essentially the history of Christian Art. Round His sacred head, encircled in early mediæval forms with the cruciform nimbus, all Christian Art revolves, as a system round a sun. He is always the great centre and object of the scene; since whether represented, according to the taste of the artist or the requirements of the patron—as Infant, Youth, or Man—as Teacher, Physician or Friend—Victim and Sacrifice—as King or Judge—He is always intended under other aspects, real or ideal, to be looked upon as God. For no philosophy, "falsely so called," intrudes into the domain of Christian Art—no subtleties of His human nature, no doubts of His Godhead, no rationalistic interpretations of His miracles. Christian Art pre-eminently illustrates faith in Christ "as God manifest in the flesh," as "the Lamb slain from the foundation of the world": and without these great fundamental truths of Christianity there is no Christian Art, either in fact or in possibility.

His Influence

316. LINDSAY

YOU will not now be surprised at claiming superiority for Christian over Classic Art, in all her three departments. If man stand higher or lower in the scale of being, according as he is Spiritual, Intellectual or Sensual, Christian Art must excel Pagan by the same rule and in the same proportion.

As men cannot rise above their principles, so the artists of Greece never rose above the religious and moral sentiments of the age. Their ideal was that of youth, grace and beauty, thought, dignity and power. Form consequently, as the expression of Mind, was what they chiefly aimed at, and in this they reached perfection. Do not for a moment suppose me insensible to Classic Art—the memories of Greece and of the Palatine are very dear to me—I cannot speak coldly of the Elgin Marbles, of the Apollo, the Venus, the Dying Gladiator, the Niobe, the Diana of Gabii, the Psyche of Naples—which comes nearer the Christian ideal than aught else of Grecian growth. But none of these completely satisfy us. The highest element of truth and beauty, the Spiritual, was beyond the soar of Phidias and Praxiteles; this truth, they felt a want—they yearned for it, and this yearning, stamped on their works, constitutes their undying charm. But they yearned in vain—Faith, Hope and Charity, those wings of immortality, as yet were not.

Herein then lies our vantage—not in our merit, not our genius, but in that we are Christians, that we start from a loftier platform, that we are raised by communion with God to a purer atmosphere, in which we see things in the light of Eternity, small as we are, but with their ulterior meanings, as shadows of deeper truths—an atmosphere which invests creation with the glow of love, and its human denizens with a beauty of expression all its own, a ray of heaven beaming on the countenance, especially of woman, which mere beauty of intellect or feeling, the highest charm attainable by Greece, can never rival. It is not, in a word, symmetry of Form or beauty of Colouring, apart or conjoined, that is required of us and that constitutes our prerogative, but in the conception by the artist, and expression to the spectator of the highest and holiest spiritual truths and emotions—and in this the vantage of the Bible over the Iliad is not more decided than that of Christian over Classic Art—than the depth, intensity, grandeur, and sweetness of the emotions at the command of Christian artists, as compared with those elicited by the ancients. Few will dispute this who have ever soared into the symbolic heaven of a Lombard or Gothic Cathedral and renewed their vows of chivalry before the S. George of Donatello— or shared the cross and the palm, the warfare and the triumph of the church of all ages in the sympathy of the Spirit, while contemplating the old Byzantine heads of Greece, the martyrdom of the Lombard Giotteschi, the Paradises of Fra Angelico, the Madonnas of Perugino, Leonardo—Bellini, the Dispute of Raphael, and the Last Judgments of Orcagna and Michaelangelo.

317. STORRS

I TRACE the grip and scope of this most spiritual but most masterful religion which comes to its fulness in the New Testament; I see its ministers compelled to know something of history, ethics, the

thought of the past, as well as of rubrics and of tithes ;
I see its cloisters coming to be crowded with diligent
writers, until the presses take their place ; I see
languages reduced to order and form that they may
receive the immortal evangel ; I see schools and
universities rising before it, education expanding, no
learning discredited, all forms of true knowledge
at last welcomed and honoured—till the entire air
of society is full of subtile intellectual stimulation,
till the new ages rise into the manifold fulness of light
in which we are embosomed, till the more inviting
realms of the world, earlier in their culture, now
turn to Christendom as having in that their only hope
for even a secondary mental progress ; I see the great
discoveries coming in this circle of nations which
barbarism so lately ruled, to enrich and empower
human society ; I hear there the poems, tender or
triumphing, which are the timbrels and the trumpets
to which the race is marching forward ; I see the
ages of intelligent faith fruitful and quickening, while
those of unbelief are barren in contrast ; I see the
vast amphitheatre filled with the light of the Book,
as Raphael's picture of Peter in prison with the light
of the angel, subduing the light of torch or of moon :—
and I say with absolute certainty, for myself, that the
power here shown is *like* a power coming for the
race, and coming from God !

Whatever else is true or not, the superlative educa-
tional force of the world appears embodied in this
system of Faith which came by peasants as its ministers,
and the son of a carpenter as its mysterious sovereign
Teacher. It lays its hand of supreme benediction
on countries and centuries at the furthest remove from
its first proclamation. It furnishes the matrix out

of which genius may be expected plenteously to spring. And sceptics themselves, with whatever learning, eloquence, or wit, appear to me but involuntary witnesses to the underlying and impenetrating impulse of this religion, which has given possibility to even their hostile culture and force.

318. WALSH

BEGINNING with St. Ambrose, the writing of a series of hymns of beautiful rhythm and of a depth of poetic meaning tempted musical genius to give them an appropriate setting in music. It has been said of some of these hymns that they must be counted among the most sublimely beautiful wedding of sense and sound to be found in the whole body of human literature. It is easy to understand then how appropriately beautiful musical numbers would naturally be found for them by the musical geniuses of the time. During the course of the following centuries of the early Middle Ages many thousands of hymns were written and many thousands of variations of musical settings were composed. Musical history continued its development along these lines all during the medieval period. Probably no greater poetry has ever been written and no greater hymns than those which are to be found in the later Middle Ages, and therefore it is not surprising to learn that the musical settings for them also were marve'lously effective and worthy accompaniments. . . . Probably no greater or more beautiful expression of grief in single notes in succession has ever been written than the chant used by the Church in the services of

Tenebræ, the Lamentations for Holy Week ; and no
more joyous succession of single notes has ever been
arranged than that of the chant for the *Exultet* on
Holy Saturday.

319. ST. AUGUSTINE

HOW deeply and greatly moved did I weep with
the sweet hymns and canticles of my Jesus !
Their voices pierced my ears and the truth distilled
into my heart and desires filled it with the ardour of
piety and the tears trickled down my cheeks and
I was happy.

320. LAMB

A COMPANY of English literary men, including
Charles Lamb, Hazlitt, Leigh Hunt, and others
one day fell to discussing persons they would like to
have met, and after naming every possible name in
the gallery of fame, whether worthy or unworthy,
Charles Lamb said in his stuttering way to the com-
pany : " There is only one person I can ever think
of after this. . . . If Shakespeare was to come
into this room, we should all rise up to meet him ;
but if that person was to come into it we should all
fall and try to kiss the hem of His garment."

321. MOMERIE

THE first thing that must strike any one who reads
carefully the history of Christ is the immense
importance He attached, not merely to His mission,
but to Himself. Every great teacher, with this single
exception, in exact proportion to his greatness, has

been willing to be cast into the shade by the glory of the doctrine which he wished to teach. Socrates declared that his only wisdom was a consciousness of ignorance, and he constantly confessed to his hearers that he was merely a fellow-seeker with them after truth and goodness. The Nazarene maintained, on the contrary, that He was the light of the world, the shepherd of the souls of men, the way to eternal life, the vine or the life-tree of humanity. It is this which distinguishes Christ from all the rest of the world's teachers.

322. DIDEROT

IN one of those evening parties of Baron d'Holbach, where the most celebrated infidels of the century used to assemble, the conversation turned freely, and in the most amusing manner, on the supposed absurdities, stupidities, and all kind of inconsistencies, of the Sacred Scriptures. The philosopher Diderot, who had taken no small part in the conversation, brought it suddenly to a close by the following remark :

"For a wonder, gentlemen, for a wonder, I know nobody, either in France or anywhere else, who could write and speak with more art and talent. Notwithstanding all the bad which we have said, and no doubt with good reason, of this devil of a book (*de ce diable de livre*), I defy you all—as many as are here—to prepare a tale so simple, and at the same time so sublime and so touching, as the tale of the passion and death of Jesus Christ ; which produces the same effect, which makes a sensation as strong and as generally felt, and whose influence will be the same, after so many centuries."

His Influence

IT is common in human history to meet with men who assert some superiority over their fellows, but they dream of nothing greater than some partial control over the actions of others for the short space of a life-time. To a few indeed it is given to influence future ages. Some have appeared who have been as levers to uplift the earth and roll it in another course. Homer by creating literature, Socrates by creating science, Cæsar by carrying civilization inland from the shores of the Mediterranean, Newton by starting science in a steady career of progress, may be said to have attained this eminence. But these men gave a single impact, like that which is considered to have first set planets in motion. Christ claims to be a perpetual attracting power, like the sun which determines their orbits. They contributed to men some discovery and passed away: Christ's discovery is Himself. To humanity, struggling with its passions and its destiny, He says, " Cling to me—cling ever closer to me." He commanded men to leave everything and attach themselves to Him ; He declared Himself King, Master, and Judge of men ; He promised to give rest to all the weary and heavy-laden ; He instructed His followers to hope for eternal life from feeding on His body and blood. Further, these enormous pretensions were advanced by One whose special peculiarity, not only among His contemporaries, but among the remarkable men that have appeared before and since, was an almost feminine tenderness and humility. The " Lamb of God " He had been called by the Baptist. Yet so clear to Him was His own dignity and importance to the race, that in the very same breath in which He asserts it in the most measured language, He alludes also to His humility. " Take my yoke upon you and learn of me ; for I am meek and lowly in heart." Meek and lowly He was ; naturally content with obscurity ; wanting the restless desire for distinction and eminence which is common in great men ; fond of what was simple and homely, of children and poor people ; occupying Himself so much with the concerns of others, with the relief of sickness and want, that the temptation to exaggerate the importance of His own thoughts and plans was not likely to master Him. And yet we find that He laid claim persistently, with the calmness of entire conviction, in opposition to the whole religious world, in spite of the offence which His own followers conceived, to a dominion more transcendent, more universal, more complete than the most delirious votary of glory ever aspired to in his dreams.

324. CARLYLE

WE understand ourselves to be risking no new assertion, but simply repeating what is already the conviction of the greatest in our age, when we say that cheerfully recognizing, gratefully appropriating, whatever Voltaire has proved or any other man has proved or shall prove, the Christian religion, once here, cannot again pass away ; that in one form or other it will endure through all time. . . . Were the memory of this faith never so obscured, as indeed in every age the coarse passions and perceptions of the world do all but obliterate it in the hearts of most, yet in every pure soul, in every poet and wise man,

it finds a new missionary, a new martyr, till the great
volume of universal history is finally closed, and man's
destinies are fulfilled on this earth. It is a height
to which the human species were fated and enabled
to attain, from which, having once attained it, they
can never retrograde.

325. THOMPSON

" **B**Y this, O singer, know we if thou see.
When men shall say to thee : Lo, Christ is here ;
When men shall say to thee : Lo, Christ is there ;
Believe them ; yea, and this—then art thou seer—
When all thy crying clear
Is but : Lo here, lo there ! ah me, lo everywhere ! "

326. MATTHEW ARNOLD

'**T**WAS August, and the fierce sun overhead
Smote on the squalid streets of Bethnal Green,
And the pale weaver, through his windows seen
In Spitalfields, look'd thrice dispirited.

I met a preacher there I knew, and said :
" Ill and o'erwork'd, how fare you in this scene ? "—
" Bravely ! " said he ; " for I of late have been
Much cheer'd with thoughts of Christ, *the living
bread.*"

O human soul ! as long as thou canst so
Set up a mark of everlasting light,
Above the howling senses' ebb and flow,

To cheer thee, and to right thee if thou roam—
Not with lost toil thou labourest through the night
Thou mak'st the heaven thou hop'st indeed thy home.

327. LONGFELLOW

GASPAR. Hail to thee, Jesus of Nazareth !
Though in a manger thou drawest thy breath,
Thou art greater than Life and Death,
    Greater than Joy or Woe !
This cross upon the line of life
Portendeth struggle, toil, and strife,
And through a region with peril rife
    In darkness shalt thou go !
Melchior. Hail to thee, King of Jerusalem !
Though humbly born in Bethlehem,
A sceptre and a diadem
    Await thy brow and hand !
The sceptre is a simple reed,
The crown will make thy temples bleed,
And in thy hour of greatest need,
    Abashed thy subjects stand !
Belshazzar. Hail to thee, Christ of Christendom !
O'er all the earth thy kingdom come !
From distant Trebizond to Rome
    Thy name shall men adore !
Peace and good-will among all men
The Virgin has returned again,
Returned the old Saturnian reign
    And Golden Age once more.
The Child Christ. Jesus, the Son of God, am I,
Born here to suffer and to die
According to the prophecy,
    That other men may live !
The Virgin. And now these clothes, that wrapped
      him, take,
And keep them precious, for his sake,
Our benediction thus we make,
    Naught else have we to give.

His Influence

WHEN thou turn'st away from ill,
Christ is this side of thy hill.

When thou turnest toward good,
Christ is walking in thy wood.

When thy heart says, " Father, pardon ! "
Then the Lord is in thy garden.

When stern Duty wakes to watch,
Then his hand is on the latch.

But when Hope thy song doth rouse,
Then the Lord is in the house.

When to love is all thy wit,
Christ doth at thy table sit.

When God's will is thy heart's pole,
Then is Christ thy very soul.

29. RICHARD LE GALLIENNE

LOUD mockers in the roaring street
Say Christ is crucified again :
Twice pierced His gospel-bearing feet,
Twice broken His great heart in vain.

I hear, and to myself I smile,
For Christ talks with me all the while.

287

No angel now to roll the stone
From off His unawaking sleep,
In vain shall Mary watch alone,
In vain the soldiers vigil keep.

Yet while they deem my Lord is dead
My eyes are on His shining head.

Ah ! never more shall Mary hear
That voice exceeding sweet and low
Within the garden calling clear ;
Her Lord is gone, and she must go.

Yet all the while my Lord I meet
In every London lane and street.

Poor Lazarus shall wait in vain,
And Bartimæus still go blind ;
The healing hem shall ne'er again
Be touched by suffering humankind.

Yet all the while I see them rest,
The poor and outcast, in His breast.

No more unto the stubborn heart
With gentle knocking shall He plead,
No more the mystic pity start,
For Christ twice dead is dead indeed.

So in the street I hear men say,
Yet Christ is with me all the day,

His Influence

IS it only the pious imaginations of successive students which make of Jesus now the source of a theology and now the founder of a Church, now peasant, now king, now the deliverer from doubt? On the contrary, the life of Jesus has, in fact, all these aspects, and indeed many more; and it is not as false interpreters, but as partial witnesses, that men stand in their own place and report that view of the gospel which presents itself to their minds. This extraordinary capacity for new adaptations, this quality of comprehensiveness in the teaching of Jesus, which so many evidences of the past illustrate, prepares us in our turn for its fresh applicability to the question which most concerns the present age. As it has happened a thousand times before, so it is likely to happen again, that the Gospel, examined afresh with a new problem in mind will seem again to have been written in large part to meet the needs of the new age. Words and deeds which other generations have found perplexing or obscure may be illuminated with meaning, as one now sees them in the light of the new social agitation and hope. It will seem, perhaps, as it has seemed so often before, that no other age could have adequately appreciated the teaching of Jesus; as if His prophetic mind must have looked across the centuries and discerned the distant coming of social conflicts and aspirations which in His own time were insignificant, but which are now universal and profound.

Such is the comprehensiveness of the teaching of Jesus. . . . It is as if one stood at night watching the moon rise from the sea, and saw the glittering band of light which leads straight to Him, as though the moon were shining for one life alone ; while in fact he knows that its comprehensive radiation is for him, and for the joy and guidance of a world besides. So the unexhausted gospel of Jesus touches each new problem and new need with its illuminating power, while there yet remain myriads of other ways of radiation toward other souls and other ages, for that Life which is the light of men.

331. JOSEPH PARKER

MAN needs Jesus Christ as a necessity and not as a luxury. You may be pleased to have flowers, but you must have bread. . . . Jesus is not a phenomenon, He is bread : Christ is not a curiosity, He is water. As surely as we cannot live without bread we cannot live truly without Christ; if we know not Christ we are not living, our movement is a mechanical flutter, our pulse is but the stirring of an animal life. It is in this way, then, that Jesus Christ is to be preached. It is even so I would preach Him now. I would call Him the water of life ; I would speak of Him as the true bread sent down from heaven ; I would tell men that it is impossible to live without Him ; I would say, with heightening passion, with glowing and ineffable love, that He only, even the holy Christ of God, can satisfy the hunger and the thirst of the soul of man. In this way I claim a distinct vocation as a preacher. I am not one amongst many who try to do the world good ; as a Christian preacher, or a preacher of Christ, I offer the *only* thing that can vitally and sufficiently touch the world's needs.

His Influence

I SEE His blood upon the rose
And in the stars the glory of His eyes,
His body gleams amid eternal snows,
His tears fall from the skies.

I see His face in every flower;
The thunder and the singing of the birds
Are but His voice—and carven by His power
Rocks are His written words.

All pathways by His feet are worn,
His strong heart stirs the ever-beating sea,
His crown of thorns is twined with every thorn,
His cross is every tree.

39

Son of Man

Behold, I see the heavens opened, and the Son of man standing on the right hand of God.—Acts 7:56

333. ST. PAUL

WHO, being in the form of God, thought it not robbery to be equal with God.

But made himself of no reputation, and took upon him the form of a servant, and was made in the likeness of men.

And being found in fashion as a man, he humbled himself, and became obedient unto death, even the death of the cross.

Wherefore God also hath highly exalted him, and given him a name which is above every name.

That at the name of Jesus every knee should bow, of things in heaven, and things in earth, and things under the earth ;

And that every tongue should confess that Jesus Christ is Lord, to the glory of God the Father.

334. À KEMPIS

I PRAISE and magnify Thee with boundless love, for Thy lowly and hidden life among men and Thy fellow villagers. Never manifesting any sign which might have led to a recognition of Thy Godhead, Thou deignedst to be called and to be considered the son of a carpenter.

Son of Man

O THOU Son of Man, who, by lifting the burdens of our humanity, hast made Thine own yoke easy and Thine own burden light, lift this life of mine into sympathy, into union with Thee. I am weary of myself, weary of the din and the battle, weary of the burden and the heat. I am seeking everywhere for a hiding-place from the storm, everywhere for a covert from the tempest. But the storm is not without me, but within ; the tempest is not in my circumstances but in me. Son of Man, save me from myself, that I may enter into Thy peace, Thine unspeakable joy. Inspire me with Thine own burden of love, that the care of self may fall from me, and that with Thy divine freedom I may be free.

O Thou divine Spirit, I have found in the Son of Man a new test of Thy presence. I used to see Thee by the vision of the eye, by the light of stars and systems, by the beauty of wood and field. But now I have lost somewhat of that ancient glory. Science has stolen the splendour of the stars, destroyed the spontaneity of the woods and fields ; I speak of law where once I spoke of will. Art Thou gone then from my modern life, Thou Spirit of the Highest ? No ; Thou art only gone into a new channel—from the stars into the soul. I see Thee now in the cross, in the tidings brought to the meek, in the binding of wounded hearts. I see Thee in my reverence for things beneath me, in my interest for pain, in my sympathy with tears. I see Thee in the elevation of every valley, in the depression of every mountain, in the crooked ways made straight and the rough places plain. I see Thee in the charity that beareth,

believeth, hopeth, endureth all things ; in the love
that seeketh not her own ; in the mercy that rejoices
against judgment, in the forgiveness that welcomes
even from the grave. These are the tests of Thy
presence. The heavens may tell of Thy glory in more
broken accents than of yore, but the strain has been
taken up by loftier harps than theirs. It has passed into
the hands of those who preach good tidings to the meek.

336. BRUCE

IT is the inalienable privilege of a living faith,
and its instinctive impulse, to declare the treasure it
finds in Jesus in its own way, and in words and ideas
thrilling with its own fresh life. In poetry and in
preaching it uses this liberty. In theology the
privilege has been little taken advantage of, the ten-
dency being to fall back on Scripture terms and
categories as alone authorized, and as alone competent
to express a true adequate doctrine concerning the
person of Jesus. Of these inspired terms the most
valuable, and therefore most frequently to be used
for the purposes of theology, are those which are
most universal in their character, and most independent
of local and temporary associations. Foremost
among the titles of Jesus possessing this character are
" Son of God " and " Son of man." The synthesis
of these two titles expresses the eternal truth of
Christianity as the universal absolute religion.

337. FORSYTH

WHEN we are asked what we mean by the
manhood of Christ, we do not mean some
stalwart dignity with which he faced and owned God

in self-respecting godliness. The "manliness of Christ," like his "bravery," is an unpleasant phrase. Nor do we mean an elemental force and passion which linked the natural side of his personality to the world with the fervour of a Titan's blood. We mean much more than his intimate and sympathetic humanness. For the essence of Humanity is conscience. It is man's moral relation to a holy God. And Christ's manhood, therefore, consists in the moral reality of his experience, his conflict, and his growth. It means his true ethical personality growing in an actual historic situation. It means that he counted in the public of his age, and really inhabited its spiritual *milieu ;* that he filled a mighty place in the social situation of his land and time, and that the immediate reference of all he said and did was to that situation, however vast, and even infinite. And above all it means that his action arose ethically out of what he was, that his carriage expressed his soul, that his vocation rested on his position, that his receptivity is the greatest human activity, that he was, first and foremost, the ever receptive Son of the holy Father, and that he only did the things which were shown him of God. His manhood was in his perfectly active receptivity. His subordination was no inferiority. His obedience was his divinest achievement.

338. W. B. PHILPOT

So closely art Thou in God's heart,
    And God so close in Thine ;
I marvel which is human part,
    And which is Thy divine.

339. TOLSTOI

THE doctrine of Jesus consisted in the elevation of the Son of man, that is, in the recognition on the part of man, that he, man, was the son of God. In his own individuality Jesus personified the man who has recognized the filial relation with God. He asked his disciples whom men said that he was— the Son of man ? His disciples replied that some took him for John the Baptist, and some for Elijah. Then came the question, *" But whom say ye that I am ? "* And Peter answered, *" Thou art the Messiah, the Son of the living God."* Jesus responded, *" Flesh and blood hath not revealed it unto thee, but My Father which is in heaven ";* meaning that Peter understood, not through faith in human explanations, but because, feeling himself to be the son of God, he understood that Jesus was also the Son of God. And after having explained to Peter that the true faith is founded upon the perception of the filial relation to God, Jesus charged his other disciples that they should tell no man that he was the Messiah. After this, Jesus told them that although he might suffer many things and be put to death, he, that is his doctrine, would be triumphantly re-established.

340. TURGENEV

I SAW myself, a youth, almost a boy, in a low-pitched wooden church. The slim wax candles gleamed, spots of red, before the old pictures of the Saints. There stood before me many people, all fair-haired peasant heads. From time to time, they began swaying, falling, rising again, like the ripe ears of wheat when the wind in summer passes over them.

Son of Man

All at once a man came up from behind and stood beside me. I did not turn towards him, but I felt that the man was Christ. Emotion, curiosity, awe overmastered me. I made an effort and looked at my neighbour. A face like everyone's, a face like all men's faces. The eyes looked a little upward, quietly and intently; the lips closed, not compressed; the upper lip as it were resting on the other; a small beard parted in two; the hands folded and still; and the clothes on him like everyone's. "What sort of Christ is this?" I thought. "Such an ordinary, ordinary man. It cannot be." I turned away, but I had hardly turned my eyes from this ordinary man when I felt again that it was really none other than Christ standing beside me. Suddenly my heart sank and I came to myself. Only then I realized that just such a face is the face of Christ— a face like all men's faces.

341. MEYNELL

O CHRIST, in this man's life
 This stranger who is Thine—in all his strife,
All his felicity, his good and ill
In the assaulted stronghold of his will;

I do confess Thee here,
Alive within this life; I know Thee near
Within this lonely conscience, closed away
Within this brother's solitary day.

Christ in his unknown heart,
His intellect unknown, this love, this art,
This battle and this peace, this destiny
That I shall never know, look upon me.

Christ in his numbered breath,
Christ in his beating heart and in his death,
Christ in his mystery! From that secret place,
And from that separate dwelling, give me grace!

342. ABBOT MARMION

THE Son of God is made flesh; He remains
what He is—perfect God. But He unites
Himself to a human nature, complete like ours,
integral in its essence, with all its native properties.
Like all of us Christ is " made of a woman." He
belongs authentically to our race. Often in the
Gospel, He calls Himself " the Son of man "; eyes
of flesh have seen Him, human hands have touched
Him. Even on the morrow of His glorious resur-
rection, He makes the incredulous Apostles verify
the reality of His human nature.

Like each of us, He has a soul, created directly by
God; a body formed of the substance of a woman,
an intelligence to know, a will to love and choose;
all the faculties that we have, memory and imagina-
tion. He has passions in the philosophical, elevated,
and noble sense of the word, in the sense excluding
all disorder and all weakness; for in Him these
passions are perfectly subject to reason and only moved
by an act of His will. His human nature is then
similar in everything to that of His brethren. . . .
Jesus has not known sin, nor that which is the source
and consequence of sin—ignorance, error, sickness, all
things unworthy of His wisdom, His dignity and
His divinity.

Son of Man

343. BROWNING

O SAUL, it shall be
A Face like my face that receives thee; a Man like
   to me,
Thou shalt love and be loved by, for ever: a Hand
   like this hand
Shall throw open the gates of new life to thee! See
   the Christ stand!

That one Face, far from vanish, rather grows,
Or decomposes but to recompose,
Becomes my universe that feels and knows.

344. CLIFFORD

WE know Jesus, in His habit as He lived, better
than He has been known by any of His followers
since the close of the first century; and we are more
sure of Him. . . . He is always modest and simple,
sober and sane, and yet radiant and magnetic through
His superhuman self-consciousness as a Revealer and
Redeemer. He seems to have such an air of common-
ness about Him that He seems to belong to everybody,
and yet so entirely original. . . . He is so completely
a part of the stock of the world's mind that we may
say that men are thinking that of all the great world-
leaders Christ is the most real, and the evidence of
His life, and of the characteristics of His person, is
so compact, so cogent, so complete as to dismiss the
last remnant of doubt as to His right to be called the
Son of Man.

345. RUSKIN

OUR preachers are continually trying in all manner of subtle ways to explain the union of the Divinity with the Manhood, an explanation which certainly involves first their being able to describe the nature of the Deity itself or, in plain words, to apprehend God. They never can explain, in any one particular, the union of the natures; they only succeed in weakening the faith of their hearers as to the entireness of either. The thing they have to do is precisely the contrary to this—to insist upon the entireness of both. We never think of Christ enough as God, never enough as Man: the instinctive habit of our minds being always to miss of the divinity, and the reasoning and enforced habit to miss of the humanity. We are afraid to harbour in our own hearts, or to utter in the hearing of others, any thought of our Lord as hungering, tired, sorrowful, having a human soul, a human will, and affected by events of human life, as a finite creature is; and yet one half of the efficiency of His atonement and the whole of the efficiency of His example depend upon His having been this to the full.

346. BISHOP BOYD CARPENTER

JESUS CHRIST takes as man a place alike in the realms of ethics and of faith. He gives to us the moral standard of life, the ethical ideal; He discloses the culminating power of the religious consciousness, for He is, in the deep harmony of his relationship with God, the mystic ideal also. While men were labouring to establish relationship with the unseen;

while some, failing and despairing, broke into angry revolt against life, and others, deceiving themselves, reached a false repose by shutting out of sight the facts of ugly moral problems; Jesus Christ, keenly alive to evil and warm to defend the weak and the oppressed, keeping the ethical standard high and the ethical perception clear, lived a life of simple and unruffled heart repose. He realizes, and we see that He realizes, the double ideal, the ideal of righteousness and of inward peace. He realizes the perfect harmony, the peace which is no counterfeit; He lives a human life, but we feel that He lives all the time in the serene atmosphere of Heaven. In Him we get a glimpse of what the soul is whose birth and being are from the eternal love. He seems something more than a soul filled with the divine; He seems to be one whose manhood is taken into God, and we no longer wonder that His utterances are sweet and satisfying; we listen to Him, and His teaching comes to us fresh as the breath of the sea and musical as the sound of falling rain.

347. J. R. LOWELL

I FOLLOWED where they led,
　　And in a hovel rude,
With naught to fence the weather from his head,
　　The King I sought for meekly stood;
A naked hungry child
　　Clung round his gracious knee,
And a poor hunted slave looked up and smiled
　　To bless the smile that set him free;
New miracles I saw his presence do,
　　No more I knew the hovel bare and poor,

The gathered chips into a woodpile grew
    The broken morsel swelled to goodly store.
I knelt and wept : my Christ no more I seek.
His throne is with the outcast and the weak.

40

Son of God

And I saw, and bare record that this is the Son of God.—John 1:34

348. ST. PAUL

WHO is the image of the invisible God, the firstborn of every creature :

For by him were all things created that are in heaven, and that are in earth, visible and invisible, whether they be thrones, or dominions, or principalities, or powers : all things were created by him, and for him :

And he is before all things, and by him all things consist.

For in him dwelleth all the fulness of the Godhead bodily.

349. MILMAN

THE first sound which reached the Pagan ear from the secluded sanctuaries of Christianity was a hymn to Christ as God.

350. BRUCE

A READY-MADE dogma concerning the divinity of Christ accepted as an ecclesiastical tradition can be of little service to us. It may very easily be of serious dis-service, acting as a veil to hide the true Jesus from the eye of the soul. The only faith concerning Jesus as the Divine Lord worth possessing is that which springs out of spiritual insight into its historical basis, and is charged with ethical significance. Such a faith calls Jesus Lord by the Holy Ghost, and is legitimate, wholesome, and fruitful in beneficent effects. What more legitimate and wholesome than to think of Jesus, the uniquely good, as the very Son of God, absolutely one with God in mind, will, and spirit? Then we are assured that Jesus is a veritable revelation of the Father. The Son hath declared Him. And the revelation is welcome. If God be like Jesus, the world has cause to be glad. The worship of Jesus as God is the worship of a goodness which inspires trust and hope in every human breast. What more legitimate and wholesome, again, than the worship of the Crucified? It means that self-sacrificing love is placed on the throne of the universe, that God does not keep aloof from the world in frigid majesty, but enters into it freely as a burden-bearer, stooping to conquer His own rebellious children. On the metaphysical side the doctrine may be encompassed with difficulty, but ethically it is worthy of all acceptation.

351. HERMANN

THE right confession of the Godhead of Jesus depends on experience of the work which God performs through Jesus on the human soul.

352. NEWMAN

WHILE our Lord is God He is also the Son of God, or rather, He is God because He is the Son of God. We are apt, at first hearing, to say that He is God though He is the Son of God, marvelling at the mystery. But what to man is a mystery, to God is a cause. He is God, not *though*, but *because* He is the Son of God. " That which is born of the flesh is flesh, that which is born of the Spirit is spirit," and that which is begotten of God is God. I do not say that we could presume thus to reason for ourselves, but Scripture draws the conclusion for us. Christ tells us Himself, " As the Father hath life in Himself, so hath He given to the Son to have life in Himself." And St. Paul says, that He is " the brightness of God's glory, and the express Image of His Person." And thus, though we could not presume to reason of ourselves that He that is begotten of God is God, as if it became us to reason at all about such ineffable things, yet, by the light of Scripture, we may. And after all, if the truth must be said, it is surely not so marvellous and mysterious that the Son of God should be God, as that there should be a Son of God at all. It is as little level to natural reason that God should have a Son, as that, if there be a Son, He must be God because He is the Son. Both are mysteries ; and if we admit with Scripture that there be an Only-begotten Son, it is even less to admit, what Scripture also teaches, that that Only-begotten Son is God because He is Only-begotten. And this is what makes the doctrine of our Lord's Eternal Sonship of such supreme importance, viz., that He is God because He is begotten of God ; and they who give up the latter truth are in the way to give up, or will be found already to have given up, the former. The great safeguard to the doctrine of our Lord's Divinity is the doctrine of His Sonship ; we realize that He is God only when we acknowledge Him to be by nature and from eternity Son.

353. THEODOR KEIM

THUS the religion of Christ goes mysteriously back to his *person*. . . . In his personal life there must have been from the very beginning and always a sentiment of human elevation, a feeling of divine love, and an aspiration after perfection in God, mighty, pure, without bitter drops of human weakness, impurity, unworthiness—a perfection such as we find elsewhere reflected only in broken and disturbed fragments. This fundamental fact alone, which with Paul we call the higher, complete, divine-human creation of the great God in the fulness of time, enables us to understand the religion which sprang from it, and the Man himself, the pure one, the sinless one, the Son of God.

Christ, in his gigantic elevation above his own and succeeding ages, " makes the impression of mysterious loneliness, superhuman miracle, divine creation."

The person of Jesus is not only a deed among the many deeds of God, but the peculiar work, the specific revelation of God. . . . Christianity is the crown of the creations of God, and Jesus is the Chosen of God, his Image, his Darling, his World-Guide and World-Shaper in the history of mankind. He is the rest, and he is the fly-wheel of the history of the world.

354. CAMPBELL

JESUS is for ever the one Master of the human race. Other masters may come and go; a few are not unworthy to stand beside Him; but He only has given us God. The creeds may fail to explain the relationship of the Father and the Son but they testify

to the discovery Jesus brought to mankind ; we have
found God in Him : to Him we owe all we know
or are able to understand of the spiritual order : He
is in very deed the Way, the Truth, and the Life.
It is really Jesus we worship when we name the name
of God. It is not that we have exalted Jesus to
share God's throne but that our very conceptions of
God have become exalted by being associated with
the person of Jesus. And yet He is of ourselves ;
only once has the world seen perfect man, and that
was in Jesus. The divinely human, the humanly
divine, He has revealed to us our own possibilities,
made us to glimpse a little of the glory that shall be
when we know as we are known. In no forensic
sense, but in simple and unescapable fact, He is Lord
of all ; our source, our goal ; our Saviour, our Judge ;
our hope of ultimate victory over all the ills of our
present lot and of entrance into everlasting habitations.

355. LAMENNAIS

A ND when I come to consider his life, his works,
his teaching, them arvellous mingling in him of
grandeur and simplicity, of sweetness and force,
that incomprehensible perfection which never for a
moment fails,—neither in the intimate familiarity
of confidence, nor in the solemnity of instructions
addressed by him to the people at large, neither in
the joyfulness of the festival at Cana, nor amid the
anguish of Gethsemane, neither in the glory of his
triumph, nor in the ignominy of his punishment,
neither on Tabor, in the midst of the splendour which
environs him, nor upon Calvary, where he expires,

abandoned by his friends, and forsaken of his Father, in inexpressible sufferings, amid the frenzied outcries and railing of his enemies :—when I contemplate this grand marvel, which the world has seen only once, and which has renewed the world, I do not ask myself if Christ was Divine : I should be rather tempted to ask myself if he were human !

356. DALE

THE Incarnation revealed and fulfilled the relations which already existed between the Son of God and mankind. From the beginning, Christ had entered into fellowship with us. When we sinned, He remained in fellowship with us still. He was in partnership with us ; the miseries of the race were His, His by His own choice, and He endured them all. It " behoved " the eternal Son of God to share the fortunes of God's earthly children. He not only became man, but submitted to all the sufferings and humiliations of our earthly condition. He endured the pains which are common to man and to inferior races. He was tried by hunger, thirst, weariness, and physical torture. He endured the sharper agonies, the deeper sorrows, which are man's special and separate inheritance, as the result of His revolt against God. He was tempted by the Devil ; He was suspected, hated, slandered. His friends were not always faithful ; one of them betrayed Him. The most appalling woe—the woe which we might have thought could never have come on the Son of God, and which to many of us seems incredible— fell upon Him : in the mysterious darkness of His

last hours, He cried, " My God, My God, why hast
Thou forsaken Me ? " That sorrow broke His
heart, and He died. He clung to us through death,
and so He saved us. Through His blood we have
remission of sins ; in His resurrection we rise to the
eternal life of God. There is solidarity between the
human race and Christ. His fellowship with us is
real ; our fellowship with Him is not less real. That
relationship between the Eternal Son of God and
us which made it possible for Him to share our
weakness and the desolation which was the result
of our sin, also makes it possible for us to share His
work in this world and His glory in the next. His
fellowship with us is the foundation of our fellowship
with Him.

357. GARVIE

THERE have been great teachers and leaders of the
souls of men, but none of them claimed to do or did
what Jesus has done. Through Moses came a law to
be obeyed ; Mohammed was the prophet of a truth
about God ; Gautama offered man the secret of a
salvation which must be secured by their own efforts.
Christ brings men to God and God to men in an
immediacy of relation, in an intimacy of communion,
in a sufficiency and an efficacy of divine grace through
human faith which is a new creation of man in his
inmost, highest life. It is because of the sufficiency
and efficacy both of His revelation of God, and His
redemption of man, the transcendence of what He
has done for man over all that other teachers and
leaders of the soul have accomplished, the absolute
quality of the relation of man to God through Him,

that we must confess that this work is not of man, even at his very best; but this God and God alone can have wrought. This cannot, of course, be demonstrated by merely intellectual arguments to those who have not had the experience of what Christ has done; but for those who have that experience, there need be no other evidence. They have the witness in themselves that He is God.

We believe that Christ is God not because He mysteriously possessed a divine nature united to a human, but because as He is as man we find God in Him, and God finds us through Him. We behold the glory of the Only Begotten of the Father in the Word incarnate, and find Him full of grace and truth. God making Himself known and even giving Himself in love to us. This and nothing less is what believing in the divinity of Christ means.

358. BROWNING

I SAY, the acknowledgment of God in Christ
　　Accepted by thy reason, solves for thee,
All questions in the earth and out of it.

359. FREDERICK WILLIAM FABER

A MID the eternal silences
　　God's endless Word was spoken;
None heard but He who always spake,
　　And the silence was unbroken.
Oh marvellous! Oh worshipful!
　　No song or sound is heard,
But everywhere and every hour,
In love, in wisdom, and in power,
The Father speaks His dear Eternal Word

Son of God

For ever in the eternal land
    The glorious Day is dawning;
For ever is the Father's Light
    Like an endless outspread morning.
Oh marvellous! Oh worshipful!
    No song or sound is heard,
But everywhere and every hour,
In love, in wisdom, and in power,
The Father speaks His dear Eternal Word!

From the Father's vast tranquillity,
    In light co-equal glowing
The kingly consubstantial Word
    Is unutterably flowing.
Oh marvellous! Oh worshipful!
    No song or sound is heard,
But everywhere and every hour,
In love, in wisdom, and in power,
The Father speaks His dear Eternal Word!

For ever climbs that Morning Star
    Without ascent or motion;
For ever is its daybreak shed
    On the Spirit's boundless ocean.
Oh marvellous! Oh worshipful!
    No song or sound is heard,
But everywhere and every hour,
In love, in wisdom, and in power,
The Father speaks His dear Eternal Word!

41

Faith in Christ

Stand fast in the faith.—I Corinthians 16:13

360. PHILLIPS BROOKS

" THEN Jesus answered and said unto her, O woman, great is thy faith; be it unto thee even as thou wilt." (Matt. xv, 28.)

You remember the story from which the words are taken. Jesus has travelled outside of the regions of the Jews, and there has come to him a Canaanitish woman asking Him to cure her poor afflicted daughter. He has hesitated and remonstrated, but at last she overcomes Him with her urgency, and He yields to her, saying, " O woman, great is thy faith; be it unto thee even as thou wilt." It would be possible to give reasons, which no doubt would be true ones, for Christ's reluctance. But I cannot but think that the truest and simplest way to look at this beautiful story, is to consider it as a record of the spiritual necessities of Jesus. The idea which seems to me to be in it is this, that Jesus gave the woman what she wanted just as soon as it was possible for Him to give it; and that, just as soon as it was possible for Him to give it, in some true sense He had to give it, it was impossible for Him to refuse it any longer. He was not holding it, as it were, behind His back, watching her face to see when was the best moment to give it to her. He was telling her of a genuine impossibility when He said, " I am not sent but unto the lost sheep of the house of Israel." He could not give her what she wanted then ; but when by her belief in Him she had crossed the line and become spiritually one of His people, then the impossibility was removed, and we may even say, I think, that He could not help helping her.

361. HENRY VAN DYKE

NEVER in a costly palace did I rest on golden bed,
Never in a hermit's cavern have I eaten idle bread.

Born within a lowly stable where the cattle round Me stood,
Trained a carpenter of Nazareth, I have toiled and found it good.

They who tread the path of labour follow where My feet have trod ;
They who work without complaining do the Holy will of God.

Where the many toil together, there am I among My own ;
When the tirèd workman sleepeth, then am I with him alone.

I, the Peace that passeth knowledge, dwell amid the daily strife,
I, the Bread of Heaven, am broken in the sacrament of life.

362. DALE

AS faith in Christ is something wholly different
from the belief that Matthew, Mark, Luke, and
John wrote the four narratives of our Lord's earthly
life contained in the New Testament, so it is wholly
different from a belief in the authenticity of these
narratives. If, when my heart is dark with the sense
of guilt, and all my strength is broken through despair
of the Divine mercy, I trust in Christ for forgiveness,
and the awful weight which crushed me is removed,
and the light breaks, and I am conscious that in the
mystery of my personal relations to the Eternal a
great change has come, and that God has absolved
me ; if, having known in past days the blessedness
of living in the presence of God, I am lonely and
desolate because no sign or intimation of the presence
of God is given me, and I trust in Christ to restore
me to God, and the vision and the power and the
glory return ; if when the springs of life seem to have
dried up, and there is apathetic indifference to all
those invisible and eternal things which once filled
me with awe, kindled fires of love for God and for
man, created an exulting hope, transfigured the
world, exalted the ideal of conduct, and inspired
strength and resolution to attempt to achieve it—
if then I trust in Christ to have pity on me, and the
" river of water of life clear as crystal, proceeding
out of the throne of God," returns to its deserted
channels, and rises and overflows its banks : if,
I say, Christ in answer to my faith does the e great
things for me, what more direct, appropriate, decisive
evidence can I have that He is the Redeemer and
Lord of men ? It is the precise kind of evidence that
I need to authenticate and confirm my faith in Him.

Faith in Christ

TO be a Christian, then, it is not enough to be a member of a Christian Church. " Many walk," says St. Paul, " of whom I have told you that they are the enemies of the cross of Christ." To be a Christian, it is not enough to profess a belief in certain propositions about Christ and His work. " Not every one that saith unto me, Lord, Lord, shall enter into the kingdom of heaven." To be a Christian it is not enough to be free from what are commonly called sins. It was to the man who had kept all the commandments from his youth that the Saviour said, " One thing thou lackest "—that one thing without which he could not enter into the kingdom of God. We sometimes think it is comparatively easy now to be a Christian—easier far than in the old times of martyrdom. But it is not. The *spirit* which was in the martyrs must be in us, or we are unworthy to bear the name of Christ. The spirit which impelled them to sacrifice themselves for Him in death, should inspire us to sacrifice ourselves for Him in life. He should be to us as He was to them— more dear than anything else the world contains. We should think it our highest joy to take up the cross of self-denial and follow Him " *whithersoever* He goeth."

This is a lofty standard. We may feel as if we could never attain it. But unless we have a sincere desire to do so, calling ourselves after the name of Christ is nothing short of blasphemy. The accusation is constantly brought against Christianity, that those who profess it are not better than their neighbours, but, on the contrary, rather worse, narrower in their sympathies, harsher in their judgments, more petty in their aims, more grossly selfish in their actions—a peculiar people indeed, but only in the sense of being peculiarly disagreeable. Woe betide us if we do anything to justify this accusation ! If Christ is nothing more to you than any ordinary historical personage ; if your heart has never been touched by the old, old story of the Cross ; if you see no beauty in a life of self-denial ; if you have no intention of making any sacrifices on behalf of your fellow-men for whom Christ died—then, for God's sake, I adjure you, do not call yourself a Christian. Why must you bring the name of Christ into contempt ? Is it not enough to treat Him with indifference ? Can you not be satisfied with ignoring Him ? What harm has He done you, that you must positively insult Him ? Will nothing content you but to crucify the Son of God afresh, and put Him to an open shame ?

364. JOHN OXENHAM

NO room !
No room !
No room for Thee,
Thou Man of Galilee !
The house is full,
Yea, overfull.
There is no room for Thee,—
Pass on ! Pass on !

Nay—see !
The place is packed.
We scarce have room
For our own selves,

Faith in Christ

So how shall we
Find room for Thee,
Thou Man of Galilee?—
   Pass on! Pass on!

But—if Thou shouldst
This way again,
And we can find
So much as one small corner
Free from guest,
Not then in vain
Thy quest.
But now—
The house is full.
Pass on!

Christ passes
On His ceaseless quest,
Nor will He rest
With any,
Save as Chiefest Guest.

*   *   *   *   *

Within my holy place
My Chiefest One is dwelling,
Not as a passing guest
But of His own houseling.
O, miracle of grace,
My whole heart's love compelling—
Within this tiny space
The Lord of All Good Life,
The Very Light of Life and Love
Is dwelling!

365. COLERIDGE

CHRISTIANITY is not a theory, or a speculation, but a life :—not a philosophy of life, but a life, and a living process. It has been eighteen hundred years in existence; and has one individual left a record like the following? "I tried it, and it did not answer. I made the experiment faithfully, according to the directions; and the result has been a conviction of my own credulity." If neither your own experience nor the history of almost two thousand years has presented a single testimony to this purport, and if you have read and heard of many who have lived and died bearing witness to the contrary and if you have yourself met with some one in whom on any other point you would place unqualified trust, who has on his own experience made report to you that He is faithful, who promised, and what He promised He has proved Himself able to perform : is it bigotry, if I fear that the unbelief which prejudges and prevents the experiment, has its source elsewhere than in the uncorrupted judgment? that not the strong free mind but the enslaved will is the true original infidel in this instance?

366. CHANNING

THERE is another evidence of Christianity, still more internal than any on which I have dwelt, and evidence to be felt rather than described, but not less real because founded on feeling. I refer to that conviction of the divine original of our religion, which springs up and continually gains strength in those who apply it habitually to their tempers and lives, and who imbibe its spirit and hopes. In such

men there is a consciousness of the adaptation of
Christianity to their noblest faculties ; a consciousness
of its exalting and consoling influences, of its power
to confer the true happiness of human nature, to
give that peace which the world cannot give ; which
assures them that it is not of earthly origin, but a ray
from the Everlasting Light, a stream from the foun-
tain of Heavenly Wisdom and Love. This is the
evidence which sustains the faith of thousands who
never read and cannot understand the learned books
of Christian apologists, who want perhaps words to
explain the ground of their belief, but whose faith
is of adamantine firmness, who hold the Gospel
with a conviction more intimate and unwavering
than mere argument ever produced.

367. BROWNING

"DOES the precept run—'Believe in good,
   In justice, truth, now understood
For the first time ? ' or—'Believe in me
Who lived and died, yet essentially
Am Lord of Life ? ' "

368. FENELON.

IF he were to come at this moment, would he find
faith on the earth—in us ? Where is our faith ?
What are the proofs of it ? Do we believe that this
life is only a short passage to a better ? Do we
believe that we must suffer with Jesus before we can
reign with him ? Do we look upon the world as a
vain show, and death as the entrance into true happi-
ness ? Do we live by faith ? Does it animate us ?
Do we enjoy the eternal truths that it presents to us ?
Do we feed our souls with them, as we nourish our

bodies with healthful aliment? Do we accustom ourselves to view everything with the eye of faith? Alas! instead of living by faith, we extinguish it in our souls. How can we truly believe what we profess to believe, and act as we act?

May we not fear, lest the kingdom of heaven be taken from us, and given to others who will bring forth more fruit? This kingdom of heaven is faith, when it dwells and reigns in the heart. Blessed are the eyes that see this kingdom; flesh and blood have not seen it; earthly wisdom is blind to it. To realize its glories, we must be born again, and to do this we must die to self.

369. BARRY

THE world is a world of facts, in which we cannot concern ourselves with fine-spun theories, made by men who have never tasted life's exceeding bitterness, never eaten their bread with tears, never known those griefs which, piercing to the heart, lay open its spiritual essence. Nor yet again is religion to be found in mere darkness. To what living faith can we betake ourselves, then, except to faith in Jesus? I know of none. The despairing creeds bring me no light; those which prate of enlightenment have no strength in them. Buddhism, Pessimism, Liberalism, are all alike in their spiritual impotence. Christianity has endured nigh upon two thousand years; and its day is not yet over. " Man must have a religion," Amiel the sceptic affirms: " Is not the Christian the best after all? The religion of sin, repentance, and reconciliation, of the new-birth and the life everlasting? " A powerful argument in a few words ! But it is the substance of Christian apologies, old or

new. Can it be refuted ? And do not its grace and
majesty go far to prove that the " Semitic miracle-
play " which Amiel put from him on his deathbed,
is no idle fiction, no empty symbolising, but the very
interposition of God Himself on the stage of history ?

370. ROBERT HUGH BENSON

NAY, but with Faith I saw my Lord and God
Walk in the fragrant garden yesterday.
Ah ! how the thrushes sang ; and, where He trod
Like spikenard lay
Jewels of dew, fresh-fallen from the sky,
While all the lawn rang round with melody.

Nay, but with Faith I marked my Saviour go,
One August noonday, down the stifling street
That reeked with filth and man ; marked from Him
flow
Radiance so sweet,
The man ceased cursing, laughter lit the child,
The woman hoped again, as Jesus smiled.

Nay, but with Faith I sought my Lord last night,
And found Him shining where the lamp was dim ;
The shadowy altar glimmered, height on height,
A throne for Him :
Seen as through lattice work His gracious Face
Looked forth on me and filled the dark with grace.

Nay then, if proof and tortured argument
Content thee—teach thee that the Lord is there,
Or risen again ; I pray thee be content,
But leave me here
With eye unsealed by any proof of thine,
With eye unsealed to know the Lord is mine.

42

His Church

Upon this rock I will build my church.
— Matthew 16:18
Christ loved the church. — Ephesians 5:25

371. LACORDAIRE

IT was not, however, enough for Him to found a doctrine and obtain faith; it was not enough to found a doctrine in contradicting all other doctrines, to found a spirit of faith in contradicting every other spirit. He had in addition to found a Church, that is to say, a society of men living by that doctrine and faith.

372. THEODORE PARKER

THE Church did not fail to espouse the cause of the people, with whom Christianity found its first adherents, its apostles and defenders. . . . It came to the Baron, haughty of soul, and bloody of hand, who sat in his cliff-tower, as a hungry raven; who broke the poor into fragments, ground them to powder, and spurned them like dust from his foot; it came between him and the captive, the serf, the slave, the defenceless maiden, and stayed the insatiate hand. Its curse blasted as lightning. Then, while nothing but the accident of distinguished birth, or the possession of animal fierceness, could save a man from the collar of the thrall, the Church took to her bosom all who gave signs of talent and piety ; sheltered them in her monasteries ; ordained them as her priests ; welcomed them to the chair of St. Peter ; and men who from birth would have been companions of the Galilean fishermen, sat on the spiritual throne of the world, and governed with a majesty which Cæsar might envy but could not equal.

373. NAPOLEON

NATIONS pass away, thrones crumble ; but the Church remains. What is, then, the power which has protected this Church, thus assailed by the furious billows of rage and the hostility of ages ? Whose is the arm which, for eighteen hundred years, has protected the Church from so many storms which have threatened to engulf it ?

Alexander, Cæsar, Charlemagne, and myself founded empires. But on what did we rest the creations of our genius ? Upon force. Jesus Christ alone founded his empire upon love ; and, at this hour, millions of men would die for him.

374. MICHELET

THE church is itself a drama. It is a petrified mystery, a Passion in stone : or, rather, it is the Sufferer himself. The whole edifice, amid the austerity of its architectural geometry, is as a living human body. The nave, extending its two arms, is the Man on the cross : the crypt, the subterranean church, is the Man in the tomb : the tower, the spire—it is still He, but erect, and rising to heaven. In the choir which declines in the direction of the nave, you see His head drooping in the agony : you recognize His blood in the vivid purple of the windows. There is something here stronger than arms of Titans : What is it ? The breath of the Spirit ! That light breath which passed before the face of Daniel, carrying away kingdom and dashing empires to pieces, it is that which has swelled these vaulted arches, and wafted these towers to the sky. It has penetrated every part of this vast body with a powerful and harmonious life, and has drawn out of a grain of mustard seed the vegetation of this marvellous tree. Ascend to those aerial deserts, to the last points of the spires, where only the slater mounts, in danger and with trembling, you will often find— left alone, under God's eye, to the stroke of the eternal winds—some delicate piece of workmanship, some masterpiece of sculptured art, in carving which the devout workman has occupied his life. Not a name is on it, not a mark, not a letter : he would have thought such a thing something subtracted from the glory of God !

375. BISHOP WOODS

" I BELIEVE in the Holy Catholic Church." That is the faith which unites us all, from the first generation until now. In a world torn with controversy as to the meaning of life, seething with every conceivable variety of opinion, religious and otherwise, there stands a world-wide society, founded

on the impregnable rock of the Incarnation, whose
very existence is due to the fact of GOD in Christ,
charged to administer Christ's sacraments, com-
missioned to deliver Christ's message, pledged to
Christ's valuation of life, committed to the setting
up of Christ's Kingdom, designed to exhibit Christ's
love to the world.

376. GARVIE

THE Church is based not on any human intentions
in time, but on the eternal purpose of God.
Related as it is to human history, it is not a product
of any human development; it was established on
earth by Jesus Christ our Lord in fulfilment of
the purpose of God; it is sustained not merely by
human volitions, but by the presence and power of
the Head, who by His Spirit is the bond of unity.
For Christ alone was the relation of Son to God
as Father unmediated by heredity or environment;
His alone was an immediate communion with God;
for all Christians the relation to God is mediated
by His grace. Even the first disciples discovered
and confessed His Messiahship in companionship
with Him and with one another. Since His Ascen-
sion His invisible Presence and intangible Power
is mediated by the Christian society. It is His body,
and His Spirit is its common possession. Accordingly,
the Christian life must be thought of as dependent
on and realised within the Christian society. The
truth and grace of the Lord Jesus Christ come to the
individual through the Christian Church, and it is
in its membership that he can more fully experience

and express that truth and grace. It is not to an isolated relation to Himself that Christ calls in His Gospel, and draws by His Spirit, but to a relation which can be received and realised only in fellowship within the Christian society. As the fullness of the Godhead dwells in Him *bodily* (Col. ii, 9), not only in His personal incarnation, but even now in His continued incarnation in the Church, the habitation of the Spirit, it is as a member of that body that the believer receives of that fullness, and grace for grace. If in the believer's consciousness the body be confined to the congregation to which he belongs, or even to the denomination to which he adheres, how much is his life impoverished, because he does not discern the whole body (I Cor. xi, 29), the unity of all believers, the communion of all the saints in the one Spirit! It is from the one Church the individual receives the gifts of Christ; it is in the one Church he makes full use of these gifts.

377. INGE

HAS the Church of Christ ever been divided in the chambers where men shut their door and pray to their Father in secret? Do we not all pray the same prayers—at least the same prayer of prayers? Has it ever been divided in the service of praise and thanksgiving? Has it ever been divided on the shelves where we keep our books of devotion? The mystics all tell the same tale. They have climbed the same mountain, and their witness agrees together. All ages, denominations, and languages are blended harmoniously in that Jacob's ladder which scales the

heavens in far other fashion than is ever dreamed oi
by the builders of Babel. Has Christendom ever
been divided in the world of letters? Do not
Biblical scholars, historians, philosophers, forget their
denominational differences and work side by side in
the cause of truth? Lastly, are we divided in
philanthropy and social service? Do we not unite,
naturally and spontaneously, in the warfare against
vice, crime and injustice? These are no slight bonds
of union. If the Church of the future will, we hope,
be co-extensive with all who love the Lord Jesus
Christ in incorruptness; if this is the goal towards
which we are moving, however slowly; if this is the
idea of the Church which already exists in the mind
of God as a fact: let us press forward thither in
heart and mind : let us anticipate that which will surely
come to pass, and which, when it has come to pass,
will make what is now the present appear in quite a
new light: let us keep that "ideal of a Christian
Church" ever before us, gazing upon it with that
eye of faith which gives substance to things hoped
for, and conviction to things not seen.

378. BISHOP BUTLER

CHRISTIANITY was left with Christians, to be
transmitted down pure and genuine, or to be
corrupted and sunk, in like manner as the religion of
nature had been before left with mankind in general.
There was, however, this difference, that by an
institution of external religion fitted for all men
(Consisting in a common form of Christian worship,
together with a standing ministry of instruction

and discipline), it pleased God to unite Christians in communities or visible churches, and all along to preserve them, over a great part of the world; and thus perpetuate a general publication of the gospel. For these communities, which together make up the catholic visible church, are, first, the repositories of the written oracles of God; and, in every age, have preserved and published them in every country, where the profession of Christianity has obtained. Hence it has come to pass, and it is a thing very much to be observed in the appointment of Providence, that even such of these communities as, in a long succession of years, have corrupted Christianity the most, have yet continually carried, together with their corruptions, the confutations of them; for they have everywhere preserved the pure original standard of it, the Scripture, to which recourse might have been had, both by the deceivers and the deceived, in every successive age. Secondly, any particular Church, in whatever place established, is like *a city that is set on an hill, which cannot be hid*, inviting all who pass by to enter into it. All persons to whom any notices of it come have, in Scripture language, *the Kingdom of God come nigh unto them*. They are reminded of that religion, which natural conscience attests the truth of; and they may, if they will, be instructed in it more distinctly, and likewise in the gracious means, whereby sinful creatures may obtain eternal life; that chief and final good, which all men, in proportion to their understanding and integrity, even in all ages and countries of the heathen world, were ever in pursuit of. And, lastly, out of these churches have all along gone forth persons, who have preached the Gospel in remote places, with greater or less good effect ; for the establishment of any profession of Christianity, however corrupt, I call a good effect, whilst accompanied with a continued publication of the Scripture, notwithstanding it may for some time be quite neglected.

379. LIDDON

DOES the kingdom of heaven exist on earth ? The Church of Christ is the living answer to that question. Boileau says somewhere that the Church is a great thought which every man ought to study. It would be more practical to say that the Church is a great fact which every man ought to measure. Probably we Christians are too familiarized with the blessed presence of the Church to do justice to her as a world-embracing institution, and as the nurse and guardian of our moral and mental life. Like the air we breathe, she bathes our whole being with influences which we do not analyse ; and we hold her cheap in proportion to the magnitude of her unostentatious service. The sun rises on us day by day in the heavens, and we heed not his surpassing beauty until our languid sense is roused by some observant astronomer or artist. The Christian Church pours even upon those of us who love her least, floods of intellectual and moral light ; and yet it is only by an occasional intellectual effort that we detach ourselves sufficiently from the tender monotony of her influences, to understand how intrinsically extraordinary is the double fact of her perpetuated existence and of her continuous expansion.

380. S. J. STONE

THE Church's one foundation
Is Jesus Christ her Lord;
She is His new creation
By water and the word:
From heaven He came and sought her
To be His holy bride;
With His own blood He bought her,
And for her life He died.

'Mid toil and tribulation,
And tumult of her war,
She waits the consummation
Of peace for evermore;
Till with the vision glorious
Her longing eyes are blest,
And the great Church victorious
Shall be the Church at rest.

43

Epilogue

Jesus Christ the same yesterday, and to-day, and for ever.—Hebrews 13:8

381. ANCIENT HYMN

JESUS CHRIST, Joyful Light of the holy! Glory of the eternal, heavenly, holy, blessed Father! Having now come to the setting of the sun, beholding the evening light, we praise the Father, and the Son, and the Holy Spirit of God. Thou art worthy to be praised of sacred voices at all seasons, O Son of God, who givest life: wherefore the universe glorifieth Thee.

382. CONSTANTINE

THUS do we render thanks to Thee, according to our feeble power, our God and Saviour, Christ; supreme Providence of the mighty Father, Who both savest us from evil, and impartest to us Thy most blessed doctrine: thus we essay, not indeed to celebrate Thy praise, but to speak the language of thanksgiving. For what mortal is he who shall worthily declare Thy praise, of Whom we learn that Thou didst from nothing call creation into being, and illumine it with Thy light: that Thou didst regulate the confusion of the elements, by the laws of harmony and order!

But chiefly we mark Thy loving-kindness in that Thou hast caused those whose hearts inclined to Thee, to desire earnestly a divine and blessed life; and hast provided that, like merchants of true blessings, they might impart to many others the wisdom and happiness which they had received—themselves, meanwhile, reaping the everlasting fruit of virtue.

383. MOULE

THIS Jesus Christ has, somehow, touched, and changed, and set free my soul, my being. He, and only He—His Name, His Person—has had a power over me which is like nothing else. The more I have seen, trusted, loved Him, the more always I have stood clear of sin, of self. I cannot but love Him still.

384. DALE

THE historical events on which our faith rests did not come to an end eighteen hundred years ago when Jesus of Nazareth was crucified; nor even when He rose from the dead: nor even when He ascended to the Father. "Even though we *have* known Christ after the flesh, yet now we know Him so no more." Through sixty generations men of every tongue and of every land and of every Church have discovered for themselves that He is living still. Penitents have received absolution from His lips. At His word an evil passion has sometimes withered to its roots; at the touch of His hand evil habits have sometimes fallen away from men as the fetters

Epilogue

fell away from Peter at the touch of the angel. More
commonly He has given to those who have trusted
Him strength to struggle with their baser life and
to subdue it—strength to achieve by vigilance and
self-discipline a righteousness which they knew was
impossible to them apart from Him. He has given
them peace in times of great trouble, courage in
the presence of great dangers ; and they knew that
the peace and courage came from Him. In prisons
and solitary places they were not alone, for He was
with them. In Christ—but in the living, personal
Christ, a great multitude that no man can number
have found God. Those who deny His supernatural
power have only begun their task when they have
stated the case against the miracles which are recorded
in the narratives of His earthly life. They have to
descend through the Christian centuries and to destroy
the trustworthiness of the long succession of penitents
and saints who have testified, on their own knowledge,
that He was living still, and that His compassions
failed not, and that His power was unspent. For the
life of every Christian man adds to the great story
of Christ new miracles of mercy and of power. The
canon is not closed. Every age contributes materials
for new Gospels. Four brief narratives contain the
record of Christ's earthly ministry, and they are
incomplete, for " many other signs did Jesus in the
presence of His disciples," and many other discourses
were spoken by Him of which the evangelists have
said nothing, but if the history were to be told of
the greater miracles of grace which He has wrought
since He ascended to the throne of God, " I suppose
that even the world itself would not contain the
books that should be written."

385. CLIFFORD

LOOKING back upon my past, upon these sixty years spent in Jesus Christ's school, I see many lessons badly learned, many blunders, innumerable faults, yet, scientifically interpreting the whole of the past, I say, with the full assurance of understanding, that all that there is in me, and has been in me, throughout these years, of any good, is due to Jesus Christ . . . whatsoever of value there has been in my life is due entirely to Him, whatsoever of service I have been able to perform for my generation owes all its inspiration, all its strength, to His indwelling. All the conceptions I have formed of God, the answers I am able to give for myself as to what is religion, human duty, human destiny, all that man may hope for, I get from Him who is the Way, the Truth, and the Life.

407. LIDDON

IF you are intellectually persuaded that in confessing the true Godhead of Jesus you have not followed a cunningly-devised fable, or the crude imagination of a semi-barbarous and distant age, then do not allow yourselves to rest content with this intellectual persuasion. A truth so sublime, so imperious, has other work to do in you besides shaping into theoretic compactness a certain district of your thought about the goodness of God and the wants of man. The Divine Christ of the Gospel and the Church is no mere actor, though He were the greatest, in the great tragedy of human history; He belongs not exclusively

Epilogue

or especially to the past ; He is " the Same yesterday, to-day, and for ever." He is at this moment all that He was eighteen centuries ago, all that He has been to our fathers, all that He will be to our children. He is the Divine and Infallible Teacher, the Healer and Pardoner of sin, the Source of all graces, the Conqueror of Satan and of death—now, as of old, and as in years to come. Now as heretofore, He is " able to save unto the uttermost them that come unto God by Him " ; now, as on the day of His triumph over death, " He opens the Kingdom of Heaven to all believers " ; now, as in the first age of the Church, He it is " that hath the key of David, that openeth, and no man shutteth ; and shutteth, and no man openeth." He is ever the Same, but, as the children of time, whether for good or evil, we move onwards in perpetual change. The hours of life pass, they do not return ; they pass, yet they are not forgotten ; " pereunt et imputantur." But the present is our own ; we may resolve, if we will, to live as men who live for the glory of an Incarnate God. Brethren, you shall not repent it, if, when life's burdens press heavily, and especially at that solemn hour when human help must fail, you are able to lean with strong confidence on the arm of an Almighty Saviour. May He in deed and truth be with you, alike in your pilgrimage through this world, and when that brief journey is drawing to its close ! May you, sustained by His Presence and aid, so pass through the valley of the shadow of death as to fear no evil, and to find, at the gate of the eternal world, that all the yearnings of faith and hope are to be more than satisfied by the vision of the Divine " King in His Beauty "

387. NEWMAN

"O TASTE, and see how gracious the Lord is." If you have hitherto thought too little of these things, if you have thought religion lies *merely* in what it certainly does consist in also, in filling your worldly station well, in being amiable, and well-behaved, and considerate, and orderly,—but if you have thought it was nothing more than this, if you have neglected to stir up the great gift of God which is lodged deep within you, the gift of election and regeneration, if you have been scanty in your devotions, in intercession, prayer, and praise, and if, in consequence, you have little or nothing of the sweetness, the winning grace, the innocence, the freshness, the tenderness, the cheerfulness, the composure of the elect of God, if you are at present really deficient in praying, and other divine exercises, make a new beginning henceforth. Start, now, and rise with Christ. See, He offers you His hand; He is rising; rise with Him. Mount up from the grave of the old Adam; from grovelling cares, and jealousies, and fretfulness, and worldly aims; from the thraldom of habit, from the tumult of passion, from the fascinations of the flesh, from a cold, worldly, calculating spirit, from frivolity, from selfishness, from effeminacy, from self-conceit and high-mindedness. Henceforth set about doing what it is so difficult to do, but what should not, must not, be left undone; watch, and pray, and meditate, that is, according to the leisure which God has given you. Give freely of your time to your Lord and Saviour, if you have it. If you have little, show your sense of the privilege by giving that little. But anyhow, show that your heart and

your desires, show that your life is with your God.
Set aside every day times for seeking Him. Humble
yourself that you have been hitherto so languid and
uncertain. Live more strictly to Him ; take His
yoke upon your shoulder ; live by rule. I am not
calling on you to go out of the world, or to abandon
your duties in the world, but to redeem the time ;
not to give hours to mere amusement or society,
while you give minutes to Christ ; not to pray to
Him only when you are tired, and fit for nothing
but sleep ; not altogether to omit to praise Him,
or to intercede for the world and the Church ; but
in good measure to realize honestly the words of the
text, to " set your affection on things above ; " and
to prove that you are His, in that your heart is risen
with Him, and your life hid in Him.

388. MAZZINI

HE came—the soul the most full of love, the most
sacredly virtuous, the most deeply inspired by
God and by the future, that men have yet seen on
earth—Jesus. He bent over the corpse of the dead
world and whispered a word of faith. Over the
clay that had lost all of man but the movement and
the form, He uttered words until then unknown,
love, sacrifice, a heavenly origin. And the dead arose.
A new life circulated through the clay which
philosophy had in vain tried to reanimate. From
that corpse arose the Christian world, the world of
liberty and equality. From that clay arose the true
Man, the image of God, the precursor of humanity.
Christ expired. All He had asked of mankind

wherewith to save them, says Lamennais, was a Cross whereon to die. But ere He died, He had announced the glad tidings to the people; to those who asked of Him whence He had received it, He answered, "From God the Father." From the height of His Cross, He had invoked Him twice. Therefore upon the Cross did His victory begin and still does it endure.

389. MATHESON

"CHRIST being raised from the dead, dieth no more," wrote St. Paul. A bold assertion; the man who made it must have been a great man. In a world of change, in an age of special changes, he declared that the human race had reached finality. This faith in the Crucified, he says, will be the last religion. Men will never outgrow it, never get beyond it. Times shall change, manners shall change, customs shall change, the order of life shall change, but this faith shall abide. The heavens shall pass away with a loud noise. A new science of the stars shall dawn. The earth shall move round the sun instead of the sun moving round the earth. But there shall be no new Christ in the firmament; His eyes shall not grow dim, His strength shall not be abated. A thousand systems shall fall at His side, but their crash shall not touch *Him*. He shall be the survivor in the struggle for existence. He shall have the dew of His youth when the world is old. He shall have the last judgment. There shall be no verdict after His, no appeal to the Cæsar of a future age. His feet shall touch the final ridge of the mountains, and the beauty of His tidings shall be a joy for ever.

Epilogue

390. OXENHAM

GOD grant us wisdom in these coming days,
And eyes unsealed, that we clear visions see
Of that new world that He would have us build,
To Life's ennoblement and His high ministry.

God give us sense,—God-sense of Life's new needs,
And souls aflame with new-born chivalries—
To cope with those black growths that foul the ways,—
To cleanse our poisoned founts with God-born
energies.

To pledge our souls to nobler, loftier life,
To win the world to His fair sanctities,
To bind the nations in a Pact of Peace,
And free the Soul of Life for finer loyalties.

Not since Christ died upon His lonely Cross
Has Time such prospect held of Life's new birth;
Not since the world of chaos first was born
Has man so clearly visaged hope of a new earth.

Not of our own might can we hope to rise
Above the ruts and failures of the past,
But, with His help Who did the first earth build,
With hearts courageous we may fairer build this last.

391. MYERS

YEA, through life, death, through sorrow and
through sinning,
Christ shall suffice me, for he hath sufficed;
Christ is the end, for Christ was the beginning,
Christ the beginning, for the end is Christ.

392. JACOPONI DA TODI

LOVE, Love, O Jesu, I have reached the goal,
 Love, Love, O Jesu, whither Thou hast led;
Love, Love, O Jesu, comfort Thou my soul,
 Love, Love, O Jesu, on her fiery bed.
Love, Love, O Jesu, Thou Who art my Goal,
 O set Thy gentle hands about my head!
 To Thee my soul is wed,
  In Love most sure,
  In Truth most pure,
 In Thy transforming Love.

Love, Love, O Love, the world's wild voices cry,
 Love, Love, O Love, the clamorous echoes spread;
Love, Love, O Love, so deep Thy treasures lie,
 We hunger more, the more we taste Thy bread:
Love, Love, O Love, Thou Circling Mystery,
 Who enters Thee at Love's deep heart is fed;
 Thou'rt Loom, and Cloth, and Thread:
  O sweet to be
  Clad all in Thee,
 And ceaseless chant of Love.

393. BONAVENTURA

TO Thee, then O Jesus, do I turn as my true and
last end. Thou art the river of life which alone
can satisfy my thirst. Without Thee all else is
barren and void. Without all else Thou alone art
enough for me. Thou art the Redeemer of those
that are lost; the sweet Consoler of the sorrowful;
the Crown of Glory for the victors; the recompense
of the Blessed. One day I hope to receive of Thy

fulness, and to sing the song of praise in my true home. Give me only on earth some few drops of consolation, and I will patiently wait Thy coming that I may enter into the Joy of my Lord.

He is the life of our life. If we would build a solid structure, it must be grounded on this Rock of Ages.

394. ST. ALOYSIUS

O CHRIST, Love's Victim, hanging high
Upon the cruel Tree
What worthy recompense can I
Make, mine own Christ, to Thee?

All my life's blood if I should spill
A thousand times for Thee,
Ah! 'twere too small a quittance still
For all thy love to me.

My sweat and labour from this day,
My sole life, let it be.
To love Thee aye the best I may
And die for love of Thee.

395. WILLIAM BLAKE

AND did those feet in ancient time
Walk upon England's mountains green?
And was the holy Lamb of God
On England's pleasant pastures seen?

And did the Countenance Divine
　　Shine forth upon our clouded hills ?
And was Jerusalem builded here
　　Among these dark Satanic Mills ?

Bring me my bow of burning gold !
　　Bring me my arrows of desire !
Bring me my spear ！ O clouds, unfold !
　　Bring me my chariot of fire !

I will not cease from mental fight,
　　Nor shall my sword sleep in my hand,
Till we have built Jerusalem
　　In England's green and pleasant land.

396. ALFRED GURNEY

A NEW world did Columbus find ?
　　Ah ! 'tis not so *that* world is found ;
God's golden harvest sheaves who bind
　　Are tillers of another ground.

No new world like the old we need ;
　　One thing suffices—one alone,
A garnered world-harvest from seed
　　The wounded Hands of Christ have sown.

No earthly Paradise avails,
　　No Eldorado in the West ;
The Spirit's Breath must fill their sails
　　Who seek the Highlands of the Blest.

Epilogue

By stripes is healing wrought, and stars
    Point ever to a central Sun ;
He flies the conquering flag, whose scars,
    Transfigured, speak of Victory won.

O Royal Heart, Thy Kingdom come !
    All else may change ; all else may go :
Not eastward, westward, is our Home,
    But *onward, upward :*—even so !

One Sign alone is love-designed,
    God's Evergreen, the Eternal Rood ;
Happy the home-seekers who find
    Its meaning plain—*a world renewed !*

397. MEYNELL

WITH this ambiguous earth
    His dealings have been told us.   These abide :
The signal to a maid, the human birth,
    The lesson, and the young Man crucified.

    But not a star of all
The innumerable host of stars has heard
How he administered this terrestrial ball.
Our race have kept their Lord's entrusted Word.

    Of his earth-visiting feet
None knows the secret, cherished, perilous,
The terrible, shamefast, frightened, whispered, sweet,
Heart-shattering secret of his way with us.

    No planet knows that this
Our wayside planet, carrying land and wave,
Love and life multiplied, and pain and bliss
Bears, as chief treasure, one forsaken grave.

Nor, in our little day,
May his devices with the heavens be guessed,
His pilgrimage to thread the Milky Way,
Or his bestowals there be manifest.

But in the eternities,
Doubtless we shall compare together, hear
A million alien Gospels, in what guise
He trod the Pleiades, the Lyre, the Bear.

O, be prepared, my soul!
To read the inconceivable, to scan
The million forms of God those stars unroll
When, in our turn, we show to them a Man.

398. ISAAC WATTS

JESUS shall reign where'er the sun
Doth his successive journeys run,
His kingdom stretch from shore to shore,
Till moons shall wax and wane no more.

For Him shall endless prayer be made,
And praises throng to crown His head:
His name, like sweet perfume, shall rise
With every morning sacrifice.

People and realms of every tongue
Dwell on His love with sweetest song;
And infant voices shall proclaim
Their early blessings on His name.

Blessings abound where'er He reigns
The prisoner leaps to loose his chains;
The weary find eternal rest;
And all the sons of want are blest.

Epilogue

Let every creature rise, and bring
Peculiar honours to our King,
Angels descend with songs again,
And earth repeat the long " Amen."

399. ST. MATTHEW

WHEN the Son of man shall come in his glory,
and all the holy angels with him, then shall
he sit upon the throne of his glory :

And before him shall be gathered all nations :
and he shall separate them one from another, as a
shepherd divideth his sheep from the goats :

And he shall set the sheep on his right hand, but
the goats on the left.

Then shall the King say unto them on his right
hand, Come, ye blessed of my Father, inherit the
kingdom prepared for you from the foundation of
the world :

For I was an hungred, and ye gave me meat :
I was thirsty, and ye gave me drink : I was a stranger,
and ye took me in :

Naked, and ye clothed me : I was sick, and ye
visited me : I was in prison, and ye came unto me.

Then shall the righteous answer him, saying,
Lord, when saw we thee an hungred, and fed thee ?
or thirsty, and gave thee drink ?

When saw we thee a stranger, and took thee in ?
or naked, and clothed thee ?

Or when saw we thee sick, or in prison, and came
unto thee ?

And the King shall answer and say unto them,
Verily I say unto you, Inasmuch as ye have done
it unto one of the least of these my brethren, ye have
done it unto me.

Then shall he say also unto them on the left hand, Depart from me, ye cursed, into everlasting fire, prepared for the devil and his angels :

For I was an hungred, and ye gave me no meat : I was thirsty, and ye gave me no drink :

I was a stranger, and ye took me not in : naked, and ye clothed me not : sick, and in prison, and ye visited me not.

Then shall they also answer him, saying, Lord, when saw we thee an hungred, or athirst, or a stranger, or naked, or sick, or in prison, and did not minister unto thee ?

Then shall he answer them, saying, Verily I say unto you, Inasmuch as ye did it not to one of the least of these, ye did it not to me.

400.   Te Deum

WE praise Thee, O God : we acknowledge Thee to be the Lord.

All the earth doth worship Thee : the Father ever-lasting.

To Thee all angels cry aloud : the heavens, and all the powers therein.

To Thee cherubin, and seraphin : continually do cry,

Holy, holy, holy : Lord God of Sabaoth ;

Heaven and earth are full of the majesty : of Thy glory.

The glorious company of the apostles : praise Thee.

The goodly fellowship of the prophets : praise Thee.

The noble army of martyrs : praise Thee.

The holy Church throughout all the world : doth acknowledge Thee ;

REFERENCES TO
AUTHORS AND SOURCES

(The numbers refer to Quotations.)

1. REV. GEORGE MATHESON, D.D. The blind preacher of Scotland. 1842–1906. From " Moments on the Mount," ch. lxi, pp. 144–6.

2. THOMAS A. KEMPIS. " Of the Imitation of Christ."

3. CHRISTINA ROSSETTI. 1830–1894. " When my heart is vexed I will complain," from " Verses." 1896.

4. REV. A. M. FAIRBAIRN, D.D. " Studies in the Life of Christ," pub. 1880, ch. i, pp. 2–3.

5. PÈRE DIDON. " Jesus Christ," Introduction.

6. St. Matthew, ch. xi, 28.

7. THE ALEXANDRIAN APOSTLE. Epistle to the Hebrews, ch. i, 1–8.

8. PÈRE LACORDAIRE. " Jesus Christ, God, God and Man," pp. 92–5.

9. PASCAL. " Thoughts on Religion," ch. xv.

10. DEAN STANLEY. " History of the Jewish Church," N. York ed., 1863. Part I, pp. 517, 519–20.

11. PRINCIPAL A. E. GARVIE, D.D. b. 1861. From " The Christian Doctrine of the Godhead," p. 114.

12. LAURENCE HOUSMAN. " The Mystery of the Incarnation," being a Disputation between Christ and the Human Form. For the Feast of the Nativity.

13. " Jesus Christ," ch. i, p. 31.

14. St. Luke, ch. i, 29, and ch. ii, 6.

15. MILTON. 1608–1674. " Ode on the Nativity."

16. " In the Bleak Mid-winter."

17. ELIZABETH BARRETT BROWNING. 1806–1861. " The Virgin Mary to the Child Jesus," stanza v.

Anthology of Jesus

18. DANTE GABRIEL ROSSETTI. 1828–1882. "Mary's Girlhood." (For a picture.)

19. GILBERT KEITH CHESTERTON. "A Christmas Carol."

20. ALICE MEYNELL. "Advent Meditation."

21. REV. A. D. MARTIN. "Aspects of the Way," Prologue, pp. 1–5.

22. "Jesus Christ, God, God and Man."

23. GEORGE HERBERT. 1593–1633. From the second part of "Christmas."

24. St. Luke, ch. i, 46–55.

25. CHARLES HADDON SPURGEON. 1834–92. "Morning by Morning or Daily Readings," p. 39. The passage by Rev. W. J. Fullerton is taken from "C. H. Spurgeon," ch. v, pp. 82–3.

26. AN EARLY ENGLISH WRITER. Lambeth MS. 853. It is a translation from the Latin, attributed to R. Rolle.

27. RICHARD CRASHAW. 1613?–1649. "To the Name above every Name, the Name of Jesus." Appeared originally in "Steps" of 1648. From Fuller Worthies Library, 1872. 100 copies printed.

28. A Hymn.

29. "Jesus Christ," Vol. I, ch. v, pp. 86–8 and 89–90.

30. "Paradise Regained," Book I.

31. MARTIN LUTHER. 1483–1546. "The Table Talk of Martin Luther." Translated and Edited by William Hazlitt, p. 106.

32. "Aspects of the Way," p. 25.

33. "Jesus Christ, God, God and Man."

34. "The Baptism." "Paradise Regained," Book I.

35. "Paradise Regained," Book I.

36. "Studies in the Life of Christ," ch. v, pp. 89–90.

37. BISHOP HANDLEY C. G. MOULE. One time Bishop of Durham. From "Scenes in the Life of Our Lord," V, "The Temptation."

38. "Jesus Christ, God, God and Man."

39. "Moments on the Mount," ch. xii, p. 23 and pp. 24–5.

40. "Meditations on the Life of Christ," p. 42.

References to Authors and Sources

41. DEAN FARRAR. "Life of Lives," chapter xvii, p. 251.

42. JOHN R. SEELEY. "Ecce Homo," ch. v.

43. REV. RICHARD S. STORRS, D.D. "The Divine Origin of Christianity," published 1884. Notes to Lecture I, p. 371.

44. DR. CHANNING. Works. Boston ed., 1843. Vol. III, pp. 130–1.

45. REV. R. W. DALE, D.D. "The Living Christ and the Four Gospels," published 1890. Lecture V, section v, p. 101.

46. "Steps."

47. "Searchings in the Silence," published 1894, ch. viii, p. 26.

48. BISHOP HEBER. 1783–1826. "Fourth Sunday after Epiphany."

49. ORIGEN. Adv. Celsus : II, xlviii.

50. TENNYSON. 1809–92. "In Memoriam," xxxi.

51. ARTHUR HUGH CLOUGH. 1819–1861. "Bethesda," Poems and Prose Remains, Vol. II, p. 188.

52. "Imago Christi," ch. vi, sec. iv, p. 122.

53. LONGFELLOW. 1807–82. "Blind Bartimeus."

54. "The Christian Doctrine of the Godhead," p. 69.

55. JOHN CHARLES EARLE. "Lo, I am with you always."

56. REV. ALEXANDER WHYTE, D.D. "The Walk, Conversation and Character of Jesus Christ our Lord," published 1905, ch. xxvi, pp. 248–9.

57. "The Life of Jesus Christ," ch. iv, p. 75.

58. "What Went Ye out for to See ? " Poetical Works.

59. JEAN JACQUES ROUSSEAU. "Emile," Oeuvres, Paris ed., 1793. Tom. IX, pp. 40–42.

60. F. C. BAUR. "Geschichte der Christ Kirche." Tubingen. 1863. Band I, S. 472 f.

61. BUNSEN. "Christianity and Mankind." London ed., 1854. Vol. VII, p. 4.

62. MONTAIGNE. "Essais," Paris ed., 1826. Tom. I, p. 178.

63. "The Divine Origin of Christianity," Lecture VII, p. 235.

64. SHELLEY. Taken from Mr. Bowyer Nichols' quotation in " Words and Days," 1895, for Christmas Day. *See* Dr. Bridges' " Spirit of Man."

65. TOLSTOI. " My Religion," p. 38.

66. " The Living Christ and the Four Gospels." Lecture III, section 5, p. 59.

67. REV. JOHN WATSON, D.D. " The Mind of the Master." 1896 ed., ch. ii, p. 28, and pp. 30 and 40.

68. THEODORE PARKER. 1810–1860. " A Discourse of Matters pertaining to Religion," Boston ed., 1847, pp. 281 and 287.

69. MISS FRANCES POWER COBBE. Died 1880. " Broken Lights," Boston ed., 1864, p. 150 ff.

70. WALTER RICHARD CASSELS. " Supernatural Religion," Vol. II, pp. 487 and 488.

71. " The Christian Doctrine of the Godhead," pp. 60–61.

72. LOUIS AUGUSTE SABATIER. " Outlines of a Philosophy of Religion based on Psychology and History." Translated by Rev. T. A. Seed. Book II, ch. ii, p. 152.

73. MATTHEW ARNOLD. " Progress."

74. PROFESSOR J. FINDLAY, D.D. " Jesus as They Saw Him," Part II, ch. vi, pp. 210–11.

75. ARCHBISHOP OF ARMAGH (DR. D'ARCY) " Ruling Ideas of our Lord." Introduction p. xii.

76. " Thoughts on Religion," ch. xiv, pp. 129–30.

77. R. L. STEVENSON. " The Pocket R.L.S.," p. 129.

78. GEORGES BERGUER. " Vie de Jésus, au point de vue psychologique," p. 218.

79. " Imago Christi," ch. vi, Sec. iii, p. 119.

80. FENELON. From " Selections from the Writings of Fénelon," by a Lady. 2nd edition, Boston, 1829, p. 266.

81. RUSKIN. " Modern Painters."

82. REV. JAMES ROBERTSON. " Our Lord's Teaching," 1895 edition, ch. xiii, p. 139.

83. St. Matthew's Gospel, xxiv, 35.

84. " Ecce Homo," ch. xxiv, pp. 263–4.

References to Authors and Sources

85. " The Mind of the Master," ch. xv, p. 319.

86. " Ruling Ideas of Our Lord," ch. viii, pp. 135–9.

87. FRANCIS THOMPSON. 1859–1907. " The Kingdom of God."

88. " Of the Imitation of Christ," Third Book, ch. lvi, p.161.

89. " Jesus Christ, God, God and Man," p. 138.

90. DANTE. 1265–1321. " Paradise," Canto 19, lines 115–20.

91. " In Memoriam." xxxvi.

92. THEDOR MIKHAILOVICH DOSTOEVSKY. "Les Frères Karamazor."

93. " Jesus and the Resurrection," ch. xii, p. 194.

94. JOHN OXENHAM. " Follow Me ! "

95. ABBOT MARMION, O.S.B., OF MAREDSOUS ABBEY. " Christ, the Life of the Soul," 1922 edition, pp. 212 and 217.

96. " Not Yours but You." 1856.

97. DINAH M. CRAIK. " Fishermen—not of Galilee."

98. DR. R. J. CAMPBELL. " The Life of Christ," Note A, p. 348.

99. " Voices of the Spirit," ch. xi, p. 28.

100. " Morning by Morning or Daily Readings," p. 173.

101. SAMUEL RUTHERFORD. 1600–1661. Lectures delivered by Principal Alexander Whyte, 1894, ch. iii, p. 27.

102. " The Descent from the Cross."

103. Epistle to the Romans, ch. viii, 35–39.

104. PROF. MOMERIE, D.Sc. " Defects of Modern Christianity," ch. vi, p. 71.

105. " Of the Imitation of Christ," ch. xi, para. 3, p. 63.

106. JOHN YOUNG. " The Christ of History," Book III, Part iv, pp. 228–9.

107. ANTHONY HORNECK, Chaplain to Charles II. From " The Crucified Jesus."

108. " Morning by Morning or Daily Readings," p. 88.

109. " Love," the last poem in " The Temple."

110. " Jesus Christ, God, God and Man."

111. " The Mind of the Master," ch. ix, pp. 191–2.

112. " My hymn," wrote Dr. George Matheson, " was composed in the Manse of Innellan on the evening of 6th June, 1882. I was at that time alone. It was the day of my sister's marriage, and the rest of the family were staying over night in Glasgow. Something had happened to me, which was known only to myself and which caused me the most severe mental suffering. The hymn was the fruit of that suffering. It was the quickest bit of work I ever did in my life. I had the impression rather of having it dictated to me by some inward voice than of working it out myself. I am quite sure that the whole work was completed in five minutes and equally sure that it never received at my hand any retouching or correction. The Hymnal Committee of the Church of Scotland desired the change of one word. I had written originally ' I climbed the rainbow in the rain.' They objected to the word ' climb ' and I put ' trace.' " p. 181, " The Life of George Matheson," by Dr. D. Macmillan, published by Hodder and Stoughton.

113. From the Library of Early English Writers. Edited by C. Horstman of Berlin. The author is possibly Richard Rolle of Hampole. Father Benson's version.

114. " Jesus and the Resurrection," ch. xi, p. 180.

115. *See* 113.

116. EDMUND SPENSER. 1552?–99. " An Hymn of Heavenly Love," verses 25 and 26.

117. JACOB BEHMEN. " Thoughts on the Spiritual Life." Translated from the German by Charlotte Ady Rainy. Published 1896. Extract from " The Way to Christ of True Repentance."

118. PHINEAS FLETCHER. 1580–1650. " The Divine Lover." Poetical Works, 1793.

119. FRANCIS QUARLES. 1592–1644. Canticles 2, 16. " My Beloved is Mine, and I am His." Prose and Verse, vol. iii, p. 91.

120. *See* 101.

121. ARTHUR EDWARD WAITE. Born 1860. " Restoration." Collected Poems, xxxi.

References to Authors and Sources

122. MINUCIUS FELIX. "Octavius": xxxvii, xxxviii.

123. DR. HORATIUS BONAR. 1808–1889.

124. RT. REV. PHILLIPS BROOKS, A.M. "Light of the World," Sermon viii, pp. 125–6.

125. "Selections from the Writings of Fénelon," by a Lady. Second edition. "On Meekness and Humility." 1829.

126. SAINT TERESA. "On Humility." Taken from passages selected by Dr. Alexander Whyte.

127. "Imago Christi," ch. xvi, sec. v, p. 310.

128. JOHN BUNYAN.

129. "Moments on the Mount," ch. xix, p. 41.

130. "Aspects of the Way," ch. viii, pp. 97 and 98.

131. EVELYN UNDERHILL (Mrs. Stuart Moore). "Immanence."

132. "The Good Shepherd," from the Spanish of Lope de Vega.

133. "The Good Shepherd."

134. Version by FRANCIS ROUS, 1579–1658, and WILLIAM BARTON, c. 1603–78.

135. RICHARD ROBERTS. "The Jesus of Poets and Prophets," ch. ii, p. 27.

136. 1822–88. From a Sonnet. "The Good Shepherd with the Kid."

137. DR. ALEX. SMELLIE. "The Shepherd Lord," a Meditation.

138. DR. JOHN CLIFFORD. "The Gospel of a World Brotherhood," chapter i, pp. 12, 13.

139. A. W. W. DALE. "The Life of R. W. Dale of Birmingham," ch. xxiv, p. 622.

140. ROBERT BROWNING. 1812–1889. "Before."

141. WILLIAM BLAKE. 1757–1827. Written 1811. Poetical Works. Edited by W. M. Rossetti.

142. MAZZINI. "Faith and the Future" in "The Duty of Man."

143. "Christ; the Life of the Soul," p. 353.

144. "Imago Christi," ch. v, sec. iv, p. 101.

145. GEORGE MACDONALD. 1824–1905. "Lost and Found."

146. "It was in Fair Bethlehem."

147. "The Mind of the Master," ch. 3, p. 56.

148. "Little Jesus Wast Thou Shy."

149. EBENEZER SHERMAN OAKLEY. From "Adveni Jesu Domine."

150. "Divine Origin of Christianity," p. 144.

151. "In the Children's Hospital," Stanzas II and III.

152. "Jesus Christ," Vol. I, Book III, ch. xii, p. 487.

153. "Imago Christi," ch. ii, sec. ii, pp. 42–3.

154. CHARLES KINGSLEY. Poems. Child's Ballad.

155. AUBREY DE VERE. 1788–1846. "The Right Use of Prayer."

156. "Aspects of the Way," ch. vi, pp. 75 and 76.

157. "Imago Christi," ch. vii, sec. iii, pp. 136–138.

158. "The Passing of Arthur."

159. PRINCIPAL FORSYTH. 1848–1920. A Sermon.

160. FATHER JOHN, of the Greek Church. "On Making Every Day Sacramental," from An Appreciation by Alexander Whyte.

161. "Imago Christi," ch. ix, sec. i, p. 168; and sec. ii, p. 171.

162. WALTER C. SMITH. 1824–1908. "Thoughts and Fancies for Sunday Evenings."

163. "Aspects of the Way," ch. iii, p. 39.

164. "Mind of the Master." 1896 edition. Ch. ii. Optimism the Attitude of Faith, pp. 232–323.

165. GIOVANNI PAPINI. "Histoire du Christ," "L'Ultime Expérience."

166. "The Christ." Fifth Lecture, pp. 141–142.

167. BLUNTSCHLI. "Das Moderne Völkerrecht." Nördlingen, 1878: S. 14.

168. LIDDON. Bampton Lectures, 1866. 5th edition. Lecture vi, p. 333.

169. "Modern Painters." "Mountain Glory."

References to Authors and Sources

170. Sermons Preached in English Churches, ch. ix, pp. 182–183.

171. ARCHBISHOP TRENCH. 1807–1886.

172. "Aspects of the Way," ch. vi, pp. 78–79.

173. "Moments on the Mount," ch. C, p. 253.

174. "Histoire du Christ."

175. H. H. MILMAN. 1791–1868. "Ride on ! ride on in majesty ! "

176. HENRY VAUGHAN. "Palm Sunday."

177. "Of the Imitation of Christ," fourth book, ch. i, 1–3, 10 ; and ch. ii, 6.

178. "The Christ." Fourth Lecture, p. 90.

179. Attributed to Princess Elizabeth during the reign of her sister Queen Mary. Sent to me by Right Rev. Msgr. Canon Barry, D.D.

180. "Meditations of the Life and Passion of Our Lord Jesus Christ," pp. 271–2.

181. From his Letters.

182. D. M. DOLBEN. 1848–1867. "Flowers for the Altar."

183. St. Matthew, ch. xxvii, 3–5. Moffatt's Translation.

184. "Jesus Christ," Vol. ii, Book v, ch. v, pp. 259–61.

185. THOMAS DE QUINCEY. "Essays on Christianity, Paganism and Superstition," Judas Iscariot.

186. SHAKESPEARE. Henry VI, Third Part, Act V, scene vii.

187. "The Trial and Death of Jesus Christ," p. 128.

188. ANONYMOUS.

189. JAMES MONTGOMERY. 1771–1854. "Go to dark Gethsemane."

190. JOHN TAULER. "Meditations on the Life and Passion of Our Lord Jesus Christ," ch. vii, pp. 51–2.

191. "Studies in the Life of Christ." 1880 edition, ch. xiv, pp. 239–40.

192. 1400. A.D. "A Devotion on the Symbols of the Passion," from MSS. edited by the Early English Text Society.

193. " The Sacrifice," from " The Temple."
194. " Hymn for Good Friday."
195. " The Look."   A Sonnet.
196. THOMAS HARDY.   b. 1840.   " In the Servants' Quarters."
197. " Morning by Morning or Daily Readings," p. 101.
198. " To the Penitent Thief on Calvary."
199. " The Mind of the Master."   1896 edition, ch. vi, pp. 126–7.
200. From his Letters.
201. H. N. OXENHAM.   1829–1888.   " The Child-Christ on the Cross."
202. R. ROLLE.   " An Introduction to the Meditation on the Passion," published in the " Library of Early English Writers."
203. " Meditations of the Life and Passion of Our Lord Jesus Christ," pp. 271–2.
204. RACHEL ANNAND TAYLOR.   " The Question."
205. EVELYN   UNDERHILL   (Mrs.   Stuart   Moore). b. 1875. " Corpus Christi."
206. NEWMAN.   Sermon xxi (Lent), " The   Cross   of Christ the Measure of the World."
207. I Corinthians, ch. xv, 1–10.
208. JOSEPHUS.   " Antiquities of the Jews."   Book xviii.

209. " Easter Even."
210. " Easter Night."
211. " Jesus Christ," Vol. II, Book V, ch. xii, pp. 364, 367.
212. " Good Friday in my Heart."
213. Poems by V.
214. " Jesus Christ, God, God and Man," pp. 65–6.
215. GOETHE.   From the Easter Hymn in " Faust."
216. COWPER.   1731–1800.   " The Walk to Emmaus."
217. " Searchings in the Silence," ch. lxiv, pp. 158–60 ; ch. lxvi, p. 157.
218. " Modern Painters," Part IV, ch. iv, para. 16.
219. " Geschichte der Christ."

References to Authors and Sources

220. " Life of R. W. Dale of Birmingham," ch. xxiv, p. 642.

221. W. R. NICOLL. 1851. " The Incarnate Saviour. A Life of Jesus Christ," ch. xx, p. 329.

222. From Part III of " Rue," 1899.

223. ARTHUR SHEARLY CRIPPS. b. 1869. " To The Black Christ." (At Easter in South Africa.)

224. ANNA BUNSTON DE BARY. " Under a Wiltshire Apple Tree."

225. " The Christian Doctrine of the Godhead," p. 90.

226. C. F. GELLERT. From a Hymn.

227. " The Christ." Third Lecture, pp. 82–3.

228. I Corinthians xv. Moffatt's Translation.

229. " The Life of Christ," ch. xi, sec. 5, p. 346.

230. KEBLE. 1792–1866. St. Thomas' Day.

231. " Jesus and the Resurrection," ch. 5, pp. 67–70.

232. MICHELANGELO. " La Nativita di Giesù Christo."

233. " The Light of the World."

234. Part of " Ascension Day."

235. " Aspects of the Way," ch. x, pp. 153–4.

236. " Christmas Eve," stanza 10.

237. ST. JULIANA. " Revelations of Divine Love recorded by Julian, Anchoress at Norwich. A.D. 1373." A version from the MS. in the British Museum edited by Grace Warrack, ch. li, pp. 120–21.

238. " The Walk, Conversation and Character of Jesus Christ our Lord," pub. 1905, ch. i, pp. 17–18.

239. " The Veteran of Heaven."

240. Sermon XXIX (Ascension). " Warfare the Condition of Victory."

241. I Peter i, 18–23.

242. SISTER TERESA GERTRUDE. Of the Blessed Sacrament. " Jesus the All-Beautiful."

243. REV. W. J. FULLERTON. " C. H. Spurgeon," ch. v, p. 94.

244. " Requests."

245. The late PRINCIPAL JOHN CAIRNS, D.D. " Life and Letters."

246. DORA GREENWELL. 1821–1882. " Songs of Salvation," 1873.

Anthology of Jesus

247. " Thousands of things do Thee employ." From " Praise."

248. DAVID LIVINGSTONE. " The Story of his Life."

249. " GOETHE. " Conversations of Goethe with Eckermann," pp. 567–8.

250. " Despised and Rejected."

251. " The Living Christ and the Four Gospels." 1890 edition. Lecture I, section 2, pp. 14–16.

252. PRINCIPAL L. P. JACKS, D.D. " Perplexity in the Christian Religion."

253. ANATOLIUS. Fifth century.

254. From her Life, by her Sister.

255. " From lines written before August 1903."

256. DR. SUTTON. Early English writer. " Colloquie of the Soul with Christ touching the Passion."

257. " The Walk, Conversation and Character of Jesus Christ Our Lord." 1905 edition, ch. xiii, p. 129.

258. " Abt Vogler," stanza ix.

259. ROBERT HERRICK. 1591–1674. " Christ took our nature."

260. " The Mystery of the Incarnation." " A Disputation between Christ and the Human Form." (For the Feast of the Nativity.)

261. " Idylls of the King." Guinevere.

262. " Aspects of the Way," ch. lx, p. 137.

263. ADAM DE SAINT VICTOR. Old Latin Hymn said to have been sung at the death-bed of William the Conqueror.

264. PRINCIPAL P. T. FORSYTH. " The Person and Place of Christ," Lecture xii.

265. FRANCIS BACON. 1561–1626. " Advancement of Learning," Book IV, cii.

266. " The Sadhu," by B. H. Streeter and A. J. Appasamy.

267. LEWES BAILY. " Practice of Piety."

268. ROBERT BURNS. 1759–1796. Stanzas on the Prospect of Death.

269. " Looking at the Cross."

References to Authors and Sources

270. From " Stories for the Pulpit."

271. ST. THOMAS AQUINAS. (From Right Rev. Msgr. Cannon Barry, D.D.)

272. " Christmas Eve."

273. " Jesu, in me Thy love inspire."

274. " A Prayer for Grace and Glory." From the Processional of the Nuns of Chester.

275. Sermon LIII. (Sundays after Trinity.) " The Shepherd of our Souls."

276. " The Light of the World." Sermon I, pp. 4–5.

277. JAMES CLARENCE MANGAN. 1803–1849. St. Patrick's Hymn before Tara.

278. " In Memoriam."

279. " Searchings in the Silence," ch. lv, p. 137.

280. Early Hymn. Vesper or " Lamplighting " Hymn used in the Greek Church, quoted by Basil, Bishop of Cæsarea, in the 4th century. Translation by John Keble.

281. FR. JOHN BANNISTER TABB. 1845–1909. " Christ and the Pagan." From " Later Poems."

282. REV. J. R. ILLINGWORTH, M.A. " Personality."

283. LUDOLPHUS DE SAXONIA. Quoted in F. Coleridge's " Vita vitæ nostræ," and Church's " Human Life," p. 192.

284. " Ecce Homo," ch. xxiv, p. 257.

285. JOHN GREENLEAF WHITTIER. 1807–1892. From the hymns " Blow, winds of God, awake and blow," and " Dear Lord and Father of mankind."

286. " Poetical Works." Edited by J. C. Smith. " A Hymn of Heavenly Beauty."

287. " Repayment."

288. " The Jesus of Poets and Prophets," ch. ix, pp. 164–5.

289. " Christ, the Life of the Soul, pp. 250–1.

290. THOMAS CHUBB. From " The True Gospel of Jesus Christ," sec. viii, pp. 55–6.

291. " The Christian Doctrine of the Godhead," ch. ii, p. 68.

292. "Outlines of a Philosophy of Religion based on Psychology and History," translated by Rev. T. A. Seed. 1897 edition. Book II, ch. ii, pp. 154-5.

293. "Meditations on the Life and Passion of Our Lord Jesus Christ," attributed to John Tauler, Dominican Friar. Translated from Latin by A. P. J. Cruikshank. 1925 edition, ch. lv, p. 339.

294. "Thoughts on the Spiritual Life," translated from the German by Charlotte Ada Rainy. 1896 edition, No. 15, "Consecration," p. 17.

295. THOMAS EDWARD BROWN. 1830-1897. "Disguises."

296. CHARLES DICKENS. "Life of Charles Dickens," by John Forster.

297. "He came unto His Own, and His Own received Him not."

298. "Emile ou de l'Education," livre iv. Œuvres complètes, Paris, 1839, tome iii, pp. 365-7.

299. NAPOLEON. Conversation with General Bertrand at St. Helena.

300. F. PECAUT. A modern French author, in a work entitled "Le Christ et la Conscience," Paris, 1859.

301. "Sartor Resartus," Book III, ch. iii.

302. From the Sermon on the "Character of Christ" (on Matt. 17, 5), in his Works. Boston edition, 1848, Vol. IV.

303. DAVID FRIEDRICH STRAUSS. From his Essay, "Vergangliches und Bleibendes im Christhum," 1838 (Freihafen, 3tes Heft, p. 47).

304. "A Discourse of Matters pertaining to Religion," Book III, ch. vi.

305. "Broken Lights." An inquiry into the present Condition and future Prospects of Religious Faith. 1864 edition, ch. vii, appendix 2.

306. ALBERT SCHWEITZER. "The Quest of the Historical Jesus," ch. xx, p. 399 and p. 401.

307. CORNELIUS TACITUS. "The Annals of Tacitus," from his Works, Book XV, Sec. xliv, p. 287.

308. "The Bampton Lectures," preached before the University of Oxford in 1866. Lecture VII, pp. 398-401.

References to Authors and Sources

309. POLYCARP. Taken from "Apostolic Fathers," in "Martyrdom of Polycarp," p. 963, by Bishop Lightfoot.

310. From Church Service. "Gaudent in caelis."

311. "Thoughts on Religion," ch. xiv, pp. 127-8.

312. RUDOLF EUCKEN. "Meaning and Value of Life."

313. "The Jesus of Poets and Prophets," ch. i, p. 20 and p. 41.

314. SIR WYKE BAYLISS. "Christ and the Christian Character," p. 46.

315. MRS. JAMESON. "History of Our Lord," 1864. Vol. I, Introduction, p. 1.

316. LORD LINDSAY. "Sketches of the History of Christian Art," vol. I, p. 3.

317. "The Divine Origin of Christianity," Lecture VII, pp. 244-5.

318. DR. JAMES J. WALSH. "The World's Debt to the Catholic Church," p. 86.

319. ST. AUGUSTINE. "Confessions."

320. CHARLES LAMB. 1775-1834. From Hazlitt's "Sketches."

321. "Inspiration and other Sermons," ch. v, p. 52.

322. DENIS DIDEROT. Original source is Stier's " Reden Jesu," Part vi, p. 496, which relates the words of Antistes Hess of Zurich.

323. "Ecce Homo," see 284.

324. See 301.

325. The end of the "Orient Ode."

326. "East London."

327. From "The Golden Legend," "The Nativity." iv, "The Wise Men of the East."

328. "Approaches."

329. "The Second Crucifixion."

330. PROF. FRANCIS GREENWOOD PEABODY. From "Jesus Christ and the Social Question," ch. i, p. 32.

331. DR. JOSEPH PARKER. "The Inner Life of Christ," vol. ii, pp. 320, 321.

Anthology of Jesus

332. JOSEPH MARY PLUNKETT. 1887–1916. " I see His Blood upon the Rose."

333. Epistle to the Philippians, ch. ii, pp. 6–11.

334. " Meditations on the Life of Christ," p. 38.

335. " Moments on the Mount," ch. xv, p. 33 ; and second paragraph from " Voices of the Spirit," ch. xxix, pp. 74–5.

336. BRUCE. From " Apologetics of Christianity Defensively Stated." Book III, ch. ii, pp. 356-7.

337. *See* 264.

338. W. B. PHILPOT. 1823–1889. No. 359, from " A Pocket of Pebbles."

339. " My Religion," p. 145.

340. TURGENEV. " Novels and Stories."

341. " The Unknown God."

342. " Christ, the Life of the Soul." Edition 1922, pp. 34–5.

343. " Saul," stanza 18.

344. REV. JOHN CLIFFORD, D.D. " Life and Letters," by Sir James Marchant.

345. " Notes on the Lord's Prayer."

346. BISHOP BOYD CARPENTER. " The Witness to the Influence of Christ," ch. ii, pp. 59–60.

347. JAMES RUSSELL LOWELL. " The Search."

348. Epistle to the Colossians, ch. i, 15–17, and ch. ii, 9.

349. " History of Christianity," p. 512.

350. " Apologetics of Christianity Defensively Stated," Book III, ch. v, pp. 404–5.

351. HERMANN. " Der Verkehr des Christen mit Gott," p. 113, 2te Aufl.

352. On " God the Son," Parochial and Plain Sermons, Vol. VI, Sermon V.

353. THEODOR KEIM. " Geschichte Jesu von Nazara," Vol. I, p. 448. The second paragraph is from Vol. III, p. 662, and the third from Vol. III, p. 667.

354. " Life of Christ," ch. xi, p. 346.

355. LAMENNAIS. From his " Essai sur l'Indifférence." Paris edition, 1823. Tom. IV, p. 449.

References to Authors and Sources

356. " Fellowship with Christ," 1891 edition, p. 7.

357. " The Christian Doctrine of the Godhead," ch. i, pp. 56–8.

358. From " A Death in the Desert."

359. 1814–1863. From " The Eternal Word."

360. " Sermons Preached in English Churches," ch. viii, pp. 157 and 158–9.

361. HENRY VAN DYKE. Quoted from Rev. Dr. Hugh Miller. " Finding the Way."

362. " The Living Christ and the Four Gospels," Lecture 2, sec. 3, p. 36.

363. " Defects of Modern Christianity," ch. iv, pp. 236-8.

364. " The Inn of Life."

365. COLERIDGE. Works, New York edition, 1853, vol. i, p. 233.

366. Works. Boston edition, 1843, vol. iii, p. 135.

367. " Christmas Eve."

368. Selections from the writings of Fénelon, by a Lady. 2nd edition, 1829, Boston, p. 242.

369. MSGR. WILLIAM CANON BARRY. b. 1849. From " Heralds of Revolt."

370. From " Christian Evidences."

371. " Jesus Christ, God, God and Man," p. 144.

372. " Discourse of Religion," Boston edition, 1842, pp. 422–4.

373. *See* 299.

374. MICHELET. " Histoire de France," Paris edition, 1855. Tom. II, pp. 662, 673 and 683.

375. THE RT. REV. THEODORE WOODS, Bishop of Winchester. " Great Tasks and Great Inspirations " ; " In the Church at Home," pp. 107 & 109.

376. " The Christian Doctrine of the Godhead."

377. DEAN INGE. " The Church and the Age."

378. An Appreciation and best passages by Alexander Whyte. " On the Church," pp. 178–80.

379. Bampton Lectures preached in 1866. Lecture 3, " Our Lord's Divinity," p. 118.

380. S. J. STONE. 1839–1900. " The Church's one foundation," a Hymn.

381. Ancient Hymn.
382. CONSTANTINE. " Orat. to Assembly, XI " (Eusebius' Life, pp. 258–9).
383. " Jesus and the Resurrection," ch. i, p. 8.
384. " Fellowship with Christ," ch. ii, pp. 41, 42, 43.
385. " Life and Letters," From His Diary.
386. Bampton Lectures, preached in 1866. Conclusion of Lecture VIII, p. 499.
387. " Parochial and Plain Sermons," Sermon XXX. " Rising with Christ." Fourth edition, pp. 258–9.
388. " Faith and the Future."
389. " Searchings in the Silence," ch. lxvi, p. 162.
390. " A New Earth."
391. F. W. H. MYERS. The end of " St. Paul."
392. JACOPONI DA TODI, the first great Italian Poet and Mystic. 1228–1306. Lauda xc. Translated by Mrs. Theodore Beck.
393. " The Month of Jesus Christ," pp. 61 and 62.
394. From the Latin, " The Sighs of St. Aloysius."
395. From " Milton." From the Preface.
396. ALFRED GURNEY. " The New World."
397. " Christ in the Universe."
398. ISAAC WATTS. " Jesus shall reign where'er the sun," a Hymn.
399. St. Matthew, ch. xxv, 31–46.
400. " Te Deum."

INDEX OF AUTHORS

[References are to pages]

Index to Authors

Fletcher, Phineas, 105
Forsyth, Principal, 140, 233, 294
Fullerton, W. J., 24, 221

Garvie, A. E., 9, 48, 64, 204, 251, 309, 325
Gellert, C. F., 205
Gertrude, Teresa Sister, 220
Goethe, 194, 224
Greenwell, Dora, 223
Gurney, Alfred, 342

Hardy, Thomas, 177
Havergal, Frances Ridley, 228
Heber, Reginald, 44
Herbert, George, 21, 98, 174, 223
Hermann, 304
Herrick, Robert, 231
Horneck, Anthony, 96
Housman, Laurence, 10, 130, 180, 201, 231, 249
Hsi, Pastor, 237

Illingworth, Rev. J. R., 245
Inge, Dean, 326

Jacks, L. P., 226
Jacoponi da Todi, 340
Jameson, Mrs., 276
John, Father, 141
Josephus, 190
Juliana, St., 213

Keble, John, 209
Keim, Theodor, 306
Kempis, Thomas à (*see* À Kempis)
Kingsley, Charles, 136

Lacordaire, 7, 20, 33, 37, 80, 98, 193, 322
Lamb, Charles, 281
Lamennais, 307
Le Gallienne, Richard, 287
Liddon, Canon, 150, 270, 329, 334

ALPHABETICAL CONTENTS

[References are to pages]

... ... is to be returned only ...